Ninja® Foodi™ Smart XL Grill
COMPLETE COOKBOOK

NINJA® Foodi™

SMART XL GRILL

COMPLETE COOKBOOK

150 RECIPES TO
SEAR, SIZZLE, AND CRISP

AUTHORIZED BY NINJA® AUTHORIZED BY

Mellanie De Leon

Photography by Hélène Dujardin

ROCKRIDGE PRESS

For general information on our other products and services or to obtain technical support, please contact our Customer Care Department within the United States at (866) 744-2665, or outside the United States at (510) 253-0500.

Rockridge Press publishes its books in a variety of electronic and print formats. Some content that appears in print may not be available in electronic books, and vice versa.

Interior and Cover Designer: Heather Krakora
Art Producer: Janice Ackerman
Editor: Anna Pulley
Production Editor: Andrew Yackira
Production Manager: Riley Hoffman

Photography © 2021 Hélène Dujardin. Food styling by Anna Hampton.

ISBN: Print 978-1-64876-865-1
eBook 978-1-64876-266-6

R0

*To my everythings: John, Jaxon, and Allexie,
who think my cooking is the best. Love you.*

CONTENTS

INTRODUCTION

I AM A *FOODIE* AT HEART. WHEN EATING OUT, I WANT TO BE ABLE TO try dishes that I haven't made in my own kitchen and find ways to recreate them back at home. When traveling, I like to explore neighborhood restaurants to taste local food and indulge in new flavors. I also love being able to prepare a meal with common ingredients, because, honestly, it can be frustrating to hunt down specialty items that aren't at the local supermarket. I love eating different foods, creating recipes, introducing unfamiliar dishes to people, and cooking for others, because I believe food brings us together.

I have owned about every indoor grill and appliance you can imagine. If you're anything like me, I'm sure you have a ton of stuff you don't need, taking up all the counter and cupboard space.

Unlike those other indoor grills, the Ninja® Foodi™ Smart XL Grill has become an appliance that I use every day and a staple in my kitchen. It is so much more than just an indoor grill. It can also air crisp, bake, roast, broil, and dehydrate foods my family and I love. The Foodi™ Grill is worth the counter space, and I proudly showcase it in the kitchen.

As a busy, working, stay-at-home mom, I'm no stranger to throwing together quick meals to feed the family. I want to be able to eat foods that cater to us, provide me convenience and ease, and don't use a lot of ingredients. Most importantly, I want the food to taste good and not take hours to prepare and cook. Thankfully, the Ninja® Foodi™ Smart XL Grill can truly do it all! Whether whipping up hot and crispy Lemon-Pepper Chicken Wings (page 94) from frozen in 40 minutes or grilling family favorites like Orange-Ginger Soy Salmon (page 215) in 12 minutes, every family can enjoy a fresh and healthy meal without having to resort to takeout.

If you can navigate a toaster or microwave oven, you'll find using the Ninja® Foodi™ Smart XL Grill to be a snap. I have personally cooked all of the recipes in this book and followed them step by step to make sure that you can enjoy a good, home-cooked meal just like I do. With 150 recipes and all the information you need, this is your definitive, official source for all things Ninja® Foodi™ Smart XL Grill.

Welcome to the *biggest* book of Ninja® Foodi™ Smart XL Grill recipes to get the most out of your new favorite kitchen appliance.

1

The Magic of the Ninja® Foodi™ Smart XL Grill

IN THIS CHAPTER, YOU WILL LEARN EVERYTHING YOU NEED TO know about the Ninja® Foodi™ Smart XL Grill appliance, including its features, the six cooking functions, its parts and accessories, and even how to grill food from frozen. You can load up the grill and simply walk away, not having to worry about continuously checking the food or having to insert an external thermometer at the right time. You will learn all the tips, tricks, and troubleshooting to help you become a pro Foodi™ Griller.

INDOOR GRILLING—AND MUCH MORE

With the Ninja® Foodi™ Smart XL Grill, you get all the perks of outdoor grilling year-round and in any weather. The Foodi™ Grill allows you to make easy, delicious, satisfying meals any night of the week. Its easy-to-use functionality and user-friendliness have changed the multicooker landscape with its ability to pack on the heat—the Foodi™ Grill cooks up to 500ºF—and to give you balanced temperature distribution that cooks food evenly. No hot spots or one part cooking faster than any other.

Whether you are unable to fire up an outdoor grill because of rain, snow, or excessive summer heat or you live in a home that does not allow for grilling on a patio or balcony or that has little outdoor space, you can still get all the benefits with the Foodi™ Grill. Indoor grilling on the Foodi™ Grill also makes for easy weeknight meals, as it's fast, efficient, and a breeze to clean up. There is no need to prep charcoal, wood pellets, or chips or worry about having enough gas or propane on hand. A quick plug-in and preheat will give you the grill results and quick cooking that you want. Plus, there is no need to fear the smoke detector going off, as the Foodi™ Grill gives you a smoke-free experience.

The Ninja® Foodi™ Smart XL Grill is low-maintenance, easy to set up, and versatile. It can be used to feed one person or the whole family.

FEATURES: HOW TO GRILL EVERYTHING

You can use the Ninja® Foodi™ Smart XL Grill all year to get delicious grill flavor in your chicken, steaks, veggies, and chops. Cyclonic Grilling Technology allows you to cook directly and quickly on the high-density Grill Grate as the air circulates around the food. Even better, the Foodi™ Grill makes it easy to grill up breakfast, lunch, and dinner, not just any time of year but every day!

The temperature-sensing Grill Grate and Smart Thermometer continuously monitor your food's temperature so you don't have to! The grill even tells you when to flip your food. You'll be able to cook the perfect Chicken Cordon Bleu Roll-Ups (page 79) just the way you like them or cook everyone's Rib Eye Steak with Rosemary Butter (page 126) just the way they want it.

With the Ninja® Foodi™ Smart XL Grill, you can get Honey-Garlic Ribs (page 148) that are juicy and tender, and you can also grill up Mom's Lemon-Pepper Salmon (page 218) and enjoy a crispy bottom but creamy, buttery, flavorful top—without worrying about flipping the tender fish. I love the ability to grill veggies like mushrooms or bell peppers alongside my steaks, and doing so with the Foodi™ Grill means I don't have to worry about smaller pieces falling through the grate of an outdoor grill.

Outdoor grilling can sometimes be a gamble. How many times have you grilled up some delicious chicken only to find it beautifully charred on the outside but almost raw on the inside? Thankfully, the Ninja® Foodi™ Smart XL Grill takes out the guesswork—no more under- or overcooking food. Whether you manually select your desired food's internal temperature or use one of the Foodi™ Grill's preset functions, your food is constantly being monitored. There are no timing worries, as the grill will automatically shut off or tell you when to remove the food when the internal temperature is reached and your desired level of doneness is achieved.

Another perk of the Foodi™ Grill is time saved. With the Ninja® Foodi™ Smart XL Grill, you don't have to worry about prepping it with charcoal or a chimney starter, waiting for it to heat up, or using special tools and utensils. What would normally take hours on an outdoor grill, such as Uncle's Famous Tri-Tip (page 133) or Burnt Ends (page 140), can now be done in a fraction of the time. And don't forget about dessert! With the Ninja® Foodi™ Smart XL Grill, you can make tasty grilled peaches and even more surprising treats, like Everyday Cheesecake (page 228).

Create the outdoor taste you love with less time and less mess. Grill season now is year-round.

Grill from Frozen

We all have those days where we forget to thaw the protein we meant to eat that night or when plans to eat out get canceled, leaving you in the lurch. Now you don't have to go into panic mode because you don't have a dinner plan B. The Ninja® Foodi™ Smart XL Grill allows you to grill meats from frozen, and this feature is especially great for fish.

If you are cooking straight from the freezer, you will only have to add a few more minutes of cook time. You will also want to flip often for items such as frozen chicken wings and to check frozen steaks to ensure they're cooked evenly. Yes, you read that right! I have grilled up frozen steaks in a pinch when I wanted a good, hearty meal. When cooking frozen protein, it is recommended to not use the Smart Thermometer to avoid damage.

Do not soak your frozen proteins in water to thaw them. But a tip I have learned is, if any frost or ice has accumulated, sprinkle a little water on the area and rub the frost away. Applying a thin layer of avocado oil works, too. If you happen to get your protein wet, I suggest patting it dry with a paper towel before cooking.

THE FUNCTIONS

The Ninja® Foodi™ Smart XL Grill has six different cooking functions: GRILL, AIR CRISP, BAKE, ROAST, BROIL, and DEHYDRATE. Along with the functions, the grill has four protein settings with temperatures preset for your desired food type: Beef/Lamb, Chicken/Turkey, Pork, and Fish. The grill also has nine doneness levels: RARE (1, 2), MEDIUM-RARE (3, 4), MEDIUM (5, 6), MEDIUM-WELL (7, 8), and WELL-DONE (9). With the Smart Thermometer correctly inserted into the meat (see page 7), the control panel displays both the target temperature (your desired doneness) and the current temperature of the food. This allows you to achieve the perfect doneness without the guesswork and enables you to see the progress of your cooking. A nice feature of the Foodi™ Grill is that its display tells you when it's time to add the food, when your unit is done preheating, and of course, when it is done cooking.

Grill. When using the GRILL function, you can create an even char, grill marks, and grilled flavor. LO (400°F) is recommended for bacon and sausages or when using thicker barbecue sauces. MED (450°F) is recommended for frozen meats, marinated items, and sauced meats. HI (500°F) is recommended for steaks, chicken, burgers, hot dogs, and meat kebabs. MAX (up to 510°F) is recommended for veggies, fruit, pizzas, fresh and frozen seafood, and veggie kebabs. The GRILL setting allows you to cook in 1-minute increments for up to 30 minutes.

Air Crisp. When using the AIR CRISP function, the rapid circulation of air makes food crunchy and crispy, similar to deep-frying but with little to no oil. This setting allows you to cook in 1-minute increments for up to 1 hour. I recommend using the AIR CRISP function when heating up frozen foods that are meant to have deep-fried texture, like French fries, fish sticks, chicken nuggets, tater tots, or pizza rolls. If I have leftovers, I enjoy reheating them using the AIR CRISP function.

Bake. The BAKE function is for baking cakes, desserts, and casseroles. The Cooking Pot works as a baking sheet, such as with cookies or brownies, or you can place another small baking pan in the pot, such as for a cheesecake. With this setting, you can cook in 1-minute increments for up to 1 hour and in 5-minute increments from 1 to 2 hours. Because the Ninja® Foodi™ Smart XL Grill uses convection-style cooking (a fan and exhaust system to move the hot air around), your food will cook faster. If using a recipe not created specifically for the Foodi™ Grill, you may want to check your food often to avoid overcooking—I recommend baking at a lower temperature for a longer amount of time to avoid burning and getting too much browning and crusting on baked goods. I also recommend covering cheesecakes with aluminum foil so they do not brown too fast.

Roast. The ROAST function cooks perfect meats, vegetables, and more. In this setting, you can cook in 1-minute increments for up to 1 hour and in 5-minute increments from 1 to 4 hours. I recommend using this function for meats and vegetables that you would similarly roast in the oven to bring heat to the food from the top and the bottom. The slower cooking of the ROAST function makes for tender and juicier large cuts of meat, like rotisserie chickens, whole fish, pot roast, and beef tenderloin, and results in perfect browning, crispiness, and tons of flavor.

Broil. When using the BROIL function, the heat source comes from the top, allowing you to add a quick finishing crisp. This setting allows you cook in 1-minute increments for up to 30 minutes. I recommend using this function when you want to cook already tender or fresh vegetables and thin cuts of meat for the perfect caramelization, crust, and sear.

Dehydrate. Using the DEHYDRATE function removes the moisture from your foods, preserving them and making them last longer. Foods dehydrate by using low and steady heat for several hours. This setting allows you to cook in 15-minute increments for up to 12 hours. I recommend using this function if you want to make your own jerky or dehydrate fruits for your own healthy snacks, such as homemade trail mix. You can rest assured that any dehydrated snacks you make with the Foodi™ Grill will have no unnecessary sugar or added preservatives. I have even dehydrated my own herbs to make them last longer, which is the next best thing to using fresh herbs in the kitchen.

THE PARTS

The Ninja® Foodi™ Smart XL Grill has six primary parts specially designed to prepare meals to perfection.

Grill Grate. The 9-by-12-inch, high-density Grill Grate gives you the char flavor and attractive grill marks we all want from a grill. The Grill Grate's unique design allows for quick grilling, and its large surface area fits up to 6 steaks, 6 burgers, or 6 fish fillets.

Crisper Basket. The 4-quart-capacity basket allows you to air-crisp up to 2 pounds of French fries or chicken wings. The Crisper Basket is used for air-crisping foods or dehydrating.

Cooking Pot. The 6-quart capacity of the pot easily fits a 3-pound roast. The Cooking Pot makes for easy cleanup of the Foodi™ Grill, as it catches all of the fat drippings from the Grill Grate and all of the crumbs from the Crisper Basket.

The Cooking Pot should always be placed in the unit when using any of the cooking functions.

Grill Hood. After the unit preheats, a nice feature of the Foodi™ Grill is that it will automatically start cooking when the grill is loaded and the hood is closed. There is no need to press the Start button again to initiate cooking. When the hood is opened so that you can flip your food or give the Crisping Basket a shake, cooking is automatically paused, then resumes when the hood is closed again.

Splatter Shield. Located on the underside of the hood, the Splatter Shield keeps the heating element clean and prevents the unit from smoking. Always ensure the Splatter Shield is installed to prevent oil buildup on the heating element. The Splatter Shield is removable for easy cleaning and is dishwasher safe.

Smart Thermometer. This leave-in thermometer with dual-sensor technology allows for more accurate cooking results as it continuously monitors your food's internal temperature in two places. Plug the thermometer into the grill, select the preset or manual thermometer buttons on the display unit, then ensure the Smart Thermometer is properly inserted in your protein. The Smart Thermometer continuously monitors your food's internal temperature and cooking process. Store your Smart Thermometer in the Smart Thermometer Storage that easily attaches to the grill unit, or store it on the refrigerator for fast access and easy remembering.

Scale It Down

The recipes in this cookbook were developed using the Ninja® Foodi™ Smart XL Grill, which has a 9-by-12-inch Grill Grate and a 4-quart Crisper Basket. Most of the recipes will work with the older Ninja® grill models, but you may need to scale down the recipe if you are feeding fewer than 6 people or cook in batches to not overcrowd the space. As always, check food often if you are worried about overcooking, and don't be afraid to cook at a lower temperature or shorten the time to get your smaller-portioned food cooked to perfection.

HOW TO PLACE THE THERMOMETER

Once you've selected your cooking function, cooking temperature, protein type, and desired level of doneness, insert the Foodi™ Smart Thermometer into the thickest part of your protein while the grill is preheating.

Steaks, Pork chops, Lamb chops, Chicken breasts, Burgers, Tenderloins, Fish fillets		
PLACEMENT	**CORRECT**	**INCORRECT**
• Insert thermometer horizontally into the center of the thickest part of the meat. • Make sure the tip of the thermometer is inserted straight into the center of the meat, not angled toward the bottom or top of it. • Make sure the thermometer is close to (but not touching) the bone and away from any fat or gristle. NOTE: The thickest part of the fillet may not be the center. It is important that the end of the thermometer hits the thickest part so desired results are achieved.		
Whole chicken		
PLACEMENT	**CORRECT**	**INCORRECT**
• Insert thermometer horizontally into the thickest part of the breast, parallel to, but not touching, the bone. • Make sure the tip reaches the center of the thickest part of the breast and doesn't go all the way through the breast into the cavity.		

DO NOT use the thermometer with frozen protein or for cuts of meat thinner than 1 inch.

BECOME A PRO FOODI™ GRILLER

Now that you know the Ninja® Foodi™ Smart XL Grill inside out, it's time to take your knowledge to the next level with these helpful tips.

Preheat the grill

Preheating the Foodi™ Grill ensures that you get the perfect crust, char, and iconic grill marks everyone raves about. Adding cold meat to a cold cooking surface results in longer cooking times. Plus, nothing beats the sound of a good sizzle.

Bring uncooked meats to room temperature

Allow your meat to come to room temperature on the counter for about 30 minutes before grilling. This will ensure the food cooks more evenly. This doesn't apply to marinated meats, however. Meats marinated for 30 minutes or more should be kept in the refrigerator. Once you're ready to grill, remove the marinated meat from the refrigerator and let it sit on the counter for about 10 minutes, so that any oil in the marinade can come back to liquid form.

Rest your meat

Once the meat is done cooking, it's tempting to take a big bite out of it right away. But when you cut too early, the juices end up on your cutting board or plate instead of staying in the meat and giving you more flavor and better texture. Allowing your meat to rest ensures that the moisture and juices that come closer to the surface during cooking are redistributed back into the meat. For steaks, I recommend resting for at least 5 minutes; for larger cuts and roasts, 10 to 20 minutes. Be patient. It is well worth the wait.

Slice against the grain

The grain is the direction of the meat fibers. When you slice with the grain, the muscle fibers are still intact, giving you a tougher slice of meat. Cutting against the grain shortens the muscle fibers, giving you a more tender bite. From the outside, you can see where the lines of the fibers are running. Once you find them, cut perpendicular to those lines.

Experiment with cooking times

If you're unsure how long something takes to cook, it is better to undercook foods and add time than to overcook foods and find that you've burned your meal or that the texture is too dry for your liking.

Add some extra glaze

If you are grilling marinated meats, set some marinade aside for later use. If you are cooking delicate meats, like salmon or other fish, and the grill suggests to flip the food, instead of flipping, you can brush on the reserved marinade to make a glaze for added flavor. You can also brush on glaze in the last 5 minutes of cooking.

Don't be afraid of fat

Use the fat drippings from grilled meats to your advantage. For instance, you can use the drippings from grilled meats for roasting vegetables—you will get a lot of flavor and seasonings added into them that way. Using the drippings is also a great way to caramelize onions if you want to top your steak with them. When grilling, I cook meats fat-side down so that the fat-cap drippings do not wash away any seasonings on the meat.

Choose the best cut

Not all steaks are created equal. It's good to know which cuts of meat lend themselves to which cooking methods. Steaks that are best for marinades include flank steaks, skirt steaks, and hanger steaks. Brisket, tri-tip, and chuck steaks are best when cooked slowly for a longer period of time. When selecting a steak for grilling, people tend to look for a good amount of marbling (fat), which is usually found in pricier cuts, such as rib eyes, strip steaks, T-bones or porterhouse steaks, and filet mignon.

NINJA TEST KITCHEN FAQ

Q: How long should I preheat?

A. Grill mode takes approximately 10 minutes to preheat. Air Crisp, Roast, and Bake take approximately 3 minutes to preheat. And the unit does not preheat in either Broil or Dehydrate modes.

Q: Can I put the accessories in the dishwasher?

A. The Cooking Pot, Grill Grate, Splatter Shield, and Crisper Basket are all dishwasher safe. The only exception is the Smart Thermometer, which should not go in the dishwasher.

Q: How do I clean the thermometer?

A. The thermometer should be handwashed only. To deep clean, soak the stainless steel tip and grip in warm, soapy water. Do not immerse the jack or cord in water or any other liquid.

Q: How would I clean the splatter shield?

A. It is recommended to clean the splatter shield after every use. Soaking it overnight will help soften the baked-on grease. After soaking, use the cleaning brush to remove grease from the stainless steel frame and front tabs.

Q: Can I cancel preheating?

A. Preheating is highly recommended but can be skipped by selecting the PREHEAT button after you press the START/STOP button.

Q: Should I add ingredients before or after preheating?

A. For best results, let the unit fully preheat before adding ingredients.

DOs and DON'Ts

DO let the unit completely preheat before placing items on the unit for cooking. While the unit is preheating, you can prep and gather all your ingredients and tools needed for grilling.

DO use proper grilling tools and accessories. You do not want to use metal utensils or metal spatulas to remove or stir food around on the Grill Grate, as they can scratch and damage the nonstick surface.

DO clean the Splatter Shield after every use. The Splatter Shield is easily removable. It is a breeze to clean by soaking it in dish soap and hot water. For tougher, baked-on grease, you can use a leave-on oven cleaner spray.

DON'T cook on a dirty Grill Grate. Make sure all parts are clean for each new use. Reusing a dirty part can create smoke from burnt bits of food left behind.

DON'T spray your Grill Grate, Crisper Basket, or Cooking Pot with oil. There is no need to spray the parts, because they all have a nonstick ceramic coating. If you wish to use oil, it is best to add the oil to the food or use it in your marinade before cooking.

DON'T cook foods with wet batter when using the AIR CRISP function. The batter will run off, and you will end up with burnt glop in the basket. I suggest freezing batter-coated food first for best results, or instead of batter, use a classic egg wash, then coat with panko, plain, or seasoned bread crumbs.

Grilled Pork Banh Mi, *page 151*

2

Your Indoor Grilling Kitchen

NOW THAT YOU KNOW THE INS AND OUTS OF YOUR NINJA® FOODI™ Smart XL Grill, it's time to get your kitchen set up for grilling. Whether you have a large kitchen or a small one, I will show you how to stock and prep your space to cook up delicious foods with the Foodi™ Grill, what tools and accessories you need, and how to grill safely and prevent cross-contamination. All this from the comfort of your kitchen—no need to run back and forth from outside, the way you would with an outdoor grill.

SETTING UP FOR SUCCESS

Before you start, there are a few tips and tricks I want to share so you'll get the most out of your experience with your Ninja® Foodi™ Smart XL Grill. These include ingredients to keep stocked in your kitchen, tools to help you be a Foodi™ Grill master, and hints for understanding the recipes in this book.

Staples & Spices

When it comes to preparing delicious and flavorful meals, you will want to make sure that you have these basic staples on hand.

My first tip is to see what you have in your pantry already. Start by throwing out any spices, seasonings, or condiments that have expired, and try to arrange ones you use more frequently in a way you can see or reach easily. If something is hard to access, you are most likely not going to use it.

Here is my list of must-have staples for the Ninja® Foodi™ Smart XL Grill:

Condiments: Barbecue sauce, whether spicy, sweet, or another flavor, helps glaze your foods. Other sauces to keep on hand include soy sauce and Worcestershire sauce, which are great bases for marinades. Vinaigrettes (such as balsamic vinaigrette), ketchup, mustards (yellow, honey, Dijon), and hot sauces help bring new flavors together and can be used to make a variety of sauces for grilling.

Oils: When cooking with the Ninja® Foodi™ Smart XL Grill, use high-smoke-point oils, such as avocado oil, canola oil, coconut oil, grape-seed oil, or vegetable oil. This ensures the grilling remains smokeless. My preference is to use avocado oil because of its versatility in cooking and its health benefits. I may use extra-virgin olive oil for lower cooking temps or when doing a quick grill for shrimp. Just remember, olive oil can smoke quickly at high heat and give grilled foods a burnt taste, so you will need to pay special attention when using olive oil with high cooking temperatures.

Spices and seasonings: Sea salt or kosher salt and black pepper (black peppercorns for freshly ground pepper) are base spices in many recipes in this book. Salt brings out the natural flavors in foods as well as enhances its palatability, and black pepper gives a mild kick to a dish as well as added depth. In this book, in recipes that don't specify sea salt or kosher salt, you can use either.

Other go-to seasonings include basil, bay leaves, thyme, oregano, and parsley. I prefer using fresh ingredients over dried if I have them, but having dried versions on hand can bring much-needed flavor to grilled foods and save you from making multiple trips to the grocery store.

For heat and versatility, reach for cayenne pepper, chili powder, cumin, curry, paprika, and red pepper flakes.

Garlic powder, garlic salt, ground ginger, onion powder, and onion salt also bring a lot of flavor to food. I like to have these dried seasonings on hand in case I run out of the fresh ingredients. When choosing dry spices, I prefer the ground or powdered versions.

For holiday cooking, baking, and desserts that need some added spice and aroma, look to allspice, cinnamon, ground cloves, and nutmeg.

Light brown sugar and granulated white sugar are good to stock up on for preparing your own marinades and sauces in addition to making desserts in your Ninja® Foodi™ Smart XL Grill.

Fresh items: I use a lot of garlic and onions in recipes for flavor. I use dried onions when I am in a pinch for time, because I do not have to slice them. Minced garlic in a jar also saves time and energy and can easily be found at local grocery stores.

Vegetables to stock include bell peppers, mushrooms, and squash, which all work excellently on the Foodi™ Grill in sides, mains, or salads, or as an easy way to add some veggies in your diet. If you are worried about fresh produce going bad, supplement it with frozen vegetables. A frozen stir-fry veggie bag works great on the grill, and so do frozen broccoli, cauliflower, bell peppers, and onions.

Tools & Extras

You are only as good as your tools when it comes to grilling. The Foodi™ Grill comes stocked with many tools, including a Smart Thermometer and Grill Brush, but here are other items that will make your grilling experience easier and tastier.

Spatula: A good silicone spatula works best with delicate meats, like fish, or to easily flip those burgers while grilling. Silicone material will also ensure you are not scraping or damaging the nonstick ceramic coating of the Grill Grate.

Tongs: Tongs are commonly used when grilling and are great for turning thick steaks, ribs, chicken, or kebabs. It is best to use tongs instead of a fork to help food retain its flavors and juiciness. As with the spatula, choose tongs with silicone grips.

Grill mitts: When removing the Grill Grate or switching parts to change from one cooking function to another, such as from GRILL to AIR CRISP, grill mitts are necessary to protect your hands from surfaces that are too hot to touch.

Basting brush: Brushing marinades, sauces, or liquids onto grilled foods helps keep them flavorful and juicy. You can also use a basting brush to coat foods like shrimp with oil or when applying an egg wash to pastry dough. I suggest using a silicone basting brush for easier cleanup—just throw it in the dishwasher when done—and because silicone stands up to high heat.

Masher: A masher, commonly used on potatoes, can be used to mash up veggies that you have grilled and turn them into, for instance, mashed cauliflower. It works great to tenderize meats, too.

Wooden spoon: Use a wooden spoon to break apart ground meats and to stir food in the Cooking Pot. It won't damage the nonstick surface, and you won't have to worry about it melting into your food.

Foodi™ Grill Accessories

Ninja has many great products and accessories you can use with your indoor grill. The Ninja® Foodi™ Smart XL Grill comes with the Grill Grate, Crisper Basket, Cooking Pot, Smart Thermometer, and Grill Brush. Many different retail packages may include different accessories, such as Kitchen Collections or Accessory Bundles, to enjoy all the options available. The following accessories are sold separately but may make your grilling experience that much better.

Griddle Plate

Turn your Grill Grate into a flat surface for griddling. The Griddle Plate covers half of the XL Grill Grate, allowing you to make your morning essentials, like eggs and pancakes, while using the other half of the Grill Grate to grill your proteins simultaneously. The nonstick ceramic coating makes for easy cleaning.

Veggie Tray

The Veggie Tray allows you to cook thinly sliced vegetables, like onions and bell peppers, or small foods, like peas and kernels of corn, that would otherwise fall between the grates of an outdoor grill. Simultaneously cook the smaller veggies using the Veggie Tray while you grill sausages, steaks, hamburgers, chicken, or pork chops. One of my favorite ways to use the Veggie Tray is to cook up French fries while grilling hamburgers.

Kebab Skewers

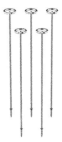

Get the most out of your grilling experience by using stainless steel Kebab Skewers to secure your meats, veggies, fruits, and even cake (see Peaches-and-Cake Skewers, page 242). No need to worry about soaking wooden skewers or ending up with burnt skewers—these tools are ready to load and use and easy to clean and store. The ring end helps you hold them while piercing and also ensures ingredients do not fall off when cooking, flipping, and removing from the grill.

Roasting Rack

The Roasting Rack fits directly inside the Cooking Pot. Roast vegetables and large pieces of meat while keeping food raised off the bottom so liquids can drip. The Roasting Rack can also keep other cooking pans elevated to protect the surface of the Cooking Pot from scratching.

Dehydrating Rack

The Dehydrating Rack allows for dehydrating multiple levels of food for homemade snacks, like jerky, chips, and dried fruits, without added sugar and preservatives. Easy to use, the wire racks can be used one at a time or you can stack them. For easier cleanup, you can line the wire racks with parchment paper.

Multi-Purpose Pan

Use the Multi-Purpose Pan for your baking needs, from making cakes or casseroles to getting the perfect pie or round pizza crust. The pan makes for easy cleaning and removal because of its nonstick ceramic coating.

How to Convert Conventional Grilling Recipes

With the Ninja® Foodi™ Smart XL Grill, you can easily recreate your favorite outdoor recipes inside! Like all recipes, if you are unsure how long a food should be cooked, knowing the desired internal cooking temperature and using the Smart Thermometer for your proteins will keep you at ease.

As you go through this book and make the recipes, take note of the flavors and combinations you like. You may find yourself adjusting the recipe to include more vegetables or more proteins based on your preferences. When you adjust conventional grilling recipes for the Ninja® Foodi™ Smart XL Grill, it is important to check your ingredients frequently to make sure you are not overcooking or undercooking food. For instance, if you increase the amount a recipe makes, you may need to increase the cook time for the greater quantity and to account for the opening and closing of the grill while checking on your food. If you adjust by using lower cooking temperatures, know that you may be lengthening the required cooking times. When using higher cooking temperatures, you may be shortening the cooking times. If you're unsure, check out the handy cheat sheet on page 249, which shows sample grill times, temperatures, tips, and flipping instructions for adjustments.

CLEANUP AND CARE

Cleaning your Foodi™ Grill is just as easy as setting it up for grilling. I'll admit, there are times I have been too tired to clean up after cooking dinner. The non-stick surface of the Foodi™ Grill saves me time and energy, as it doesn't require much scrubbing to get the grease or food debris off. The nonstick feature also means that since foods don't really stick to it, you don't have to worry much about rushing to clean it right after dinner.

Before you begin cleaning, first allow the Foodi™ Grill to cool down to room temperature and unplug the unit. Once cooled, remove the Grill Grate, Cooking Pot, Crisper Basket, or any other Foodi™ Grill accessories used during cooking, along with the Splatter Shield. Soak them in warm water mixed with dishwashing liquid. If additional scrubbing is necessary to remove any food residue or grease, use the Grill Brush that is included with your unit. The brush makes scrubbing in between the grooves easier without damaging the ceramic coating. The opposite end of the cleaning brush can be used to scrape off baked-on foods and sauces. Also, all of these parts are dishwasher safe.

Use a warm, damp cloth to wipe the outer unit, the display screen, and the inner unit, as the appliance should not be soaked in water. Be sure to clean in between the hinges of the hood, where grease may collect. The Splatter Shield may appear to have discoloration after many uses. If that's the case, it can be placed in boiling water for 10 minutes or soaked overnight with dish soap and then cleaned with the Grill Brush.

ABOUT THE RECIPES

With few exceptions, the recipes in this book will serve between 4 and 8 people using easily accessible ingredients you can find at your local supermarket. All cooking will be done only on your Ninja® Foodi™ Smart XL Grill, and most recipes use 10 or fewer ingredients (not including the staples of oil, water, salt, and black pepper) to make things even easier for you.

Labels

As appropriate, recipes use the following labels to accommodate certain dietary needs: **Dairy-Free**, **Gluten-Free**, **Nut-Free**, and **Vegan** or **Vegetarian**. To make things easy, you will also find labels for meals made with no more than **5 Ingredients** (aside from oil, water, salt, and pepper), meals that are made in **Under 30 Minutes**, and meals that are **Family Favorites** that you can be sure will leave all tummies happy.

Tips

Each recipe in this book has one, sometimes two, of the following tips:

Substitution tip: You may not always have all the ingredients on hand and don't have the time to run to the store, or you may need to accommodate an allergy or dietary restriction. This tip offers substitutions for recipe ingredients.

Variation tip: This tip includes ideas for changing up the dish's flavor profile.

Did you know? This tip provides interesting information about a particular ingredient used in the recipe.

Hack it: This tip makes the recipe even easier by providing shortcuts or making prep work more efficient.

I hope you find these tips and tricks to be useful as you navigate and learn how to use your Ninja® Foodi™ Smart XL Grill. Whether you are just learning to cook, finding new ways to eat more at home, or working more with less time to cook, I hope you find my recipes to be easy to follow, tasty, and fun to prepare.

Avocado Eggs, *page 24*

3

Breakfast & Brunch

Avocado Eggs

This quick and easy breakfast dish is protein-packed and also provides you with some of the healthiest "good fat" you can eat, leaving you full and satisfied. To remove the pit from an avocado, tap the heel of your knife blade into the pit and twist gently. Safety tip: You can also use a spoon to scoop out the pit.

5 INGREDIENTS / DAIRY-FREE / GLUTEN-FREE / NUT-FREE / UNDER 30 MINUTES / VEGETARIAN

PREP TIME: 10 minutes

COOK TIME: 10 minutes

ACCESSORIES: Grill Grate

VARIATION TIP: You can use egg whites if you are watching your cholesterol. If you want grill marks on the avocados, place them cut-side down on the grill for 5 minutes without the egg. Halfway through cooking or when the Foodi™ Grill says to flip, flip the avocados, add the cracked egg, and cook for the remaining 5 minutes.

4 ripe avocados, divided

3 tablespoons extra-virgin olive oil

1 teaspoon salt

½ teaspoon freshly ground black pepper

8 small eggs

Hot sauce or salsa, for garnish (optional)

1. Insert the Grill Grate and close the hood. Select GRILL, set the temperature to HI, and set the time to 10 minutes. Select START/STOP to begin preheating.

2. While the unit is preheating, cut the avocados in half lengthwise and remove the pits, but leave the skin on. You may need to scoop out some of the green flesh so the egg fits once added. Set the extra flesh aside to use as an additional topping later.

3. In a small bowl, whisk together the olive oil, salt, and pepper. Brush the seasoned olive oil on the flesh of the avocados. Then, crack an egg into the center of each avocado half.

4. When the unit beeps to signify it has preheated, place the avocados on the grill, egg-side up. Close the hood and grill for 10 minutes.

5. Cooking is complete when the egg whites are firm. Remove the avocados from the grill. Garnish with the reserved avocado and top with your favorite hot sauce or salsa, if desired.

Blueberry Dump Cake

Blueberries are a tiny, powerful fruit. Having many health benefits for cardiovascular and cognitive function, blueberries are also rich in antioxidants. As an added bonus, baking this dump cake will make the kitchen smell amazing! You'll enjoy the rich, sweet, blueberry taste with a buttery crumble on top. It's one of the easiest things to bake in your grill.

5 INGREDIENTS / NUT-FREE / VEGETARIAN

PREP TIME: 10 minutes

COOK TIME: 25 minutes

ACCESSORIES: Cooking Pot

VARIATION TIP: Want to change up the flavor? Use a lemon cake mix to bring some tartness to the blueberries, or switch out the blueberries with some fresh sliced strawberries. If fresh fruits are not in season, you can also use canned pie filling.

3 cups fresh blueberries

½ cup granulated sugar

1 (16-ounce) box yellow cake mix

8 tablespoons (1 stick) unsalted butter, melted

1. Select BAKE, set the temperature to 300°F, and set the time to 25 minutes. Select START/STOP to begin preheating.

2. While the unit is preheating, wash and pat dry the blueberries. Then place them and the sugar into the Cooking Pot and mix to coat the fruit with the sugar.

3. In a large bowl, mix together the cake mix and melted butter. Stir until the cake mix is no longer a powder but crumbly like a streusel. Cover the blueberry-sugar mixture with the cake crumble.

4. When the unit beeps to signify it has preheated, place the Cooking Pot in the unit. Close the hood and bake for 25 minutes.

5. Baking is complete when the fresh blueberries have bubbled and the cake crumble is golden brown. Serve.

Bread Pudding

This bread pudding is a comforting dish that you can assemble the night before. When you wake up, you'll have an easy breakfast that is ready to place on the grill. This is an easy recipe that is great when you aren't sure what to do with that loaf of bread that's going stale, so nothing goes to waste.

NUT-FREE / VEGETARIAN

PREP TIME: 10 minutes, plus 30 minutes to chill

COOK TIME: 30 minutes

ACCESSORIES: Grill Grate / Cooking Pot

SUBSTITUTION TIP: Instead of French bread, you can use a loaf of Texas toast or even plain white bread. It's best to use stale bread, as it doesn't have a lot of moisture. If you have only fresh bread available, dry it out by placing the cubed bread in the Cooking Pot using the Grill function for 10 minutes, then let the bread cool down to room temperature before preparing the recipe.

1 loaf (about 1 pound) day-old French bread, cut into 1-inch cubes

3 large eggs

4 tablespoons (½ stick) unsalted butter, melted

1 cup milk

¾ cup heavy (whipping) cream, divided

2 cups granulated sugar, divided

1 tablespoon cinnamon

1 teaspoon vanilla extract

8 ounces cream cheese, at room temperature

1. Line the inside bottom and sides of the Cooking Pot with aluminum foil. This will wrap the bread pudding, so make sure it fits the sides of the Cooking Pot.

2. Place the bread cubes in the Cooking Pot.

3. In a large bowl, whisk together the eggs, melted butter, milk, ½ cup of heavy cream, 1 cup of sugar, cinnamon, and vanilla. Evenly pour the mixture over the bread cubes. Place another foil layer on top of the bread cubes, then fold over all the foil ends to seal all around. Place the Cooking Pot in the refrigerator for at least 30 minutes, or overnight, for the bread to absorb the liquid.

4. Insert the Grill Grate and close the hood. Select GRILL, set the temperature to HI, and set the time to 30 minutes. Select START/STOP to begin preheating.

5. While the unit is preheating, prepare your frosting. In a large bowl, whisk together the cream cheese, remaining 1 cup of sugar, and remaining ¼ cup of heavy cream until smooth. Set aside.

6. When the unit beeps to signify it has preheated, place the Cooking Pot with the foil-wrapped bread pudding on top of the Grill Grate. Close the hood and cook for 30 minutes.

7. When cooking is complete, remove the pot from the grill. Use grill mitts to carefully open up the top foil lining. Drizzle the frosting over the bread pudding. Allow the bread pudding to cool before serving.

Brie and Apple Tart

SERVES 4

Soft, dreamy, and oh-so creamy! This is an easy dish that impresses all and comes together in a snap. Cut into the flaky crust and watch the cheese ooze out. Brie paired with sugared apples satisfies both sweet and savory cravings.

NUT-FREE / UNDER 30 MINUTES / VEGETARIAN

PREP TIME: 10 minutes

COOK TIME: 10 minutes

ACCESSORIES: Grill Grate

HACK IT: Use the top of the Brie cheese box to make an outline in the center of your pastry dough, so you'll know where to place the apple filling.

SUBSTITUTION TIP: Your favorite jam can be used in place of the homemade apple filling.

1 sheet ready-to-bake puff pastry (thawed, if frozen)

1 small apple, cored and thinly sliced

3 tablespoons honey

1 teaspoon light brown sugar, packed

1 (8-ounce) round Brie cheese

2 tablespoons unsalted butter, melted

1. Insert the Grill Grate and close the hood. Select GRILL, set the temperature to LO, and set the time to 10 minutes. Select START/STOP to begin preheating.

2. While the unit is preheating, unroll the pastry dough on a flat surface. Place the apple slices in the center of the dough. Drizzle the honey over the apples and sprinkle the brown sugar on top. Unwrap the Brie and place it on top of the apple slices. Fold the ends of the pastry around the Brie, similar to wrapping up a package, making sure to fully enclose the Brie and apples. Using a basting brush, brush the pastry all over with the melted butter.

3. When the unit beeps to signify it has preheated, place the pastry on the grill. Close the hood and grill for 10 minutes.

4. When cooking is complete, the pastry will be a nice golden brown. The Brie may leak out while cooking, and this is okay. The filling will be hot, so be sure to let it cool for a few minutes before serving.

Breakfast Chilaquiles

If you like enchiladas, you're going to love chilaquiles! It is a Mexican dish made with fried tortillas covered in salsa and topped with cheese and eggs, making it an easy and fast breakfast. There is less work in chilaquiles than in making enchiladas—no rolling necessary—and you can put those leftover tortilla chips to good use. This is one of my favorite dishes to make because it all comes together in less than 30 minutes.

GLUTEN-FREE / NUT-FREE / UNDER 30 MINUTES / VEGETARIAN

PREP TIME: 10 minutes

COOK TIME: 15 minutes

ACCESSORIES: Cooking Pot

SUBSTITUTION TIP: Don't have queso fresco? Use feta crumbles or cotija cheese. There is no wrong way to eat this dish. You can also use red onion, other kinds of shredded cheese, and thinly sliced radishes, or fry up your own corn tortillas at home in place of the chips.

4 cups tortilla chips (40 to 50 chips)

1 (10- to 14-ounce) can red chile sauce or enchilada sauce

6 large eggs

¼ cup diced onion, for garnish

½ cup crumbled queso fresco, for garnish

Chopped fresh cilantro, for garnish

1. Select GRILL, set the temperature to HI, and set the time to 15 minutes. Select START/STOP to begin preheating.

2. While the unit is preheating, add the tortilla chips to the Cooking Pot and pour the red chile sauce over them.

3. When the unit beeps to signify it has preheated, place the Cooking Pot in the unit. Crack the eggs, one at a time, over the tortilla chips, making sure they're evenly spread out. Close the hood and cook for 15 minutes.

4. Cooking is complete when the egg whites are firm with a runny yellow center. Garnish with the onion, queso fresco, and fresh cilantro, and serve.

Chorizo Sausage and Eggs

Chorizo is a spicy and fatty sausage popular in Mexico. It gets a lot of its flavor from red chiles and spices. You can find it in the sausage or meats section at the grocery store. Mexican chorizo links sometimes have an inedible casing that must be removed prior to cooking. This meal is easy to prepare, and you can have breakfast ready in under 30 minutes.

5 INGREDIENTS / GLUTEN-FREE / NUT-FREE / UNDER 30 MINUTES

PREP TIME: 10 minutes

COOK TIME: 20 minutes

ACCESSORIES: Cooking Pot

VARIATION TIP: If you prefer your eggs not so runny, you can pour scrambled eggs on top instead of having sunny-side-up eggs. Once cooking is done, stir the eggs.

½ **onion, diced**

2 **pounds chorizo, casings removed if using links**

6 **large eggs**

1 **large tomato, diced**

Chopped fresh cilantro, for garnish

1. Insert the Cooking Pot and close the hood. Select GRILL, set the temperature to HI, and set the time to 20 minutes. Select START/STOP to begin preheating.

2. When the unit beeps to signify it has preheated, place the onion in the pot. Then place the chorizo on top of the onion. Use a wooden spoon or silicone spatula to break the sausage apart into bite-size pieces. Close the hood and cook for 15 minutes.

3. After 15 minutes, open the hood and stir the sausage and onion. Crack the eggs on top of the mixture and add the diced tomato. Close the hood and cook for 5 minutes more.

4. When cooking is complete, garnish with the cilantro and serve. You can also serve with your favorite flour or corn tortillas for breakfast tacos.

Cinnamon Sugar Roll-Ups

SERVES 4

This is a simple recipe made with only four ingredients. It goes great with coffee or tea and is perfect for brunch. Puff pastry has become a new freezer staple in my house, allowing me to whip up a quick breakfast treat that is sweet, like these cinnamon sugar roll-ups. You can also make your roll-ups savory by filling them with spinach and cheese or making them into mini turnovers.

5 INGREDIENTS / FAMILY FAVORITE / NUT-FREE / UNDER 30 MINUTES / VEGETARIAN

PREP TIME: 5 minutes

COOK TIME: 10 minutes

ACCESSORIES: Grill Grate

VARIATION TIP: Along with the cinnamon-and-sugar coating, spread a little cream cheese on the pastry before adding the cinnamon sugar. And if you don't have pastry dough on hand, you can flatten and roll out white bread, similar to Cream Cheese–Stuffed French Toast (page 37).

1 sheet frozen puff pastry, thawed

3 tablespoons cinnamon

5 tablespoons granulated sugar

2 tablespoons unsalted butter, melted, divided

1. Insert the Grill Grate and close the hood. Select GRILL, set the temperature to LO, and set the time to 10 minutes. Select START/STOP to begin preheating.

2. While the unit is preheating, unroll the pastry dough on a flat surface. In a small bowl, combine the cinnamon and the sugar. Brush 1 tablespoon of butter over the surface of the pastry. Then sprinkle on the cinnamon sugar evenly.

3. Carefully roll the pastry into a log. Using a sharp knife, cut the log into 1- to 2-inch slices. Lightly brush the top and bottom of the roll-ups with the remaining 1 tablespoon of butter.

4. When the unit beeps to signify it has preheated, place the roll-ups on the Grill Grate. Close the hood and grill for 5 minutes.

5. After 5 minutes, open the hood and flip the roll-ups. Close the hood and cook for 5 minutes more.

6. When cooking is complete, the roll-ups will be a nice golden brown. Serve.

Country-Fried Steak and Eggs

Country-fried steak and eggs is an iconic breakfast meal for good reason. It's a hearty dish that I cook when I need something that will last me until dinnertime. The crispy, crunchy coating that is usually deep-fried is made healthier in this recipe by cooking it on the Foodi™ Grill.

NUT-FREE / UNDER 30 MINUTES

PREP TIME: 10 minutes

COOK TIME: 16 minutes

ACCESSORIES: Grill Grate / Cooking Pot

HACK IT: If you like some spice or want a kick in your homemade gravy, add 1 teaspoon of your favorite hot sauce. Make this meal a filling dinner by serving it alongside some Green Beans with Sun-Dried Tomatoes and Feta (page 181) and mashed potatoes.

For the country-fried steak

1 cup milk

2 large eggs

2 cups all-purpose flour

2 teaspoons salt

1 teaspoon freshly ground black pepper

1 teaspoon garlic powder

1 teaspoon onion powder

¼ teaspoon cayenne pepper

¾ teaspoon paprika

4 (8-ounce) cube or round steaks

For the eggs and gravy

4 to 8 large eggs

4 tablespoons (½ stick) unsalted butter

4 tablespoons all-purpose flour

½ cup heavy (whipping) cream

¼ teaspoon salt

¼ teaspoon freshly ground black pepper

To make the country-fried steak

1. Create an assembly line with 3 shallow dishes. In the first dish, whisk together the milk and eggs. In the second dish, combine the flour, salt, black pepper, garlic powder, onion powder, cayenne pepper, and paprika. Place a steak in the flour mixture to coat both sides, then dip it into the egg mixture to coat both sides. Dip the steak back in the flour mixture, coating both sides. Place the coated steaks in the third shallow dish.

2. Insert the Grill Grate and close the hood. Select GRILL, set the temperature to HI, and set the time to 6 minutes. Select START/STOP to begin preheating.

3. When the unit beeps to signify it has preheated, place all 4 steaks on the Grill Grate. Close the hood and cook for 3 minutes.

CONTINUED ▶

4. After 3 minutes, open the hood and flip the steaks. Close the hood and cook for 3 minutes more.

5. When grilling is complete, transfer the steaks to a plate. Using grill mitts, remove the Grill Grate from the unit, leaving any excess fat drippings from the Grill Grate in the Cooking Pot.

To make the eggs and gravy

6. Select AIR CRISP, set the temperature to 400°F, and set the time to 10 minutes. Select START/STOP and then press the PREHEAT button to skip preheating. Crack the eggs in the Cooking Pot. Close the hood and cook for 5 minutes, until the egg whites are opaque and firm. Remove the eggs from the pot.

7. Place the butter and flour in the Cooking Pot with the remaining fat drippings. Stir with a wooden spoon or silicone whisk until the butter has melted. Pour in the heavy cream and add the salt and pepper. Stir until completely mixed.

8. Close the hood and cook for 3 minutes. After 3 minutes, open the hood, stir the gravy, then close the hood to cook for 2 minutes more.

9. When cooking is complete, stir the gravy again and let it sit until you're ready to serve. To serve, pour the gravy over the country-fried steaks next to the eggs.

Egg and Bacon Nests

If you are limiting your carbohydrate intake, or if you're looking for a portable breakfast option, these are a good way to enjoy breakfast on the go or bring a new variation to egg bites. You can store these egg and bacon nests in a resealable bag in the refrigerator for an easy, low-carb, grab-and-go snack.

5 INGREDIENTS / DAIRY-FREE / GLUTEN-FREE / NUT-FREE

PREP TIME: 10 minutes

COOK TIME: 30 minutes

ACCESSORIES: Grill Grate

HACK IT: Silicone muffin tins work best—they are easier to clean up and make for a better nonstick surface. If you want a variety of flavors, fill each muffin cup with different veggies, like bell peppers, broccoli, or diced tomatoes.

3 tablespoons avocado oil

12 slices bacon

12 eggs

Salt

Freshly ground black pepper

1. Insert the Grill Grate and close the hood. Select GRILL, set the temperature to HI, and set the time to 30 minutes. Select START/STOP to begin preheating.

2. While the unit is preheating, brush the avocado oil in the bottom and on the sides of two 6-cup muffin tins. Wrap a bacon slice around the inside of each muffin cup, then crack an egg into each cup. Season to taste with salt and pepper.

3. When the unit beeps to signify it has preheated, place one muffin tin in the center of the Grill Grate. Close the hood and grill for 15 minutes.

4. After 15 minutes, remove the muffin tin. Place the second muffin tin in the center of the Grill Grate, close the hood, and grill for 15 minutes.

5. Serve immediately or let cool and store in resealable bags in the refrigerator for up to 4 days.

Cream Cheese–Stuffed French Toast

This French toast stuffed with cream cheese is easier to make than pancakes! One of the best things about French toast is how easy it is to customize it to your liking. Switch up the toppings by adding your favorite fresh fruits, powdered sugar, and maple syrup, or fill it with jam instead of cream cheese. You can even replace the white bread with whole wheat or cinnamon-raisin bread.

NUT-FREE / UNDER 30 MINUTES

PREP TIME: 10 minutes

COOK TIME: 6 minutes

ACCESSORIES: Grill Grate

SUBSTITUTION TIP: If whipped cream cheese is not available, you can use an 8-ounce package of cream cheese at room temperature, mixed with 1 tablespoon vanilla extract (or any other flavoring extract, like strawberry syrup) and ⅓ cup powdered sugar.

- 2 large eggs
- 1 cup milk
- 1 teaspoon cinnamon
- 1 teaspoon light brown sugar, packed
- 1 teaspoon vanilla extract
- 1 (8-ounce) package whipped cream cheese (flavored or plain)
- 12 slices white bread

1. Insert the Grill Grate and close the hood. Select GRILL, set the temperature to HI, and set the time to 6 minutes. Select START/STOP to begin preheating.

2. While the unit is preheating, in a small bowl, whisk together the eggs, milk, cinnamon, brown sugar, and vanilla.

3. Spread a thick layer of cream cheese on one side of 6 bread slices. Top each with the remaining 6 bread slices. Dip the sandwich into the egg mixture, making sure to coat both sides completely.

4. When the unit beeps to signify it has preheated, place the French toast sandwiches on the Grill Grate. Close the hood and grill for 3 minutes.

5. After 3 minutes, open the hood and flip the French toast. Close the hood and continue cooking for 3 minutes more.

6. When cooking is complete, remove the French toast from the grill and serve.

Fluffy Pancake Sheet

SERVES 4

This take on traditional pancakes means you no longer have to worry about timing them just right when flipping to get perfect, golden pancakes. Let the Foodi™ Grill do all of the work for you! Make this fluffy pancake sheet, cut it up into squares, and let everyone choose their favorite toppings. You can even make it a pancake bar with a toppings station.

5 INGREDIENTS / FAMILY FAVORITE / NUT-FREE / UNDER 30 MINUTES / VEGETARIAN

PREP TIME: 5 minutes

COOK TIME: 12 minutes

ACCESSORIES: Cooking Pot

VARIATION TIP: Top the pancake sheet with fresh fruit, like strawberries, blueberries, or bananas, during the last 5 minutes of baking. Sprinkle on some powdered sugar and serve with additional fresh fruit and whipped cream.

3 cups pancake mix	Nonstick cooking spray
1½ cups milk	Unsalted butter, for topping
2 eggs	Maple syrup, for topping

1. Insert the Cooking Pot and close the hood. Select BAKE, set the temperature to 350ºF, and set the time to 12 minutes. Select START/STOP to begin preheating.

2. While the unit is preheating, in a large bowl, whisk together the pancake mix, milk, and eggs.

3. When the unit beeps to signify it has preheated, spray the Cooking Pot with cooking spray. Pour the batter into the pot. Close the hood and cook for 12 minutes.

4. When cooking is complete, cut the pancake into squares. Top with the butter and maple syrup and serve.

Everything Bagel Breakfast Bake

Everything-bagel seasoning is a blend of poppy seeds, sesame seeds, dried garlic, dried onion, and salt. You'll find that it brings a lively flavor to anything you put it on. But if you prefer a different or plain bagel breakfast bake, you can always use those, too. Similar to a bread pudding recipe, all these ingredients are combined for an easy casserole dish you can prepare the night before and have ready to bake the next morning.

NUT-FREE / VEGETARIAN

PREP TIME: 5 minutes, plus 25 minutes to rest

COOK TIME: 25 minutes

ACCESSORIES: Cooking Pot

VARIATION TIP: Make it like a bagel sandwich by adding pieces of cooked ham or bacon, eggs, or sausage, and swap out the cream cheese for your favorite cheese.

6 large eggs

2 cups milk

½ cup heavy (whipping) cream

4 everything bagels, cut into 1-inch cubes (or bagel flavor of choice)

2 cups cherry tomatoes

1 pound cream cheese, cut into cubes

1. In a large bowl, whisk together the eggs, milk, and heavy cream.

2. Add the bagel cubes to the egg mixture. Set aside to rest for 25 minutes.

3. After 25 minutes, insert the Cooking Pot and close the hood. Select BAKE, set the temperature to 375°F, and set the time to 25 minutes. Select START/STOP to begin preheating.

4. While the unit is preheating, slice the cherry tomatoes into thirds.

5. When the unit beeps to signify it has preheated, pour the bagel mixture into the Cooking Pot. Top with the sliced cherry tomatoes and evenly place the cream cheese cubes over the top. Close the hood and bake for 25 minutes.

6. When cooking is complete, remove the pot from the grill and serve.

Grilled Breakfast Burritos

This is a yummy breakfast that consists of bacon, hash browns, cheese, and all the fixings wrapped up in a grilled tortilla. Loaded with all this goodness, you'll be fully fueled to start your day. These also make a great meal prep dish, as you can freeze the assembled, uncooked burritos for up to 1 month. (Just leave out the sour cream and avocado until they're ready to serve.) These are even perfect for those dinners when you crave breakfast.

NUT-FREE / UNDER 30 MINUTES

PREP TIME: 5 minutes

COOK TIME: 15 minutes

ACCESSORIES: Cooking Pot / Grill Grate

SUBSTITUTION TIP: Instead of bacon, you can use deli meats, like ham, roasted turkey, or roast beef.

4 large eggs

12 slices bacon, cut into 1-inch pieces

1 cup frozen shredded hash browns

1 cup shredded Monterey Jack cheese

4 (10-inch) flour tortillas

2 tablespoons extra-virgin olive oil

4 tablespoons sour cream, for topping

1 avocado, pitted and diced, for topping

1. Insert the Cooking Pot and close the hood. Select AIR CRISP, set the temperature to 390°F, and set the time to 15 minutes. Select START/STOP to begin preheating.

2. While the unit is preheating, in a medium bowl, whisk the eggs. Add the bacon, frozen hash browns, and cheese to the eggs and stir to combine.

3. When the unit beeps to signify it has preheated, pour the egg mixture into the Cooking Pot. Close the hood and cook for 10 minutes.

4. While the eggs are cooking, place the tortillas on top of the Grill Grate.

5. After 10 minutes, open the hood and use a silicone spatula to scramble the eggs and ensure the bacon is cooked. Remove the pot from the unit. Top the center of each tortilla with the scrambled egg mixture. Roll one end of the tortilla over the eggs, fold in the sides, and finish rolling the tortilla. Brush the olive oil over the burritos and place them seam-side down on the Grill Grate. Place the Grill Grate into the unit. Close the hood and cook for the remaining 5 minutes.

6. When cooking is complete, transfer the burritos to plates. Top with the sour cream and avocado and serve.

Grilled Kielbasa and Pineapple Kebabs

SERVES 4

These sweet and savory kebabs are perfect any time of year and come together easily for a quick breakfast or snack. I remember having something similar in my childhood, except little smoked sausages were cooked in a crockpot for hours with pineapple juice and teriyaki sauce. These kebabs are bigger and cook in a fraction of the time.

5 INGREDIENTS / DAIRY-FREE / NUT-FREE

PREP TIME: 10 minutes, plus 10 minutes to marinate

COOK TIME: 12 minutes

ACCESSORIES: Grill Grate / Ninja® Foodi™ Grill Kebab Skewers

VARIATION TIP: Switch out the soy sauce and brown sugar for ½ cup of your favorite barbecue sauce mixed with 4 tablespoons pineapple juice from the pineapple can. If pineapples are in season, using fresh pineapple works great for the grill.

- ½ cup soy sauce
- ¼ cup light brown sugar, packed
- 2 (8-ounce) cans pineapple chunks, drained
- 2 (12-ounce) packages kielbasa sausages, cut into ½-inch slices

1. In a large bowl, mix together the soy sauce, brown sugar, and pineapple chunks until the sugar is dissolved. Add the sausage slices and set aside for 10 minutes.

2. Thread the kielbasa and pineapple onto 10 to 12 skewers, alternating meat and fruit. Set aside any glaze that remains in the bowl.

3. Insert the Grill Grate and close the hood. Select GRILL, set the temperature to HI, and set the time to 12 minutes. Select START/STOP to begin preheating.

4. When the unit beeps to signify it has preheated, place half of the skewers on the Grill Grate. Brush them with extra glaze. Close the hood and grill for 3 minutes.

5. After 3 minutes, open the hood and flip the skewers. Close the hood and cook for 3 minutes more. After a total of 6 minutes, remove the skewers. Repeat with the remaining skewers.

6. When cooking is complete, remove the skewers from the grill and serve.

Ham and Cheese Cups

MAKES 12 CUPS

Stand aside, bread bowls. I present to you these cups, where ham is the vessel that holds the meal together. The beauty about these easy breakfast cups is that you can fill them up with your favorite protein or cheese and top them off with veggies. If you like easy, on-the-go breakfasts and snacks, be sure to check out Egg and Bacon Nests (page 35), too.

5 INGREDIENTS / GLUTEN-FREE / NUT-FREE / UNDER 30 MINUTES

PREP TIME: 10 minutes

COOK TIME: 20 minutes

ACCESSORIES: Grill Grate

VARIATION TIP: You can also use any kind of deli or cooked meat in place of the ham.

12 large eggs

3 tablespoons avocado oil

12 slices deli ham

1 cup shredded cheese of choice

Salt

Freshly ground black pepper

1. Insert the Grill Grate and close the hood. Select GRILL, set the temperature to HI, and set the time to 20 minutes. Select START/STOP to begin preheating.

2. While the unit is preheating, in a large bowl, beat the eggs. Brush the avocado oil in the bottom and on the sides of two 6-cup muffin tins. Line each muffin cup with a slice of ham. Spoon the eggs evenly into each cup. Top with the shredded cheese and season with salt and pepper.

3. When the unit beeps to signify it has preheated, place one muffin tin on the Grill Grate. Close the hood and grill for 10 minutes.

4. After 10 minutes, open the hood and remove the muffin tin. Place the second muffin tin on the Grill Grate, close the hood, and cook for 10 minutes.

5. When cooking is complete, remove the cups from the tins and serve.

Mini Caprese Pizzas

Caprese salad is my all-time favorite. Something about the combination of tomatoes, basil, balsamic vinegar, and cheese make me crave it all the time. Pizzas are, likewise, delicious any time of day and feel especially decadent for breakfast! These mini caprese pizzas are sure to please, and their small size makes them easy to share, if you're feeling generous.

5 INGREDIENTS / NUT-FREE / UNDER 30 MINUTES / VEGETARIAN

PREP TIME: 10 minutes

COOK TIME: 10 minutes

ACCESSORIES: Grill Grate

HACK IT: Want to make perfect circles? Use a glass, small ramekin, or small bowl to cut out the mini pizza shape.

SUBSTITUTION TIP: If you do not have fresh mozzarella, using preshredded mozzarella works just fine.

1 (14-ounce) package refrigerated pizza dough

2 tablespoons extra-virgin olive oil

2 large tomatoes, thinly sliced

8 ounces fresh mozzarella cheese, cut into thin discs

12 fresh basil leaves

Balsamic vinegar, for drizzling or dipping

1. Insert the Grill Grate and close the hood. Select GRILL, set the temperature to MED, and set the time to 10 minutes. Select START/STOP to begin preheating.

2. While the unit is preheating, lay the pizza dough on a flat surface. Cut out 12 small round pizzas 1½ to 2 inches diameter each. Brush both sides of each dough round with the olive oil.

3. When the unit beeps to signify it has preheated, place the dough rounds on the Grill Grate, 4 across, in 3 rows. Close the hood and grill for 5 minutes.

4. After 5 minutes, open the hood and flip the rounds. Top each round with the tomato and cheese slices. Close the hood and cook for 5 minutes more.

5. When cooking is complete, remove the pizzas from the Grill Grate. Top each with the basil. When ready to serve, drizzle each pizza with the balsamic vinegar, or keep the vinegar on the side in a small bowl for dipping.

Pesto Egg Croissantwiches

Pesto has that yummy pine nut, garlic, and basil flavor mixed with Parmesan cheese; it goes great with eggs. You will want to get a taste of this sauce in every bite, so be generous when spreading! The pesto is also a great complement to the tasty and flaky croissant. If you don't want to use jarred pesto, make your own using the recipe in Herb and Pesto Stuffed Pork Loin (page 146).

5 INGREDIENTS / UNDER 30 MINUTES / VEGETARIAN

PREP TIME: 5 minutes

COOK TIME: 8 minutes

ACCESSORIES: Cooking Pot / Grill Grate

SUBSTITUTION TIP: If croissants are not available, butter up some regular white toast. You'll still be able to enjoy that buttery flavor.

4 large eggs

4 croissants

8 tablespoons pesto

1. Insert the Cooking Pot and close the hood. Select GRILL, set the temperature to HI, and set the time to 8 minutes. Select START/STOP to begin preheating.

2. While the unit is preheating, in a small bowl, whisk together the eggs.

3. When the unit beeps to signify it has preheated, pour the beaten eggs into the Cooking Pot. Close the hood and cook for 4 minutes.

4. While the eggs are cooking, split the croissants. Place the croissant halves on top of the Grill Grate.

5. After 4 minutes, open the hood and scramble the eggs with a spatula. Spoon the scrambled eggs onto the bottom halves of the croissants. Remove the Cooking Pot from the unit.

6. Insert the Grill Grate into the unit. Spoon 2 tablespoons of pesto on top of each egg-topped croissant, then top each sandwich with the croissant top. Close the hood and cook for 4 minutes.

7. When cooking is complete, the croissant crust should be toasted. Serve.

Spinach and Mushroom Florentine Hash

SERVES 4

Here is an easy, all-in-one dish loaded with eggs, cheese, spinach, and mushrooms on a bed of crispy hash browns. Frozen hash browns make this a quick meal and a staple for those weekday breakfasts or weekend brunches that need to be cooked to perfection in a short amount of time.

GLUTEN-FREE / NUT-FREE / UNDER 30 MINUTES / VEGETARIAN

PREP TIME: 5 minutes

COOK TIME: 15 minutes

ACCESSORIES: Cooking Pot

VARIATION TIP: You can make this hash with any of your favorite veggies or proteins. Change up the flavor by using different cheeses, too.

3 cups frozen shredded hash browns

5 eggs, divided

1 cup shredded cheese of choice

½ teaspoon garlic powder

8 ounces mushrooms, sliced

1 cup fresh spinach

1. Select AIR CRISP, set the temperature to 390°F, and set the time to 15 minutes. Select START/STOP to begin preheating.

2. While the unit is preheating, in a large bowl, combine the frozen hash browns, 2 eggs, and the shredded cheese. Transfer the mixture to the Cooking Pot, pressing it into the bottom of the pot in an even layer.

3. When the unit beeps to signify it has preheated, insert the Cooking Pot. Close the hood and cook for 10 minutes.

4. While the hash browns are cooking, in a medium bowl, whisk together the remaining 3 eggs and garlic powder. Stir in the mushrooms and spinach.

5. After 10 minutes, open the hood and pour the egg and veggie mixture on top of the hash brown bed. Close the hood and cook for 5 minutes more.

6. When cooking is complete, the eggs should be set. Serve with optional additional toppings, like sour cream, fresh sliced avocados, and your favorite hot sauce, if you like.

Stuffed Bell Peppers with Italian Maple-Glazed Sausage

Did you know that bell peppers are actually a fruit? They're not only tasty but versatile, too. You can eat them raw in salads and dips, grill them, broil them, and stuff them. In this recipe, the crunchy peppers pair well with the sweet and savory sausage, giving your usual breakfast routine a twist.

5 INGREDIENTS / DAIRY-FREE / GLUTEN-FREE / NUT-FREE

PREP TIME: 10 minutes

COOK TIME: 28 minutes

ACCESSORIES: Grill Grate / Cooking Pot

DID YOU KNOW? It is best to cook the sausage before stuffing it in the bell peppers. Adding raw sausage inside a bell pepper will result in a watery mess.

2 pounds ground Italian sausage or links

1 cup light brown sugar, packed

6 bell peppers (any color)

1 cup water

12 tablespoons (¾ cup) maple syrup, divided

1. Insert the Cooking Pot and close the hood. Select GRILL, set the temperature to HI, and set the time to 8 minutes. Select START/STOP to begin preheating.

2. While the unit is preheating, remove the sausage from the casings if using links.

3. When the unit beeps to signify it has preheated, place the sausage and brown sugar in the Cooking Pot. Use a wooden spoon or potato masher to break the sausage apart and mix it with the brown sugar. Close the hood and cook for 8 minutes.

4. While the sausage is cooking, cut the top off each bell pepper and remove the seeds. Then slice the bell peppers in half lengthwise.

5. When cooking is complete, spoon the sausage into each bell pepper cup. Add the water to the Cooking Pot. Place 6 bell pepper halves on the Grill Grate, and place the Grill Grate in the unit.

6. Select GRILL, set the temperature to HI, and set the time to 20 minutes. Select START/STOP and then press the PREHEAT button to skip preheating. Close the hood and cook for 5 minutes.

CONTINUED ▶

7. After 5 minutes, open the hood and drizzle 1 tablespoon of maple syrup in each bell pepper cup. Close the hood and cook 5 minutes more. After 5 minutes, remove the stuffed peppers and place the remaining 6 stuffed peppers on the Grill Grate. Repeat this step to cook.

8. When cooking is complete, remove the peppers from the grill and serve.

Supersized Family Pizza Omelet

SERVES 4

This combines my two favorite pastimes, omelets and pizza! Just like a traditional pizza, this is something you can customize to fit what you and your family like. Add more veggies or make it a "meatza" with more pepperoni, sausage, chicken, and bacon bits.

5 INGREDIENTS / GLUTEN-FREE / NUT-FREE / UNDER 30 MINUTES

PREP TIME: 5 minutes

COOK TIME: 10 minutes

ACCESSORIES: Grill Grate / Cooking Pot

VARIATION TIP: Stuff your omelet instead. When the egg sheet is done cooking, add your toppings to one half, fold over, and then place on top of the Grill Grate.

10 large eggs

1 tablespoon Italian seasoning

½ cup pizza or marinara sauce

1 cup shredded mozzarella cheese

2 ounces pepperoni slices (about 24 slices)

1. Insert the Cooking Pot and close the hood. Select GRILL, set the temperature to HI, and set the time to 10 minutes. Select START/STOP to begin preheating.

2. While the unit is preheating, in a medium bowl, whisk together the eggs and Italian seasoning.

3. When the unit beeps to signify it has preheated, pour the egg mixture into the Cooking Pot. Close the hood and cook for 5 minutes.

4. Place the Grill Grate next to the unit on top of the counter. After 5 minutes, open the hood and use a spatula to fold the egg sheet in half, then place it on top of the Grill Grate.

5. Place the Grill Grate into the unit. Top the omelet with the pizza sauce, mozzarella cheese, and pepperoni slices. Close the hood and cook for 5 minutes more.

6. When cooking is complete, the cheese will be melted. Remove the omelet from the grill and serve.

Goat Cheese Bruschetta with Tomatoes, *page 59*

4

Sides, Snacks & Appetizers

Avocado Egg Rolls

SERVES 4

Fans of avocados and egg rolls go crazy for this one! Inspired by a favorite restaurant I used to go to all the time, I can now make these at home for a fraction of the price. Plus, it's healthier on the grill, so it's a win-win. Enjoy these crispy, golden egg rolls with the cilantro dipping sauce from Carne Asada Tacos (page 111). If you want to make these vegan, try Nasoya egg roll wrappers.

DAIRY-FREE / FAMILY FAVORITE / NUT-FREE / UNDER 30 MINUTES / VEGETARIAN

PREP TIME: 10 minutes

COOK TIME: 10 minutes

ACCESSORIES: Grill Grate

VARIATION TIP: Want to add more crunch or texture to the filling? Add already-cooked bacon crumbles and make this a BAT (bacon, avocado, tomato) egg roll. Need more protein in your diet? Add some diced deli meat and make it a sandwich egg-roll-up. Of course, then the egg rolls are no longer vegetarian!

4 avocados, pitted and diced

½ white onion, diced

⅓ cup sun-dried tomatoes, chopped

1 (16-ounce) package egg roll wrappers (about 20 wrappers)

¼ cup water, for sealing

4 tablespoons avocado oil

1. Insert the Grill Grate and close the hood. Select GRILL, set the temperature to LO, and set the time to 10 minutes. Select START/STOP to begin preheating.

2. While the unit is preheating, place the diced avocado in a large bowl. Add the onion and sun-dried tomatoes and gently fold together, being careful to not mash the avocado.

3. Place an egg roll wrapper on a flat surface with a corner facing you (like a diamond). Add 2 to 3 tablespoons of the filling in the center of the wrapper. The amount should be about 2½ inches wide. Gently lift the bottom corner of the wrapper over the filling, fold in the sides, and roll away from you to close. Dip your finger into the water and run it over the top corner of the wrapper to seal it. Continue filling, folding, and sealing the rest of the egg rolls.

4. When the unit beeps to signify it has preheated, brush the avocado oil on all sides of the egg rolls. Place the egg rolls on the Grill Grate, seam-side down. Close the hood and grill for 5 minutes.

5. After 5 minutes, open the hood and flip the egg rolls. Give them another brush of avocado oil. Close the hood and cook for 5 minutes more.

6. When cooking is complete, the wrappers will be golden brown. Remove from the grill and serve.

Bacon-Wrapped Onion Rings and Spicy Aioli

SERVES 4

Onion rings are a favorite of many—me included—but have you ever tried them wrapped in bacon? These make a filling appetizer, a quick snack, or a fun way to dress up your burger. Dip these in the spicy aioli or your favorite barbecue sauce.

DAIRY-FREE / FAMILY FAVORITE / GLUTEN-FREE / NUT-FREE / UNDER 30 MINUTES

PREP TIME: 10 minutes

COOK TIME: 10 minutes

ACCESSORIES: Grill Grate

DID YOU KNOW? Do not use thick-cut bacon, as it will require longer cooking time and also makes it harder to ensure the bacon cooks evenly.

HACK IT: Soak the onion rings in your favorite barbecue sauce for 15 minutes and then wrap them with bacon. This can get a little messy, but you'll add a nice glaze and tons of flavor to your onion rings.

For the onion rings
3 large white onions

2 (1-pound) packages thin-sliced bacon

For the spicy garlic aioli sauce
1 cup mayonnaise

¼ teaspoon garlic powder

1 tablespoon sriracha

1 teaspoon freshly squeezed lemon juice

To make the onion rings

1. Insert the Grill Grate and close the hood. Select GRILL, set the temperature to MED, and set the time to 10 minutes. Select START/STOP to begin preheating.

2. While the unit is preheating, cut both ends off the onions. Slice each onion crosswise into thirds and peel off the outer layer of onion skin. Separate the onion rings, keeping two onion layers together to have a stable and firm ring. Wrap each onion ring pair with a slice of bacon. The bacon should slightly overlap itself as you wrap it all the way around the onion ring. Larger rings may need 2 slices of bacon.

3. When the unit beeps to signify it has preheated, place the onion rings on the Grill Grate. Close the hood and grill for 10 minutes. Flipping is not necessary.

4. When cooking is complete, the bacon will be cooked through and starting to crisp. If you prefer the bacon crispier or even close to charred, continue cooking to your liking.

To make the spicy garlic aioli sauce

5. While the onion rings are cooking, in a small bowl, whisk together the mayonnaise, garlic powder, sriracha, and lemon juice. Use more or less sriracha depending on your preferred spice level. Serve with the bacon onion rings.

Candied Brussels Sprouts with Bacon

SERVES 4

This is a fun way to eat your veggies. These Brussels sprouts are an easy side that pairs well with most chicken, steak, and pork dishes. Brussels sprouts weren't a favorite of mine until I discovered this recipe. When you add bacon, you bring out saltiness, and when you add brown sugar and maple syrup, you bring out sweetness for a delicious combo.

5 INGREDIENTS / DAIRY-FREE / GLUTEN-FREE / NUT-FREE / UNDER 30 MINUTES

PREP TIME: 5 minutes

COOK TIME: 20 minutes

ACCESSORIES: Crisper Basket / Cooking Pot

HACK IT: Add the avocado oil to the Brussels sprouts bag and shake to coat. One fewer bowl to wash! If you prefer your Brussels sprouts crispier, you can slice them in half first.

VARIATION TIP: Want to add some variety or don't want it too sweet? Use balsamic vinegar instead of maple syrup.

2 pounds Brussels sprouts, ends trimmed

2 tablespoons avocado oil

¼ cup light brown sugar, packed

8 ounces thick-cut bacon, cut into bite-size pieces

3 tablespoons maple syrup

1. Insert the Crisper Basket and close the hood. Select AIR CRISP, set the temperature to 390°F, and set the time to 20 minutes. Select START/STOP to begin preheating.

2. While the unit is preheating, put the Brussels sprouts in a large bowl, drizzle with the avocado oil, and toss to coat.

3. In a medium bowl, rub the brown sugar into the bacon pieces.

4. When the unit beeps to signify it has preheated, place the Brussels sprouts in the Crisper Basket and sprinkle the bacon bits on top. Close the hood and cook for 10 minutes.

5. After 10 minutes, open the hood and flip the Brussels sprouts. Drizzle the maple syrup over the sprouts. Close the hood and cook for 10 minutes more. If you like, you can turn the Brussels sprouts a second time when there are 5 minutes of cooking time remaining.

6. When cooking is complete, remove the Brussels sprouts from the grill and serve. If you want your Brussels sprouts crispier and more browned, continue cooking to your liking.

Cheesy Garlic Bread

SERVES 4

Complete your meal with this cheesy garlic bread. Serve this up with your favorite pasta dish or soup, or pair it with a rack of ribs. If you want something a little more substantial, make it a meal by dipping this cheesy garlic bread in marinara sauce for impromptu pizzas.

FAMILY FAVORITE / NUT-FREE / UNDER 30 MINUTES / VEGETARIAN

PREP TIME: 10 minutes

COOK TIME: 8 minutes

ACCESSORIES: Grill Grate

SUBSTITUTION TIP: If you do not have minced garlic available, use 4 teaspoons of garlic powder instead.

VARIATION TIP: Vary the cheese in your garlic bread. Choose two different cheeses, using 1 cup of each.

1 loaf (about 1 pound) French bread

8 tablespoons (1 stick) unsalted butter, at room temperature

1 tablespoon minced garlic

1 teaspoon garlic powder

1½ cups shredded mozzarella cheese

½ cup shredded Colby Jack cheese

1 teaspoon dried parsley

1. Insert the Grill Grate and close the hood. Select GRILL, set the temperature to MED, and set the time to 8 minutes. Select START/STOP to begin preheating.

2. While the unit is preheating, cut the French bread in half lengthwise. In a small bowl, mix together the butter, garlic, and garlic powder until well combined. Spread the garlic butter on both bread halves. Top each half with the mozzarella and Colby Jack cheeses. Sprinkle the dried parsley on top.

3. When the unit beeps to signify it has preheated, place the cheese-topped bread on the Grill Grate. Close the hood and grill for 8 minutes.

4. When cooking is complete, the cheese will be melted and golden brown. Remove the bread from the grill and serve.

Creamy Artichoke Dip with Pita Chips

SERVES 4

You will be the new master dip maker with this easy, creamy artichoke dip. When you're not sure what to bring to the next gathering or serve as an appetizer, make this highly requested dip. The dip is best served warm. Then be prepared to make more, as it quickly disappears!

FAMILY FAVORITE /
NUT-FREE / UNDER
30 MINUTES / VEGETARIAN

PREP TIME: 10 minutes

COOK TIME: 15 minutes

ACCESSORIES: Cooking
Pot / Grill Grate

SUBSTITUTION TIP: If you do not have mini pitas, you can use regular pitas sliced into 8 wedges. Many local supermarkets sell lavash bread that can also be used in place of pitas. Or crisp up a baguette, as I do in Goat Cheese Bruschetta with Tomatoes (page 59).

HACK IT: Prep this dip ahead of time and store it in the refrigerator. When your guests arrive, place it on the Foodi™ Grill, and you can easily serve it in 15 minutes!

8 ounces cream cheese,
  at room temperature

1 (13-ounce) can marinated
  artichoke quarters, drained
  and coarsely chopped

½ cup sour cream

½ cup grated Parmesan
  cheese

¼ teaspoon garlic powder

2 cups shredded mozzarella

1 (6-ounce) package mini
  pita bread rounds

Extra-virgin olive oil

Chopped fresh chives,
  for garnish

1. Insert the Cooking Pot and close the hood. Select GRILL, set the temperature to MED, and set the time to 15 minutes. Select START/STOP to begin preheating.

2. While the unit is preheating, place the cream cheese, artichokes, sour cream, Parmesan cheese, garlic powder, and mozzarella cheese in a 9-by-5-inch loaf pan. Stir until well combined.

3. When the unit beeps to signify it has preheated, place the pan in the Cooking Pot. Close the hood and cook for 5 minutes.

4. After 5 minutes, open the hood and stir the dip with a wooden spoon, holding onto the loaf pan with grill mitts. Close the hood and cook for 7 minutes more.

5. Meanwhile, place the Grill Grate next to the Foodi™ Grill. Put the pita rounds in a large bowl and drizzle with the olive oil. Toss to coat. Place the pita rounds on the Grill Grate.

6. After 7 minutes, open the hood. Remove the pan of artichoke dip from the Cooking Pot. Place the Grill Grate into the unit. Close the hood and cook for the remaining 3 minutes.

7. Cooking is complete when the pita chips are warm and crispy. Garnish the dip with the fresh chives and serve.

Garlic Fries

I live in the Garlic Capital of the World. Gilroy, California, is known for its garlic crop and hosts an annual festival that showcases all sorts of garlic products and specialty garlic foods. So it made sense to include a garlic fries recipe in honor of the wonderful aromatic.

5 INGREDIENTS / DAIRY-FREE / GLUTEN-FREE / NUT-FREE / VEGAN

PREP TIME: 10 minutes, plus 30 minutes to soak

COOK TIME: 20 minutes

ACCESSORIES: Crisper Basket / Cooking Pot

HACK IT: Short on time? Use frozen French fries and air-crisp them at 400°F for 20 to 25 minutes.

SUBSTITUTION TIP: Instead of fresh garlic, you can use 5 teaspoons jarred minced garlic or more to adjust for flavor. Or take these to the next level and add shredded Parmesan cheese to make these garlic fries fully loaded!

2 large Idaho or russet potatoes (1½ to 2 pounds)

1 head garlic (10 to 12 cloves)

4 tablespoons avocado oil, divided

1 teaspoon sea salt

Chopped fresh parsley, for garnish

1. Cut the potatoes into ¼-inch-thick slices. Place the slices in a large bowl and cover with cold water. Set aside for 30 minutes. This will ensure the potatoes cook well and crisp up perfectly. While the potatoes are soaking, mince the garlic cloves.

2. Drain the potatoes and pat dry using paper towels. In a large bowl, toss the potato slices with 2 tablespoons of avocado oil.

3. Insert the Cooking Pot and Crisper Basket and close the hood. Select AIR CRISP, set the temperature to 390°F, and set the time to 20 minutes. Select START/STOP to begin preheating.

4. While the unit is preheating, in a small bowl, combine the remaining 2 tablespoons of avocado oil with the minced garlic.

5. When the unit beeps to signify it has preheated, put the fries in the Crisper Basket. Close the hood and cook for 10 minutes.

6. After 10 minutes, open the hood and give the basket a shake to toss the fries. Close the hood and continue cooking for 5 minutes. Open the hood again and give the basket a shake. Close the hood and cook for 5 minutes more.

7. When cooking is complete, the fries will be crispy and golden brown. If you like them extra-crispy, continue cooking to your liking. Transfer the fries to a large bowl and drizzle with the garlic oil. Toss and season with the salt. Garnish with the parsley and serve.

Goat Cheese Bruschetta with Tomatoes

SERVES 4

Goat cheese, called chèvre *in French, is known for its soft, spreadable texture along with its tart and tangy flavor. Entertain your guests with this restaurant-quality appetizer. It is suggested that those who are lactose intolerant may be able to tolerate goat cheese better, as it has lower lactose content and may be easier to digest.*

NUT-FREE / UNDER 30 MINUTES / VEGETARIAN

PREP TIME: 15 minutes

COOK TIME: 8 minutes

ACCESSORIES: Grill Grate

VARIATION TIP: Want to add more sweetness? Use fresh slices of strawberries instead of cherry tomatoes to bring new flavors to your taste buds. Goat cheese can also be found in different flavors, such as garlic and herb butter, honey infused, or mixed with blueberries. Feel free to change it up!

8 ounces cherry tomatoes (about 35)

8 fresh basil leaves

1 tablespoon balsamic vinegar

1 (8-ounce) baguette

½ cup extra-virgin olive oil

2 tablespoons garlic powder

8 ounces goat cheese (unflavored)

1. Insert the Grill Grate and close the hood. Select GRILL, set the temperature to HI, and set the time to 8 minutes. Select START/STOP to begin preheating.

2. While the unit is preheating, quarter the cherry tomatoes. Slice the basil leaves into very thin ribbons. Place the tomatoes and basil in a medium bowl. Add the balsamic vinegar and toss to coat.

3. Slice the baguette into ½-inch slices. In a small bowl, whisk together the olive oil and garlic powder. Brush both sides of the baguette slices with the olive oil mixture.

4. When the unit beeps to signify it has preheated, place half the baguette slices on the Grill Grate in a single layer. Close the hood and cook for 4 minutes. After 4 minutes, remove the baguettes from the grill and set aside on a plate. Place the remaining slices on the Grill Grate. Close the hood and cook for 4 minutes.

5. When cooking is complete, spread a layer of goat cheese on the baguette slices. Top with the tomato-basil mixture and serve.

Grilled Blooming Onion

SERVES 4

No need to cry over this onion! These blooming onions resemble flowers, and you peel each onion "petal" off to enjoy every crunchy bite. Amaze your guests with this creation that makes it look and feel like you're dining out. Plus, feel less guilt knowing that it's grilled instead of fried.

NUT-FREE / UNDER 30 MINUTES / VEGETARIAN

PREP TIME: 10 minutes

COOK TIME: 12 minutes

ACCESSORIES: Grill Grate

HACK IT: Bigger is definitely better. Choose the largest onion you can find so it opens up nicely on its own.

VARIATION TIP: Watching your carbohydrate content? You can sub out the flour for a half-and-half combo of almond flour and pork "panko" (a bread crumb substitute made of finely ground pork rinds), which would also make this dish gluten-free (but not vegetarian).

2 large yellow onions

1 cup milk

2 large eggs

1 teaspoon paprika

1 teaspoon cayenne pepper

1 teaspoon garlic powder

1 teaspoon onion powder

2 cups all-purpose flour

Salt

Freshly ground black pepper

Nonstick cooking spray

1. Insert the Grill Grate and close the hood. Select GRILL, set the temperature to LO, and set the time to 12 minutes. Select START/STOP to begin preheating.

2. While the unit is preheating, cut off both ends of the onions, keeping the root end as intact as possible. Peel off the outer layer of skin. With the root facing up, begin cutting your petals: Starting from ¼ inch below the root end (do not cut through the root), cut downward to slit the onion into 4 equal sections, and then again in between each cut so there are 8 equal sections, and then again to make 16 petals. Turn the onion upside down so the root is now on the bottom, and the petals should begin to open.

3. In a large bowl, whisk together the milk and eggs. Carefully place the blooming onion in the mixture to soak.

4. In a separate large bowl, combine the paprika, cayenne pepper, garlic powder, onion powder, and flour. Season with salt and pepper. Transfer the blooming onion to the bowl with the seasonings. Using your hands, carefully sift some of the mixture into the cracks of the onion, making sure the petals are coated well. Shake off any excess.

5. When the unit beeps to signify it has preheated, generously spray the onion with cooking spray and place it, petals facing up, on the Grill Grate. Close the hood and grill for 10 minutes.

6. After 10 minutes, open the hood and check for crispiness and if the onion is browned to your liking. To continue cooking, generously spray the onion with more cooking spray. Close the hood and continue cooking for 2 minutes more, or until the onions have browned and crisped up to your desired doneness. Remove the onion from the grill and serve.

Queso Bomb

SERVES 6

This is an easy campfire recipe that that can now be enjoyed indoors. This one-pot dish is fast and is best served warm. It's a perfect game-day or party snack that's sure to please any crowd. You'll want to be sure that everyone has a bowl of their own, because no one will want to share.

**FAMILY FAVORITE /
GLUTEN-FREE / NUT-FREE /
UNDER 30 MINUTES**

PREP TIME: 5 minutes

COOK TIME: 15 minutes

ACCESSORIES: Cooking Pot

VARIATION TIP: Not into chips and dip? Serve this queso bomb as sausage and cheese burritos! Use the mixture to fill flour tortillas, add shredded lettuce, and top with sour cream and your favorite hot sauce.

1 (1-pound) block
  easy-melt cheese

1 pound ground country
  breakfast sausage
  (not links)

2 tablespoons minced garlic

2 cups shredded Mexican
  cheese blend or
  three-cheese blend

1 (10-ounce) can diced
  tomatoes with green chiles

1 (10- to 13-ounce) bag
  tortilla chips

1. Insert the Cooking Pot and close the hood. Select GRILL, set the temperature to MED, and set the time to 15 minutes. Select START/STOP to begin preheating.

2. While the unit is preheating, slice the cheese block into 3-inch sections.

3. When the unit beeps to signify it has preheated, place the sausage and garlic in the Cooking Pot. Using a wooden spoon or spatula, break the sausage apart. Close the hood and cook for 5 minutes.

4. After 5 minutes, open the hood and stir the sausage. Add the pieces of easy-melt cheese, then add the shredded cheese blend in an even layer. Pour the diced tomatoes and green chiles with their juices into the pot. Close the hood and cook for 5 minutes.

5. After 5 minutes, stir the sausage and cheese together. Close the hood and cook 5 minutes more.

6. When cooking is complete, the cheese will be fully melted. Serve warm with tortilla chips.

Jalapeño Poppers

SERVES 4

When selecting jalapeños, I look for ones that are shiny and smooth skinned, with no white freckles or lines on the pepper, as these indicate the stress and heat the pepper has experienced. Jalapeños have oils that may irritate your hands and eyes, so be careful when you are removing the seeds and membranes. Removing them diminishes the heat, so these poppers can be enjoyed by those who have a low spice tolerance. People tell me all the time, "I can't believe these aren't as spicy as I thought they would be!"

GLUTEN-FREE / NUT-FREE / UNDER 30 MINUTES

PREP TIME: 10 minutes

COOK TIME: 10 minutes

ACCESSORIES: Grill Grate

SUBSTITUTION TIP: If you are not into bacon, feel free to dress each jalapeño popper with Italian-style bread crumbs, or use your favorite chips instead—just smash them up to top these poppers. Try adding ranch or barbecue-flavored chips for a different flavor.

VARIATION TIP: Use your favorite store-bought spinach-artichoke dip instead of this cream cheese filling.

8 jalapeños

4 ounces cream cheese, at room temperature

¼ cup grated Parmesan cheese

¼ cup shredded cheddar cheese

½ teaspoon garlic powder

8 slices thin-cut bacon

1. Insert the Grill Grate and close the hood. Select GRILL, set the temperature to HI, and set the time to 10 minutes. Select START/STOP to begin preheating.

2. While the unit is preheating, slice the jalapeños in half lengthwise and scoop out the seeds and membranes.

3. In a small bowl, combine the cream cheese, Parmesan cheese, cheddar cheese, and garlic powder. Scoop the cheese mixture evenly into each jalapeño half.

4. Slice the bacon in half lengthwise so you have 16 strips. Wrap each jalapeño half with a bacon slice, starting from the bottom end and wrapping around until it reaches the top of the jalapeño.

5. When the unit beeps to signify it has preheated, place the jalapeños on the Grill Grate, filling-side up. Close the hood and grill for 10 minutes.

6. When cooking is complete, the bacon will be cooked and beginning to crisp. If you prefer your bacon crispier or charred, continue cooking to your liking. Remove the poppers from the grill and serve.

Maple Butter Corn Bread

SERVES 4

Corn bread goes well with all different kinds of grilled meats, such as a rack of ribs (page 148) smothered in barbecue sauce. This corn bread, with the added creamed corn and maple butter, brings the dish to a whole new level.

FAMILY FAVORITE / NUT-FREE / VEGETARIAN

PREP TIME: 15 minutes

COOK TIME: 40 minutes

ACCESSORIES: Cooking Pot

VARIATION TIP: Add a little heat to this corn bread by adding some sliced jalapeños to the batter. Be sure to remove the seeds and membranes. If you do not want to serve butter alongside the corn bread, add 1 tablespoon brown sugar to your corn bread mix for a slight hint of sweetness.

For the corn bread

1 cup all-purpose flour

1 cup yellow cornmeal

2 teaspoons baking powder

1 teaspoon salt

1¼ cups milk

⅓ cup canola oil

1 large egg

1 (14.75-ounce) can cream-style sweet corn

Cooking spray

For the maple butter

1 tablespoon light brown sugar, packed

1 tablespoon milk

8 tablespoons (1 stick) unsalted butter, at room temperature

1 tablespoon maple syrup

To make the corn bread

1. Insert the Cooking Pot and close the hood. Select BAKE, set the temperature to 350ºF, and set the time to 40 minutes. Select START/STOP to begin preheating.

2. While the unit is preheating, in a large bowl, combine the flour, cornmeal, baking powder, salt, milk, oil, egg, and sweet corn. Mix until just combined. Grease a 9-by-5-inch loaf pan with cooking spray and pour in the corn bread batter.

3. When the unit beeps to signify it has preheated, place the pan in the Cooking Pot. Close the hood and cook for 40 minutes. If using a metal loaf pan, check the corn bread after 30 minutes, as metal pans may cook faster than glass. Bake until golden brown and the mix is completely baked through.

4. When cooking is complete, the corn bread should be golden brown and a toothpick inserted into the center of the corn bread comes out clean. Remove the pan from the grill and set aside to cool.

CONTINUED ▶

Maple Butter Corn Bread continued

continued

To make the maple butter

5. In a small bowl, whisk together the brown sugar and milk until the sugar is dissolved. Add the butter and continue whisking. Add the maple syrup and continue whisking until fully combined.

6. Cut the corn bread into slices, top with the butter, and serve.

Mozzarella Sticks

SERVES 4

Who can resist that cheese pull? Making this family favorite from scratch is easier than you think. Plus, cooking it on the Foodi™ Grill ensures you can still get that perfect deep-fried crunchy coating texture with less mess and without having to worry about hot oil splattering. Mozzarella sticks are always a good party appetizer or a great after-school snack for the kids.

5 INGREDIENTS / FAMILY FAVORITE / NUT-FREE / VEGETARIAN

PREP TIME: 10 minutes, plus 30 minutes to freeze

COOK TIME: 8 minutes

ACCESSORIES: Grill Grate

HACK IT: If you are pressed for time and cannot freeze the coated mozzarella sticks, you can still grill them after immediately coating them. They may melt and ooze out of the coating somewhat, but they can be easily removed from the Grill Grate using a spatula. Freezing the sticks helps keep them intact. You can always store these in the freezer ahead of time and grill them when ready to eat.

2 large eggs

2 cups plain bread crumbs

2 tablespoons Italian seasoning

10 to 12 mozzarella cheese sticks

Marinara sauce, for dipping

1. In a large bowl, whisk the eggs. In a separate large bowl, combine the bread crumbs and Italian seasoning.

2. Dip each cheese stick in the egg and then dip it in the bread crumbs to evenly coat. Place the breaded mozzarella sticks on a baking sheet or flat tray, then freeze for 30 minutes.

3. Insert the Grill Grate and close the hood. Select GRILL, set the temperature to MED, and set the time to 8 minutes. Select START/STOP to begin preheating.

4. When the unit beeps to signify it has preheated, open the hood and place the mozzarella sticks on the Grill Grate. Close the hood and grill for 8 minutes.

5. When cooking is complete, the mozzarella sticks will be golden brown and crispy. If you prefer browner mozzarella sticks, continue cooking to your liking. Serve with the marinara sauce on the side.

Sweet Potato Fries with Honey-Butter Sauce

As their name implies, sweet potatoes can naturally add some sweetness to a meal, along with some color and added nutrients like beta-carotene. These sweet potato fries are perfect to pair with Blackened Chicken (page 91) or Rib Eye Steak with Rosemary Butter (page 126). You'll want to dip your fries in this honey butter, or let the butter melt over them right out of the Crisper Basket.

GLUTEN-FREE / NUT-FREE / UNDER 30 MINUTES / VEGETARIAN

PREP TIME: 10 minutes

COOK TIME: 20 minutes

ACCESSORIES: Crisper Basket

HACK IT: If you prefer crispier fries, you can skip using the Crisper Basket and lay the sweet potatoes in a single layer in the Cooking Pot. Just make sure they do not touch each other.

For the sweet potato fries

- **2 medium sweet potatoes, cut into ¼-inch-thick slices**
- **3 teaspoons avocado oil**
- **1 teaspoon salt**
- **½ teaspoon paprika**
- **½ teaspoon garlic powder**
- **¼ teaspoon freshly ground black pepper**

For the honey butter

- **1 tablespoon honey**
- **1 teaspoon powdered sugar**
- **8 tablespoons (1 stick) salted butter, at room temperature**

To make the sweet potato fries

1. Insert the Crisper Basket and close the hood. Select AIR CRISP, set the temperature to 400°F, and set the time to 20 minutes. Select START/STOP to begin preheating.

2. In a large bowl, drizzle the sweet potatoes with the avocado oil and toss to coat. In a small bowl, mix together the salt, paprika, garlic powder, and pepper. Sprinkle the seasoning over the sweet potatoes and toss gently to coat.

3. When the unit beeps to signify it has preheated, place the sweet potato fries in the Crisper Basket. Close the hood and cook for 10 minutes.

CONTINUED ▶

4. After 10 minutes, open the hood and shake the basket. Close the hood and cook for 5 minutes more. Open the hood again and shake the basket. If the fries are to your desired crispness, then remove them. If not, close the hood and cook up to 5 minutes more.

To make the honey butter

5. In a small bowl, whisk together the honey and powdered sugar until the sugar is dissolved. Add the butter and continue whisking. Serve alongside the fries.

One-Pot Nachos

In my kitchen, I am all about having fewer dishes to clean up, and these one-pot nachos fit this goal perfectly. I remember my aunt making a similar version of this nacho casserole, and it was a sure hit at family get-togethers. After making this so many different times and in so many different ways, I've learned there is no wrong way to make this easy dish. Make it your own and add all your favorite toppings.

GLUTEN-FREE / NUT-FREE / UNDER 30 MINUTES

PREP TIME: 5 minutes

COOK TIME: 10 minutes

ACCESSORIES: Cooking Pot

SUBSTITUTION TIP:
Watching calories and fat content? Swap out the full-fat dairy for low-fat or fat-free. Switch the ground beef with lean ground turkey or substitute the tortilla chips with sliced bell peppers.

---

1 pound ground beef

1 (1-ounce) packet taco seasoning mix

1 (16-ounce) can refried beans

1 (14.5-ounce) can diced tomatoes, drained

2 cups sour cream

3 cups shredded Mexican cheese blend

2 cups shredded iceberg lettuce

1 cup sliced black olives

Sliced scallions, both white and green parts, for garnish

1 (10- to 13-ounce) bag tortilla chips

1. Insert the Cooking Pot and close the hood. Select GRILL, set the temperature to MED, and set the time to 10 minutes. Select START/STOP to begin preheating.

2. When the unit beeps to signify it has preheated, place the ground beef in the Cooking Pot and sprinkle it with the taco seasoning. Using a wooden spoon or spatula, break apart the ground beef. Close the hood and cook for 5 minutes.

3. After 5 minutes, open the hood and stir the ground beef to mix a little more with the taco seasoning. Evenly spread the ground beef across the bottom of the pot. Add the refried beans in an even layer over the meat, then an even layer of the diced tomatoes. Close the hood and cook for 5 minutes more.

4. When cooking is complete, remove the Cooking Pot from the unit and place it on a heatproof surface. Add an even layer each of sour cream, shredded cheese, shredded lettuce, and olives on top. Garnish with scallions and serve with the tortilla chips.

Twice Air-Crisped Potatoes

These potatoes have a crispy skin with the perfect blend of creamy and buttery mash inside. Baked potatoes can be a little boring, but this extra-crispy version of the classic spud side is sure to please. It's the perfect complement to grilled chicken, pork chops, or a thick, juicy steak.

GLUTEN-FREE / NUT-FREE / VEGETARIAN

PREP TIME: 15 minutes

COOK TIME: 40 minutes

ACCESSORIES: Crisper Basket

VARIATION TIP: Add bacon bits on top and garnish with some fresh chives. Not into bacon? Mix in diced broccoli with the potato filling during the last 10 minutes of cooking.

4 medium Idaho or russet potatoes

Extra-virgin olive oil

Kosher salt

8 tablespoons (1 stick) unsalted butter, at room temperature

½ cup sour cream

1 cup shredded cheddar cheese

Freshly ground black pepper

1. Insert the Crisper Basket and close the hood. Select AIR CRISP, set the temperature to 400°F, and set the time to 40 minutes. Select START/STOP to begin preheating.

2. While the unit is preheating, rinse and scrub the potatoes. Poke each potato several times with a fork. Brush a generous amount of olive oil over the potatoes and season well with salt.

3. When the unit beeps to signify it has preheated, place the potatoes in the Crisper Basket. Close the hood and cook for 30 minutes.

4. After 30 minutes, open the hood and remove the potatoes. Place on a plate and set aside.

5. Slice the potatoes in half lengthwise. Use a fork to carefully scoop out the insides of the potatoes without damaging the skins. Put the potato flesh in a large bowl. Add the butter, sour cream, and cheddar cheese. Using a spatula, carefully fold the mixture until the butter melts. Scoop the filling into the potato skins. Season each potato half with salt and pepper.

6. Place the loaded potatoes back into the Crisper Basket. Close the hood and cook for 10 minutes more.

7. When cooking is complete, the potato skins will be crispy and the cheese will be melted and infused into the potatoes. Remove the potatoes from the grill and serve.

Salsa Verde Chicken Enchiladas, *page 98*

5
Poultry

Adobo Chicken

Adobo chicken is a popular Filipino dish that gets its flavors from soy sauce, vinegar, and garlic. Although it is typically cooked by braising the meat, I'm bringing this family favorite onto the Foodi™ Grill! Growing up, I watched my mom make her adobo chicken, and to this day, I've never seen her measure out her seasonings. When I asked if she could help me recreate this dish, she told me, "You add a little bit of this and a little bit of that!" So, while I have given you exact measurements, don't let it stop you. Grab all the seasonings you can in your cabinet and go wild.

DAIRY-FREE / NUT-FREE

PREP TIME: 10 minutes, plus 1 hour to marinate

COOK TIME: 15 minutes

ACCESSORIES: Grill Grate

VARIATION TIP: Not into drumsticks? Use chicken thighs or chicken wings. Adobo is best when using bone-in cuts, as it helps this dish become more flavorful. Using pork for adobo is also popular.

2 tablespoons soy sauce

2 tablespoons rice vinegar

1 tablespoon balsamic vinegar

¼ teaspoon freshly ground black pepper

4 garlic cloves, minced

½ teaspoon peeled minced fresh ginger

Juice of ½ lemon

¼ teaspoon granulated sugar

3 bay leaves

Pinch Italian seasoning (optional)

Pinch ground cumin (optional)

3 pounds chicken drumsticks

1. In a large bowl, whisk together the soy sauce, rice vinegar, balsamic vinegar, pepper, garlic, ginger, lemon juice, sugar, bay leaves, Italian seasoning (if using), and cumin (if using). Add the drumsticks to the marinade, making sure the meat is coated. Cover and refrigerate for at least 1 hour. If you have the time, marinate the chicken overnight to let all the flavors settle in.

2. Insert the Grill Grate and close the hood. Select GRILL, set the temperature to MED, and set the time to 15 minutes. Select START/STOP to begin preheating.

3. When the unit beeps to signify it has preheated, place the chicken drumsticks on the Grill Grate. Brush any leftover marinade onto the drumsticks. Close the hood and grill for 8 minutes.

4. After 8 minutes, open the hood and flip the drumsticks. Close the hood and continue cooking for 7 minutes more.

5. When cooking is complete, remove the drumsticks from the grill and serve.

Buttermilk Ranch Chicken Tenders

These super crispy and tender chicken strips have a perfect blend of creamy ranch flavor in every bite. Soaking the chicken in seasoned buttermilk helps tenderize the meat so you don't have to pound it with a mallet, and it infuses both buttermilk and ranch seasoning into the chicken. I love this recipe so much because the Foodi™ Grill does all the work for you.

FAMILY FAVORITE / NUT-FREE / UNDER 30 MINUTES

PREP TIME: 10 minutes, plus 30 minutes to marinate

COOK TIME: 10 minutes

ACCESSORIES: Grill Grate

VARIATION TIP: Turn these strips into chicken nuggets or chicken bites by cutting them into smaller pieces. The kids love them as much as the adults do!

2 cups buttermilk

1 (0.4-ounce) packet ranch seasoning mix

1½ pounds boneless, skinless chicken breasts (about 3 breasts), cut into 1-inch strips

2 cups all-purpose flour

¼ teaspoon paprika

¼ teaspoon garlic powder

¼ teaspoon baking powder

2 teaspoons salt

2 large eggs

¼ cup avocado oil, divided

1. In a large bowl, whisk together the buttermilk and ranch seasoning. Place the chicken strips in the bowl. Cover and let marinate in the refrigerator for 30 minutes.

2. Create an assembly line with 2 large bowls. Combine the flour, paprika, garlic powder, baking powder, and salt in one bowl. In the other bowl, whisk together the eggs. One at a time, remove the chicken strips from the marinade, shaking off any excess liquid. Dredge the chicken strip in the seasoned flour, coating both sides, then dip it in the beaten egg. Finally, dip it back into the seasoned flour bowl again. Shake any excess flour off. Repeat the process with all the chicken strips, setting them aside on a flat tray or plate once coated.

3. Insert the Grill Grate and close the hood. Select GRILL, set the temperature to MED, and set the time to 10 minutes. Select START/STOP to begin preheating.

4. While the unit is preheating, use a basting brush to generously coat one side of the chicken strips with half of the avocado oil.

CONTINUED ▶

5. When the unit beeps to signify it has preheated, place the chicken strips on the grill, oiled-side down. Brush the top of the chicken strips with the rest of the avocado oil. Close the hood and grill for 5 minutes.

6. After 5 minutes, open the hood and flip the chicken strips. Close the hood and continue cooking for 5 minutes more.

7. When cooking is complete, the chicken strips will be golden brown and crispy. Remove them from the grill and serve.

Chicken Cordon Bleu Roll-Ups

SERVES 4

Crispy, creamy, and juicy all in one! These chicken roll-ups are stuffed with ham and Swiss cheese, then dipped in a creamy, sweet Dijon mustard. This dish is typically pan-fried, but grilling them on the Foodi™ Grill is just as easy and equally crunchy with very little prep.

NUT-FREE / UNDER 30 MINUTES

PREP TIME: 10 minutes

COOK TIME: 15 minutes

ACCESSORIES: Grill Grate

VARIATION TIP: If you are watching your carbohydrate content or want to keep this gluten-free, use pork rind crumbs in place of bread crumbs. They crisp up just as nicely.

1 tablespoon garlic powder

1 tablespoon onion powder

1½ pounds boneless, skinless chicken breasts (about 3 breasts)

6 ounces thin-sliced deli ham

6 ounces Swiss cheese, sliced

2 large eggs

1 cup plain bread crumbs

¼ cup sour cream

3 tablespoons Dijon mustard

¼ teaspoon granulated sugar or honey

1. Insert the Grill Grate and close the hood. Select GRILL, set the temperature to MED, and set the time to 15 minutes. Select START/STOP to begin preheating.

2. In a small bowl, combine the garlic powder and onion powder.

3. Cut each chicken breast in half from the side (parallel to the cutting board) to create 6 thinner, flatter chicken breasts. Lightly coat the chicken all over with the garlic-and-onion mixture.

4. Layer 3 or 4 slices of ham on top of each piece of chicken, and top with about 1 ounce of cheese. Starting at the short end, roll the chicken breasts to wrap the ham and cheese inside. Secure the chicken roll-ups with toothpicks.

5. In a large bowl, whisk the eggs. Put the bread crumbs in a separate large bowl. Dip the chicken roll-ups in the egg and then into the bread crumbs until fully coated.

6. When the unit beeps to signify it has preheated, place the roll-ups on the Grill Grate. Close the hood and grill for 7 minutes, 30 seconds.

CONTINUED ▶

7. After 7 minutes, 30 seconds, open the hood and flip the roll-ups. Close the hood and continue cooking for 7 minutes, 30 seconds more.

8. While the roll-ups are cooking, in a small bowl, combine the sour cream, Dijon mustard, and sugar and stir until the sugar is dissolved.

9. When cooking is complete, remove the roll-ups from the grill and serve with the sauce, for dipping.

Turkey Jerky

Making your own jerky at home is fun. Unlike store-bought, this jerky contains no added preservatives or unwanted ingredients, making it a healthier and more cost-effective option. This homemade version provides a great protein-packed snack that you can bring along on road trips, on hikes, or to work or school. Try this out with turkey and then explore with different proteins.

DAIRY-FREE / NUT-FREE

PREP TIME: 40 minutes, plus overnight to marinate

COOK TIME: 3 to 5 hours

ACCESSORIES: Crisper Basket

HACK IT: You can dehydrate two layers of jerky at a time by placing the first layer in the Cooking Pot and then inserting the Crisper Basket for your second layer.

1 pound turkey breast, very thinly sliced

1 cup soy sauce

2 tablespoons light brown sugar, packed

2 tablespoons Worcestershire sauce

½ teaspoon garlic powder

½ teaspoon onion powder

½ teaspoon red pepper flakes

1. In a resealable bag, combine the turkey, soy sauce, brown sugar, Worcestershire sauce, garlic powder, onion powder, and red pepper flakes. Massage the turkey slices so all are fully coated in the marinade. Seal the bag and refrigerate overnight.

2. An hour before you plan to put the turkey in the dehydrator, remove the turkey slices from the marinade and place them between two paper towels to dry out and come to room temperature.

3. Once dried, lay the turkey slices flat in the Crisper Basket in a single layer. Insert the Crisper Basket in the Cooking Pot and close the hood. Select DEHYDRATE, set the temperature to 150ºF, and set the time to 5 hours. Select START/STOP.

4. After 3 hours, check for desired doneness. Continue dehydrating for up to 2 more hours, if desired.

5. When cooking is complete, the jerky should have a dry texture. Remove from the basket and serve, or store in a resealable bag in the refrigerator for up to 2 weeks.

Cilantro-Lime Chicken Thighs

With the cilantro and zesty lime flavor of this recipe, you'll get a winner, winner, chicken dinner cooked in 15 minutes! This easy cilantro-lime marinade results in chicken that always comes out juicy and tender. Chicken thighs are a rich and flavorful dark meat. You will want to keep the skin on your chicken with this one—it will crisp up nicely on the Foodi™ Grill.

DAIRY-FREE / NUT-FREE / UNDER 30 MINUTES

PREP TIME: 10 minutes, plus 1 hour to marinate

COOK TIME: 15 minutes

ACCESSORIES: Grill Grate

SUBSTITUTION TIP:
Bone-in, skin-on chicken thighs are cheaper than boneless and skinless because of the labor that goes into the cutting. Swap out the chicken thighs for chicken breast if you prefer a leaner cut. Cooking times may change slightly, so use the Smart Thermometer to ensure the chicken is cooked to an internal temperature of 165°F. If key limes aren't available, you can use regular limes. For a gluten-free version, replace the soy sauce with an equal amount of coconut aminos or tamari.

½ **cup extra-virgin olive oil**

4 **tablespoons light brown sugar, packed**

4 **tablespoons soy sauce**

Juice of 2 key limes

Zest of 1 key lime

2 **teaspoons sea salt**

½ **teaspoon freshly ground black pepper**

2 **tablespoons minced garlic**

½ **cup chopped fresh cilantro**

3 **pounds bone-in, skin-on chicken thighs**

1. In a large bowl, whisk together the olive oil, brown sugar, soy sauce, lime juice, lime zest, salt, pepper, minced garlic, and cilantro. Place the chicken thighs in the marinade and turn so the meat is fully coated. Cover the bowl and refrigerate for at least 1 hour or up to overnight.

2. Insert the Grill Grate and close the hood. Select GRILL, set the temperature to LO, and set the time to 15 minutes. Select START/STOP to begin preheating.

3. When the unit beeps to signify it has preheated, place the chicken thighs skin-side up on the Grill Grate. Brush some of the marinade on the chicken. Close the hood and grill for 8 minutes.

4. After 8 minutes, open the hood and flip the chicken. Close the hood and continue cooking for 7 minutes more.

Creamy Tuscan Chicken

SERVES 4

When I was learning how to cook, this was one of the first dishes I experimented with in a slow cooker. I was never a big fan of chicken breasts, but because this dish is so creamy and delicious, I soon became a fan of preparing chicken breasts with creamy sauces. Over time, I evolved to cooking more with chicken thighs because juicy and creamy became my favorite combo. And now, using the Foodi™ Grill makes for quick cooking.

GLUTEN-FREE / NUT-FREE / UNDER 30 MINUTES

PREP TIME: 10 minutes

COOK TIME: 15 minutes

ACCESSORIES: Cooking Pot

VARIATION TIP: Replace the sun-dried tomatoes with 12 chopped garlic cloves for a creamy, garlic lovers' chicken dish. If you want to make this dish even creamier, add 4 ounces cream cheese with the sauce in step 6.

2 tablespoons garlic powder

1 tablespoon paprika

2 teaspoons salt

1 teaspoon freshly ground black pepper

2 pounds boneless, skinless chicken thighs

Avocado oil

1 cup heavy (whipping) cream

¼ cup grated Parmesan cheese

1 cup chicken broth

2 teaspoons minced garlic

¼ cup sun-dried tomatoes, drained

2 cups fresh spinach

Fresh chopped basil or cilantro, for garnish (optional)

1. Insert the Cooking Pot and close the hood. Select GRILL, set the temperature to MED, and set the time to 15 minutes. Select START/STOP to begin preheating.

2. While the unit is preheating, in a small bowl, combine the garlic powder, paprika, salt, and pepper. Lightly coat both sides of the chicken thighs with the seasoning and lightly drizzle with the avocado oil.

3. When the unit beeps to signify it has preheated, place the chicken in the Cooking Pot. Close the hood and cook for 2 minutes.

4. After 2 minutes, open the hood and flip the chicken. Close the hood and cook for 3 minutes more.

5. While the chicken is cooking, in a medium bowl, combine the heavy cream, Parmesan cheese, chicken broth, garlic, and sun-dried tomatoes.

6. After 3 minutes, open the hood and pour in the cream sauce. Close the hood and cook for 5 minutes more. After 5 minutes, open the hood and stir in the spinach. Close the hood and continue cooking for 5 minutes more.

7. When cooking is complete, open the hood and stir one more time. Close the hood and let the cream sauce sit for 5 minutes before removing the Cooking Pot.

8. Serve over basmati rice or with flatbread or naan. Garnish with fresh basil leaves or fresh cilantro, if desired.

Crispy Chicken Parmigiana

SERVES 4

Also known as chicken Parmesan or just chicken Parm, this crispy breaded chicken topped with marinara sauce and cheese is ready in under 30 minutes. Enjoy this quick weeknight meal by itself or over spaghetti.

FAMILY FAVORITE / NUT-FREE / UNDER 30 MINUTES

PREP TIME: 10 minutes

COOK TIME: 15 minutes

ACCESSORIES: Grill Grate

VARIATION TIP: Use fresh mozzarella instead of Parmesan. Top the chicken with the marinara sauce and fresh mozz during the last 5 minutes of cooking. Cook until the cheese has melted.

2 large eggs

2 cups panko bread crumbs

½ cup shredded Parmesan cheese

1 tablespoon Italian seasoning

1 teaspoon garlic powder

1½ pounds boneless, skinless chicken breasts (about 3 breasts), halved lengthwise

3 cups marinara sauce, hot

½ cup grated Parmesan cheese

1. Insert the Grill Grate and close the hood. Select GRILL, set the temperature to MED, and set the time to 15 minutes. Select START/STOP to begin preheating.

2. While the unit is preheating, create an assembly line with 2 large bowls. In one bowl, whisk the eggs. In the other bowl, combine the panko bread crumbs, shredded Parmesan cheese, Italian seasoning, and garlic powder. Dip each chicken breast in the egg and then into the bread crumb mix until fully coated. Set the coated chicken on a plate or tray.

3. When the unit beeps to signify it has preheated, place the chicken on the Grill Grate. Close the hood and grill for 8 minutes.

4. After 8 minutes, open the hood and flip the chicken. Close the hood and continue cooking for 7 minutes more.

5. When cooking is complete, remove the chicken from the grill and top with the marinara sauce and grated Parmesan cheese.

Garlic Brown-Butter Chicken with Tomatoes

SERVES 4

My two favorites put together—garlic and brown butter! I've typically prepared this sauce as a quick dressing for pasta, but here I'm changing that up to offer a lighter meal with chicken and tomatoes. The buttery taste infused with garlic brings a toasted, nutty, and sweet flavor to the chicken.

GLUTEN-FREE / NUT-FREE / UNDER 30 MINUTES

PREP TIME: 10 minutes

COOK TIME: 15 minutes

ACCESSORIES: Cooking Pot / Grill Grate

HACK IT: Cooking with butter may cause some smoke in your grill. After the machine beeps to signify it is done grilling, leave the hood closed for 5 minutes. If you open it right away, the smoke will escape. Additionally, keeping the hood closed will allow the garlic brown butter to settle in the chicken.

4 boneless, skinless chicken breasts

Extra-virgin olive oil

½ teaspoon paprika

½ teaspoon sea salt

12 tablespoons (1½ sticks) unsalted butter

4 garlic cloves, minced

2 tablespoons light brown sugar, packed

½ teaspoon garlic powder

6 ounces cherry tomatoes

1. Insert the Cooking Pot and close the hood. Select GRILL, set the temperature to MED, and set the time to 15 minutes. Select START/STOP to begin preheating.

2. While the unit is preheating, drizzle the chicken breasts with olive oil, then lightly sprinkle both sides with the paprika and salt.

3. When the unit beeps to signify it has preheated, place the butter and garlic in the Cooking Pot. Insert the Grill Grate on top and place the chicken breasts on the Grill Grate. Close the hood and grill for 8 minutes.

4. After 8 minutes, open the hood and use grill mitts to remove the Grill Grate and chicken. Add the brown sugar, garlic powder, and tomatoes to the butter and garlic and stir.

5. Transfer the chicken to the Cooking Pot, making sure you flip the breasts. Coat the chicken with the brown butter sauce. Close the hood and cook for 7 minutes more.

6. When cooking is complete, remove the chicken and place on a plate. Spoon the sauce over and serve.

Grilled Cornish Hens

Cornish hens are thought of as "mini chickens," which means grilling them is faster and easier than roasting a larger chicken. Cornish hens typically weigh 1 to 2 pounds, so each person can enjoy their own or easily split them in half. Experiment with your seasonings and use what you have in your pantry. I always say, if the marinade or seasoning smells good, it's most likely going to taste good!

DAIRY-FREE / GLUTEN-FREE / NUT-FREE / UNDER 30 MINUTES

PREP TIME: 10 minutes

COOK TIME: 20 minutes

ACCESSORIES: Grill Grate / Smart Thermometer

HACK IT: Instead of using the GRILL function for these Cornish hens, you can use the AIR CRISP function. Just set the temperature to 360°F and the time to 25 minutes, flipping the hens halfway through cooking to get super crispy skin.

½ cup avocado oil

1 teaspoon dried oregano

½ teaspoon freshly ground black pepper

1 teaspoon garlic salt

2 tablespoons minced garlic

1 teaspoon chopped fresh thyme

1 teaspoon chopped fresh parsley

1 teaspoon chopped fresh rosemary

2 (1-pound) Cornish hens

1 large yellow onion, halved

4 garlic cloves, peeled

1. Plug the thermometer into the unit. Insert the Grill Grate and close the hood. Select GRILL, set the temperature to LO, then select PRESET. Use the arrows to the right to select CHICKEN. The unit will default to WELL to cook poultry to a safe temperature. Select START/STOP to begin preheating.

2. While the unit is preheating, place the Smart Thermometer into the thickest part of the breast of one of the hens. In a small bowl, whisk together the avocado oil, oregano, pepper, garlic salt, minced garlic, thyme, parsley, and rosemary. Cut a few small slits in the skin of each Cornish hen. Rub the seasoning oil all over the skin and between the skin and meat where you made the slits. Place an onion half and 2 garlic cloves inside the cavity of each hen.

3. When the unit beeps to signify it has preheated, place the hens on the Grill Grate. Close the hood and cook.

4. When the Foodi™ Grill tells you, open the hood and flip the hens. Close the hood and continue to cook.

5. When cooking is complete, remove the hens from the grill and let sit for 5 minutes. Serve.

Soy-Garlic Crispy Chicken

SERVES 4

Sweet, sticky, and crunchy chicken! My husband and I used to frequently visit a Korean restaurant that specialized in similar chicken wings with a soy-garlic sauce plus all-you-can-eat steamed white rice and salad. I had to find a way to make this at home, and this is it!

DAIRY-FREE / NUT-FREE / UNDER 30 MINUTES

PREP TIME: 10 minutes

COOK TIME: 20 minutes

ACCESSORIES: Grill Grate

SUBSTITUTION TIP: If you do not have oyster sauce on hand, hoisin sauce can be substituted. These sauces are thicker than soy sauce, and hoisin sauce is sweeter than oyster sauce. If none of these sauces are available, feel free to omit them from this recipe. Want to add some kick? Add 1 teaspoon red pepper flakes and adjust according to your desired heat level.

20 to 24 chicken wings

2 tablespoons cornstarch

¼ cup soy sauce

½ cup water

1 tablespoon sesame oil

1 teaspoon peeled minced fresh ginger

1 teaspoon garlic powder

1 teaspoon onion powder

1 tablespoon oyster sauce

2 tablespoons honey

1 tablespoon rice vinegar

1 tablespoon light brown sugar, packed

1. Insert the Grill Grate and close the hood. Select GRILL, set the temperature to MED, and set the time to 20 minutes. Select START/STOP to begin preheating.

2. While the unit is preheating, pat the chicken wings dry with a paper towel and place them in a large bowl. Sprinkle the wings with the cornstarch and toss to coat.

3. In a separate large bowl, whisk together the soy sauce, water, sesame oil, ginger, garlic powder, onion powder, oyster sauce, honey, rice vinegar, and brown sugar until the sugar is dissolved. Place half the sauce in a small bowl and set aside.

4. When the unit beeps to signify it has preheated, place the chicken wings on the Grill Grate. Close the hood and cook for 10 minutes.

5. After 10 minutes, open the hood and flip the wings. Using a basting brush, brush the soy-garlic sauce from the small bowl on the chicken wings. Close the hood and cook for 10 minutes more.

6. When cooking is complete, remove the wings from the grill and place in the large bowl with the remaining soy-garlic sauce. Toss and coat the wings with the sauce, then serve.

Blackened Chicken

SERVES 4

Don't worry, this chicken isn't burnt—just flavor packed! The crust seals in all the spices, transforming ordinary chicken breast into something juicy and oh-so flavorful! Blackened chicken is great over a big bowl of Alfredo pasta or with a side of Sweet Potato Fries with Honey-Butter Sauce (page 69). Note that the chicken grills up at a high heat along with the butter, so there may be smoke.

GLUTEN-FREE / NUT-FREE / UNDER 30 MINUTES

PREP TIME: 10 minutes

COOK TIME: 10 minutes

ACCESSORIES: Grill Grate

VARIATION TIP: Want to kick up the heat? Increase the amount of cayenne pepper (up to 1 tablespoon) to turn up the spice level.

1 tablespoon paprika

1 tablespoon garlic powder

1 tablespoon onion powder

1 tablespoon freshly ground black pepper

1 teaspoon Italian seasoning

1 teaspoon salt

½ teaspoon ground cumin

½ teaspoon cayenne pepper

4 tablespoons (½ stick) unsalted butter, melted

¼ cup avocado oil

4 boneless, skinless chicken breasts (about 2 pounds), halved crosswise

1. Insert the Grill Grate and close the hood. Select GRILL, set the temperature to HI, and set the time to 10 minutes. Select START/STOP to begin preheating.

2. In a small bowl, combine the paprika, garlic powder, onion powder, black pepper, Italian seasoning, salt, cumin, and cayenne pepper.

3. In a separate small bowl, whisk together the butter and avocado oil. Lightly coat the chicken breasts on both sides with the butter-and-oil mixture, and then season both sides with the spice mix to get a nice coating.

4. When the unit beeps to signify it has preheated, open the hood and place the seasoned chicken on the Grill Grate. Close the hood and grill for 5 minutes.

5. After 5 minutes, open the hood and flip the chicken. Close the hood and cook for 5 minutes more.

6. When cooking is complete, remove the chicken from the grill and serve.

Grilled Turkey Pesto Sandwiches

I like calling these "grown-up grilled cheese sandwiches," as I've stuffed them with turkey and added some flavorful pesto to make them cheesy and buttery! Eating one makes me feel like I ordered it from a fancy deli, when in fact, I've actually just used leftover turkey from Thanksgiving or bought some thick-sliced deli meat from the store. Revamp your sandwich game with these grilled turkey pesto sandwiches.

5 INGREDIENTS / UNDER 30 MINUTES

PREP TIME: 5 minutes

COOK TIME: 6 minutes

ACCESSORIES: Grill Grate

VARIATION TIP: To make these extra cheesy, mix the pesto sauce with 4 tablespoons cream cheese. Add a sliced tomato or switch out the Monterey Jack cheese for any cheese you prefer, such as Havarti, provolone, or Swiss cheese.

- 4 tablespoons (½ stick) unsalted butter, at room temperature
- 8 slices sourdough bread
- 4 tablespoons jarred pesto
- 1 (16-ounce) package deli turkey meat (4 slices per sandwich)
- 4 slices Monterey Jack cheese

1. Insert the Grill Grate and close the hood. Select GRILL, set the temperature to LO, and set the time to 6 minutes. Select START/STOP to begin preheating.

2. While the unit is preheating, spread about ½ tablespoon of butter on the outside of each bread slice. Flip the slices over so the buttered sides are down. Spread about ½ tablespoon of pesto on the unbuttered side of each slice. Place 4 slices of turkey and 1 slice of cheese on top of the pesto on half of the bread slices. Close each sandwich with the other 4 slices, butter-side up.

3. When the unit beeps to signify it has preheated, place the sandwiches on the Grill Grate. Close the hood and cook for 3 minutes.

4. After 3 minutes, open the hood and flip the sandwiches. Close the hood and cook for 3 minutes more.

5. When cooking is complete, the bread will be lightly browned and toasted and the cheese will be melted. Remove from the grill and serve.

Lemon and Rosemary Chicken

A simple, 5-ingredient meal that doesn't skip out on the flavor. Serve this delicious chicken with your favorite veggies to keep your meal light, or serve it over rice or pasta for a heartier meal. Either way, it's perfect for a quick weeknight meal or for a date night.

5 INGREDIENTS / DAIRY-FREE / GLUTEN-FREE / NUT-FREE / UNDER 30 MINUTES

PREP TIME: 10 minutes

COOK TIME: 15 minutes

ACCESSORIES: Grill Grate

VARIATION TIP: Cook the chicken thighs in the Cooking Pot, and instead of slicing the lemon, squeeze the lemon juice into the pot so it can be soaked up by the chicken. Add extra rosemary to the Cooking Pot to infuse the lemon juice with its flavor.

3 pounds bone-in, skin-on chicken thighs

4 tablespoons avocado oil

2 tablespoons lemon-pepper seasoning

1 tablespoon chopped fresh rosemary

1 lemon, thinly sliced

1. Insert the Grill Grate and close the hood. Select GRILL, set the temperature to LO, and set the time to 15 minutes. Select START/STOP to begin preheating.

2. Coat the chicken thighs with the avocado oil and rub the lemon-pepper seasoning and rosemary evenly over the chicken.

3. When the unit beeps to signify it has preheated, place the chicken thighs on the Grill Grate, skin-side up. Place the lemon slices on top of the chicken. Close the hood and grill for 8 minutes.

4. After 8 minutes, open the hood and remove the lemon slices. Flip the chicken and place the lemon slices back on top. Close the hood and cook for 7 minutes more.

5. When cooking is complete, remove the chicken from the grill and serve.

Lemon-Pepper Chicken Wings

Even when you have nothing defrosted, you can go from frozen out of the bag to perfectly grilled and extra crispy in 45 minutes! I like to have wings in the freezer because meals like this save me from having to order takeout. Everyone can enjoy the classic lemon-pepper flavor without the spice or heat that comes from traditional Buffalo wings.

5 INGREDIENTS / FAMILY FAVORITE / GLUTEN-FREE / NUT-FREE

PREP TIME: 5 minutes

COOK TIME: 40 minutes

ACCESSORIES: Grill Grate

VARIATION TIP: You can eat these as plain wings or coat them with grated Parmesan cheese and garlic for garlic-Parmesan wings. These wings make a good base and can be dipped in your favorite sauces.

20 to 24 frozen chicken wings

4 tablespoons extra-virgin olive oil

4 tablespoons (½ stick) unsalted butter, melted

3 tablespoons lemon-pepper seasoning

1. Place the frozen wings in a large bowl. Drizzle with the olive oil and toss so the wings are well coated.

2. Insert the Grill Grate and close the hood. Select GRILL, set the temperature to MED, and set the time to 40 minutes. Select START/STOP to begin preheating.

3. When the unit beeps to signify it has preheated, place the chicken wings on the Grill Grate. Close the hood and cook for 30 minutes.

4. After 30 minutes, open the hood and flip the chicken. Close the hood and cook for 10 minutes more.

5. When cooking is complete, remove the wings from the grill and place in a large bowl.

6. In a small bowl, combine the butter and lemon-pepper seasoning. Pour this over the wings and toss to coat. Serve with celery and carrot sticks along with your favorite ranch or blue cheese dressing.

Sweet Chili Turkey Kebabs

SERVES 4

Kebabs are easy to grill and quick to whip up. And since they're on a stick, they make for a fun meal. Bonus: You don't have to eat them with a fork and spoon, so there are fewer dishes to clean. This recipe requires that you skewer the turkey first and then marinate it, versus the more common method of marinating first and then skewering. Enjoy these sweet and sticky kebabs for your next meal.

DAIRY-FREE / NUT-FREE

PREP TIME: 10 minutes, plus 30 minutes to marinate

COOK TIME: 12 minutes

ACCESSORIES: Grill Grate / Ninja® Foodi™ Grill Kebab Skewers

HACK IT: Most grocery stores sell already-made sweet chili sauce. If you have a bottle of it, you can skip the marinating step. Skewer your turkey chunks, season with salt and pepper, and brush with olive oil before placing on top of the grill. After 6 minutes, pour the sweet chili sauce into a small bowl and use a basting brush to brush both sides to coat the meat. Continue cooking and serve more sweet chili sauce on the side, for dipping.

2 pounds turkey breast, cut into 1-inch cubes

¼ cup honey

1 tablespoon extra-virgin olive oil

2 tablespoons apple cider vinegar

2 tablespoons soy sauce

Juice of 1 lime

1 teaspoon red pepper flakes

1. Place 5 or 6 turkey cubes on each of 8 to 10 skewers. In a zip-top bag, combine the honey, olive oil, vinegar, soy sauce, lime juice, and red pepper flakes. Shake to mix well. Place the turkey skewers in the marinade and massage to coat the meat. Seal the bag and let marinate at room temperature for 30 minutes or in the refrigerator overnight.

2. Insert the Grill Grate and close the hood. Select GRILL, set the temperature to MED, and set the time to 12 minutes. Select START/STOP to begin preheating.

3. When the unit beeps to signify it has preheated, place half of the skewers on the Grill Grate. Brush extra glaze on the skewers. Close the hood and grill for 3 minutes.

4. After 3 minutes, open the hood and flip the skewers. Close the hood and cook for 3 minutes more.

5. After 3 minutes, remove the skewers from the grill. Repeat steps 3 and 4 for the remaining skewers.

6. When cooking is complete, remove the kebabs from the grill and serve.

Stuffed Spinach Chicken Breast

SERVES 6

Cooking chicken breasts can be tricky because they can go from perfectly cooked and juicy to overcooked in no time. Long gone are those days, as the Foodi™ Grill helps keep your meats juicy and flavorful. Chicken dinners no longer have to be boring. Once you nail down this recipe, you'll find yourself stuffing your chicken with all sorts of things!

GLUTEN-FREE / NUT-FREE / UNDER 30 MINUTES

PREP TIME: 10 minutes

COOK TIME: 12 minutes

ACCESSORIES: Grill Grate

VARIATION TIP: Want to add texture? Replace the spinach with 2 cups chopped broccoli (fresh or thawed if frozen).

6 ounces cream cheese, at room temperature

1 teaspoon salt

½ teaspoon freshly ground black pepper

¼ cup mayonnaise

2 teaspoons garlic powder

½ cup grated Parmesan cheese

3 cups loosely packed spinach

1 teaspoon red pepper flakes (optional)

6 (6- to 8-ounce) boneless, skinless chicken breasts, butterflied (see page 118)

Avocado oil

1. Insert the Grill Grate and close the hood. Select GRILL, set the temperature to HI, and set the time to 12 minutes. Select START/STOP to begin preheating.

2. While the unit is preheating, in a large bowl, combine the cream cheese, salt, pepper, mayonnaise, garlic powder, Parmesan cheese, spinach, and red pepper flakes (if using). Spread the mixture inside the chicken breasts evenly. Close the breasts (like a book), enclosing the stuffing. Drizzle both sides of the chicken breasts with avocado oil for a nice coating.

3. When the unit beeps to signify it has preheated, place the chicken breasts on the Grill Grate. Close the hood and grill for 6 minutes.

4. After 6 minutes, open the hood and flip the chicken. Close the hood and cook for 6 minutes more.

5. When cooking is complete, open the hood and remove the chicken breasts from the grill. Serve.

Salsa Verde Chicken Enchiladas

SERVES 4

These enchiladas are covered with cheese, sour cream, and tangy salsa verde (green salsa). An easy dish to prep and serve, it is also easily customizable with all of your favorite toppings and fillings. Even better, you don't have to be the perfect tortilla roller to make these.

FAMILY FAVORITE / NUT-FREE

PREP TIME: 15 minutes

COOK TIME: 20 minutes

ACCESSORIES: Grill Grate / Cooking Pot

VARIATION TIP: Use red enchilada sauce instead of salsa verde.

HACK IT: Use a fajita seasoning packet to season the chicken instead of making your own seasoning.

1 tablespoon chili powder

1 teaspoon onion powder

1 teaspoon garlic powder

1 teaspoon ground cumin

2 teaspoons salt

3 boneless, skinless chicken breasts (about 1½ pounds)

Extra-virgin olive oil

1 (16-ounce) jar salsa verde

2 cups shredded Mexican-style cheese blend

6 (8-inch) flour tortillas

Diced tomatoes, for topping

Sour cream, for topping

1. Insert the Grill Grate and close the hood. Select GRILL, set the temperature to MED, and set the time to 12 minutes. Select START/STOP to begin preheating.

2. While the unit is preheating, in a small bowl, combine the chili powder, onion powder, garlic powder, ground cumin, and salt. Drizzle the chicken breasts with the olive oil and season the meat on both sides with the seasoning mixture.

3. When the unit beeps to signify it has preheated, place the chicken breasts on the Grill Grate. Close the hood and cook for 6 minutes.

4. After 6 minutes, open the hood and flip the chicken. Close the hood and cook for 6 minutes more.

5. When cooking is complete, open the hood and use grill mitts to remove the Grill Grate and chicken breasts. Let the chicken breasts cool for about 5 minutes. Use two forks to shred the chicken, or cut it into small chunks.

6. To assemble the enchiladas, place a generous amount of chicken on a tortilla. Lift one end of the tortilla and roll it over and around the chicken. Do not fold in the sides of the tortilla as you roll. Place the enchilada, seam-side down, in the Cooking Pot. Repeat with the remaining 5 tortillas and the rest of the chicken. Pour the salsa verde over the enchiladas, completely covering them. Top the salsa with the shredded cheese.

7. Select BAKE, set the temperature to 350°F, and set the time to 8 minutes. Select START/STOP and then press the PREHEAT button to skip preheating. Close the hood and cook for 8 minutes.

8. When cooking is complete, remove the enchiladas from the pot and serve topped with the diced tomatoes and sour cream.

Turkey Meatballs with Cranberry Sauce

SERVES 4

Turkey and cranberry sauce don't have to be served only during the holidays. These sweet, tangy, and juicy meatballs can be cooked up any time of year to bring holiday joy to any gathering. I like serving these on a platter with toothpicks ready to go for a perfect party appetizer.

DAIRY-FREE / FAMILY FAVORITE / NUT-FREE / UNDER 30 MINUTES

PREP TIME: 10 minutes

COOK TIME: 20 minutes

ACCESSORIES: Grill Grate

SUBSTITUTION TIP: Saltine crackers can be used in place of bread crumbs.

VARIATION TIP: Make homemade cranberry sauce by boiling ½ cup water with 1 cup granulated sugar and 4 cups fresh cranberries. Continue mixing and stirring until the cranberries pop and the sauce thickens. Add a splash of orange juice. Serve warm or chilled with the turkey meatballs.

2 tablespoons onion powder

1 cup plain bread crumbs

2 large eggs

2 tablespoons light brown sugar, packed

1 tablespoon salt

2 pounds ground turkey

1 (14-ounce) can cranberry sauce

1. In a large bowl, mix together the onion powder, bread crumbs, eggs, brown sugar, and salt. Place the ground turkey in the bowl. Using your hands, mix the ingredients together just until combined (overmixing can make the meat tough and chewy). Form the mixture into 1½- to 2-inch meatballs. This should make 20 to 22 meatballs.

2. Insert the Grill Grate and close the hood. Select GRILL, set the temperature to MED, and set the time to 20 minutes. Select START/STOP to begin preheating.

3. When the unit beeps to signify it has preheated, place the meatballs on the Grill Grate. Close the hood and cook for 10 minutes.

4. After 10 minutes, open the hood and flip the meatballs. Close the hood and cook for 10 minutes more.

5. When cooking is complete, remove the meatballs from the grill. Place the cranberry sauce in a small bowl and use a whisk to stir it into more of a thick jelly sauce. Serve the meatballs with the sauce on the side.

Teriyaki Chicken

SERVES 4

Teriyaki-flavored anything is my ultimate family-favorite kind of meal. We love eating this teriyaki chicken with a side of white rice or broccoli, and it is always better than takeout. There's no marinating required for this quick and easy meal.

DAIRY-FREE / FAMILY FAVORITE / NUT-FREE / UNDER 30 MINUTES

PREP TIME: 10 minutes

COOK TIME: 20 minutes

ACCESSORIES: Grill Grate

VARIATION TIP: If you want your teriyaki sauce thicker and want to pour it directly on top of your chicken, versus cooking with it, you can cook the chicken thighs on the Grill Grate and the teriyaki sauce in the Cooking Pot. At the halfway point, when you flip the chicken, use grill mitts to remove the Grill Grate, and check and stir the sauce in the Cooking Pot. When cooking is complete, pour the sauce over the chicken to serve.

½ cup soy sauce

¾ cup light brown sugar, packed

1 cup water

1 teaspoon garlic powder

1 teaspoon peeled minced fresh ginger

¼ teaspoon cornstarch (optional)

6 boneless, skinless chicken thighs (about 2 pounds)

1. Insert the Grill Grate and close the hood. Select GRILL, set the temperature to HI, and set the time to 10 minutes. Select START/STOP to begin preheating.

2. While the unit is preheating, in a large bowl, combine the soy sauce, brown sugar, water, garlic powder, ginger, and cornstarch (if using). Transfer about one-quarter of the sauce to a small bowl and set aside. Place the chicken thighs in the large bowl and coat with the teriyaki marinade. Set aside for about 5 minutes, or until the grill has been preheated.

3. When the unit beeps to signify it has preheated, place the chicken thighs on the Grill Grate. Close the hood and cook for 5 minutes.

4. After 5 minutes, open the hood and flip the chicken. Using a basting brush, glaze the chicken with the reserved teriyaki marinade, and carefully pour any remaining marinade over the chicken. Close the hood and cook for 5 minutes more.

5. When cooking is complete, remove the chicken from the grill and serve with your favorite veggies and a side of rice.

Yellow Coconut Chicken Curry

SERVES 4

You don't have to be a lover of spicy food to enjoy coconut curry. Adding coconut milk will balance the heat of the curry to give a sweeter, more mild taste for this creamy dish. Yellow curry is my favorite dish to order at a Thai restaurant, and I'm a firm believer that it always tastes best the next day, as the flavors have time to settle in.

DAIRY-FREE / NUT-FREE / UNDER 30 MINUTES

PREP TIME: 10 minutes

COOK TIME: 15 minutes

ACCESSORIES: Cooking Pot

VARIATION TIP: To make this a vegetarian dish, switch out the chicken for potatoes and carrots, and replace the chicken bouillon with vegetable bouillon! You may need to adjust the cooking time to make sure the potatoes and carrots cook until fork-tender.

½ **small yellow onion**

1 **large tomato**

2 **pounds boneless, skinless chicken thighs**

2 **tablespoons minced garlic**

1 **tablespoon chicken bouillon powder (1 cube)**

1 **tablespoon light brown sugar, packed**

2 **tablespoons yellow curry powder**

1 **teaspoon salt**

½ **teaspoon freshly ground black pepper**

2 **tablespoons fish sauce (optional)**

1 **(13-ounce) can full-fat unsweetened coconut milk**

Chopped fresh basil or cilantro, for garnish

1. Insert the Cooking Pot and close the hood. Select GRILL, set the temperature to MED, and set the time to 15 minutes. Select START/STOP to begin preheating.

2. While the unit is preheating, dice the onion and tomato and set both aside separately. Cut the chicken thighs into 1-inch cubes.

3. When the unit beeps to signify it has preheated, put the onion and garlic in the Cooking Pot. Add the chicken and stir with a wooden spoon. Close the hood and cook for 5 minutes.

4. After 5 minutes, open the hood and add the chicken bouillon, brown sugar, curry powder, tomato, salt, pepper, and fish sauce (if using). Close the hood and cook for 5 minutes.

5. After 5 minutes, open the hood and pour in the coconut milk. Stir to combine. Close the hood and cook 5 minutes more.

6. When cooking is complete, open the hood and stir one more time. Close the hood and let the coconut curry sit for 5 minutes before removing from the Cooking Pot.

7. Serve over basmati rice or with flatbread or naan. Garnish with the basil or cilantro.

Stuffed-Onion Burgers, *page 130*

6

Beef

Bacon Burger Meatballs

SERVES 4

These flavor-packed meatballs give you a bacon cheeseburger taste in every bite. What I love most is that all the condiments are already in the meatballs. Juicy on the inside and crispy on the outside, you can serve these by themselves or pile them up on hamburger buns to enjoy an extra-extra-loaded meatball burger!

**FAMILY FAVORITE /
GLUTEN-FREE / NUT-FREE /
UNDER 30 MINUTES**

PREP TIME: 10 minutes

COOK TIME: 20 minutes

ACCESSORIES: Grill Grate

VARIATION TIP: You can give these meatballs a breaded texture by dipping them in 2 beaten eggs and then in 3 cups of bread crumbs before grilling.

1 white onion, diced

1 pound thick-cut bacon (12 to 16 slices), cooked and crumbled

8 ounces cream cheese, at room temperature

4 tablespoons minced garlic

¼ cup ketchup

¼ cup yellow mustard

¼ cup gluten-free Worcestershire sauce

3 eggs

2 pounds ground beef

1. In a large bowl, mix together the onion, bacon crumbles, cream cheese, garlic, ketchup, mustard, Worcestershire sauce, and eggs. Add the ground beef and, using your hands, mix the ingredients together until just combined, being careful to not overmix. Form the mixture into 1½- to 2-inch meatballs. This should make 20 to 22 meatballs.

2. Insert the Grill Grate and close the hood. Select GRILL, set the temperature to MED, and set the time to 20 minutes. Select START/STOP to begin preheating.

3. When the unit beeps to signify it has preheated, place the meatballs on the Grill Grate. Close the hood and cook for 10 minutes.

4. After 10 minutes, open the hood and flip the meatballs. Close the hood and cook for 10 minutes more.

5. When cooking is complete, remove the meatballs from the grill and serve.

Beef and Scallion Rolls

SERVES 4

In this dish, juicy steak is wrapped around scallions, then covered in a sweet and salty glaze. A version of this recipe was one of the first meals I made when I was learning how to cook. I found a recipe in an old cookbook during my first year in college and almost burned it because I had unknowingly set the oven to broil. With the Foodi™ Grill, you'll be able to grill up these beef rolls with no worries.

DAIRY-FREE / FAMILY FAVORITE / UNDER 30 MINUTES

PREP TIME: 10 minutes

COOK TIME: 10 minutes

ACCESSORIES: Grill Grate

VARIATION TIP: Want to use a different veggie? Change it up by using asparagus, green beans, carrots, or a combo of them all.

HACK IT: If you place the steak between two pieces of plastic wrap or parchment paper, you can tenderize the meat with a mallet or rolling pin, which makes it easier to roll. You may be able to find thinly sliced Milanesa steak or extra-thin top round steak at your local grocery store, too. You can also use a ready-made teriyaki sauce or marinade instead of making your own, to save time.

1 pound skirt steak, very thinly sliced (12 slices)

Salt

Freshly ground black pepper

6 scallions, both white and green parts, halved lengthwise

2 tablespoons cornstarch

¼ cup water

¼ cup soy sauce

2 tablespoons light brown sugar, packed

1 teaspoon peeled minced fresh ginger

1 teaspoon garlic powder

1. Insert the Grill Grate and close the hood. Select GRILL, set the temperature to HI, and set the time to 10 minutes. Select START/STOP to begin preheating.

2. While the unit is preheating, season each steak slice with salt and pepper. With one of the longer sides of a steak slice closest to you, place a scallion length at the bottom, and roll away from you to wrap the scallion. Sprinkle cornstarch on the outer layer of the rolled-up steak. Repeat for the remaining steak slices, scallions, and cornstarch.

3. In a small bowl, mix together the water, soy sauce, brown sugar, ginger, and garlic until the sugar is dissolved.

4. When the unit beeps to signify it has preheated, dip each beef roll in the soy sauce mixture and place it on the Grill Grate, seam-side down. Close the hood and grill for 5 minutes.

5. After 5 minutes, open the hood and flip the beef rolls. Brush each roll with the marinade. Close the hood and cook for 5 minutes more.

6. When cooking is complete, remove the beef rolls from the grill and serve.

Beef Steak Fajitas

SERVES 4

When making fajitas, I love using different-colored bell peppers to get the contrasting tastes of sweetness from red bell peppers, bitterness from green bell peppers, and fruitiness from yellow bell peppers. Plus, it's always fun to eat your colors! I like to marinate the meat and slice the peppers and onion the night before so it becomes a quick weeknight meal that is cooked and ready on the Foodi™ Grill in less than 15 minutes.

DAIRY-FREE / FAMILY FAVORITE / NUT-FREE

PREP TIME: 10 minutes, plus 15 minutes to marinate

COOK TIME: 25 minutes

ACCESSORIES: Grill Grate / Smart Thermometer

SUBSTITUTION TIP: Make this vegetarian and sub out the beef for more veggies, like sliced mushrooms and zucchini, and even add in some cubes of firm tofu for added protein. If hanger steak is not available, use skirt steak or flank steak.

¼ **cup avocado oil**

2 **tablespoons soy sauce**

Juice of 2 limes

1 **tablespoon chili powder**

1 **teaspoon onion powder**

1 **teaspoon garlic powder**

1 **teaspoon ground cumin**

1 **teaspoon paprika**

2 **teaspoons salt**

2 **pounds hanger steak**

1 **green bell pepper, cut into strips**

1 **red bell pepper, cut into strips**

1 **yellow bell pepper, cut into strips**

1 **white onion, sliced**

8 **to 10 (10-inch) flour tortillas**

1. In a large bowl, whisk together the avocado oil, soy sauce, lime juice, chili powder, onion powder, garlic powder, cumin, paprika, and salt. Add the hanger steak, making sure it is fully covered with the marinade. Marinate for at least 15 minutes. Or, if you want to marinate the meat overnight, combine the marinade ingredients in a resealable bag, add the steak, massage the marinade into the steak, seal, and refrigerate. (If marinating overnight, also store the bell peppers and onion in a separate resealable bag in the refrigerator.)

2. Plug the thermometer into the unit. Insert the Grill Grate and close the hood. Select GRILL, set the temperature to HI, then select PRESET. Use the arrows to the right to select BEEF, then choose desired doneness. Insert the Smart Thermometer into the thickest part of the steak. Select START/STOP to begin preheating.

3. When the unit beeps to signify it has preheated, place the steak on the Grill Grate. Close the hood to begin cooking. The Foodi™ Grill will tell you when to flip the steak and when the internal temperature has been reached (15 minutes is for well-done steak).

4. When cooking is complete, use grill mitts to remove the Grill Grate and steak. Let the steak rest while the vegetables cook.

5. Put the bell peppers and onion in the Cooking Pot. Select GRILL, set the temperature to HI, and set the time to 10 minutes. Select START/STOP and then press PREHEAT to skip preheating. Close the hood and cook for 5 minutes.

6. After 5 minutes, open the hood and stir the peppers and onion with a wooden spoon. Close the hood and cook for 5 minutes more.

7. When cooking is complete, thinly slice the steak against the grain. Serve in the tortillas with the bell peppers and onion. Garnish with your favorite toppings, such as shredded cheese, pico de gallo, sour cream, and guacamole.

Carne Asada Tacos

Tacos are not just for Tuesdays when you can grill up your own marinated, thinly sliced steaks any night of the week. Carne asada means "grilled meat" in Spanish, and for this recipe, I like to use skirt steak. This is a simple but flavorful recipe served with warm tortillas and creamy cilantro sauce. You can also swap out the sauce for fresh salsa, if desired.

NUT-FREE

PREP TIME: 10 minutes, plus 15 minutes to marinate

COOK TIME: 15 minutes

ACCESSORIES: Grill Grate / Smart Thermometer

HACK IT: If the skirt steak is too thin (less than 1 inch thick), grill the steak on high for 7 to 10 minutes.

VARIATION TIP: Change it up and marinate pork for some crispy pork carnitas tacos.

For the tacos

¼ **cup avocado oil**

¼ **cup soy sauce**

¼ **cup orange juice**

3 **tablespoons white wine vinegar**

3 **tablespoons minced garlic**

Juice of 2 limes

1 **teaspoon ground cumin**

1 **teaspoon salt**

1 **teaspoon freshly ground black pepper**

1 **teaspoon onion powder**

½ **cup chopped fresh cilantro**

2 **pounds skirt steak at least 1 inch thick**

10 **corn tortillas**

For the creamy cilantro sauce

¼ **cup mayonnaise**

¼ **cup sour cream**

¼ **cup minced fresh cilantro, including stems**

Juice of 1 lime wedge, or more as desired

¼ **teaspoon paprika**

¼ **teaspoon onion powder**

To make the tacos

1. In a large bowl, whisk together the avocado oil, soy sauce, orange juice, vinegar, garlic, lime juice, cumin, salt, pepper, onion powder, and cilantro. Add the steak, making sure it is fully coated with the marinade. Set aside to marinate for 15 minutes.

2. Plug the thermometer into the unit. Insert the Grill Grate and close the hood. Select GRILL, set the temperature to HI, then select PRESET. Use the arrows to the right to select BEEF, then choose desired doneness. Insert the Smart Thermometer into the thickest part of the steak. Select START/STOP to begin preheating.

CONTINUED ▶

3. When the unit beeps to signify it has preheated, place the steak on the Grill Grate. Close the hood to begin cooking. The Foodi™ Grill will tell you when to flip the steak and when the desired internal temperature has been reached (15 minutes is for well-done steak).

To make the creamy cilantro sauce

4. While the steak is cooking, in a small bowl, combine the mayonnaise, sour cream, cilantro, lime juice, paprika, and onion powder.

5. When cooking is complete, remove the steak from the grill. Let it rest for 10 minutes before slicing against the grain. Serve in the tortillas and dress with the creamy cilantro sauce.

Chimichurri Skirt Steak

SERVES 6 TO 8

When making your own chimichurri sauce, you want to use all fresh ingredients, not dried herbs, to get the most vibrant flavors. Most days, I want just the classic taste of beef, but chimichurri sauce adds garlic flavor along with tanginess from red wine vinegar, bringing steak to a whole new level. If you have never added chimichurri sauce to your grilled steak, now is the time to try it.

DAIRY-FREE / GLUTEN-FREE / UNDER 30 MINUTES

PREP TIME: 15 minutes

COOK TIME: 15 minutes

ACCESSORIES: Grill Grate / Smart Thermometer

VARIATION TIP: Want to add some spice to your chimichurri sauce? Dice up some chiles and add according to your desired heat levels. You can also use ½ teaspoon red pepper flakes.

1 cup finely chopped fresh cilantro

1 cup finely chopped fresh parsley

1 shallot, finely chopped

3 garlic cloves, minced

2 teaspoons red wine vinegar

½ cup extra-virgin olive oil

2 (2-pound) skirt steaks

Salt

1. Plug the thermometer into the unit. Insert the Grill Grate and close the hood. Select GRILL, set the temperature to HI, then select PRESET. Use the arrows to the right to select BEEF, then choose MED (6) or desired doneness. Insert the Smart Thermometer into the thickest part of one of the steaks. Select START/STOP to begin preheating.

2. While the unit is preheating, in a small bowl, combine the cilantro, parsley, shallot, garlic, red wine vinegar, and olive oil. Mix well and set aside.

3. When the unit beeps to signify it has preheated, season the steaks with salt, then place them on the Grill Grate. Close the hood to begin cooking. The Foodi™ Grill will tell you when to flip the steak and when the desired internal temperature has been reached.

4. When cooking is complete, remove the steaks. Let them rest for 10 minutes before slicing against the grain. Spoon the chimichurri sauce over the top and serve.

Coffee-Rubbed Steak

SERVES 4

I never thought that adding coffee to my steak would make it as delicious as it does, but one try and I think you'll be converted, too. The slight acidity and roasted flavor of the coffee come together so well with the spices and seasonings, along with a hint of sweetness. This is a must-try and must-do!

DAIRY-FREE / GLUTEN-FREE / NUT-FREE / UNDER 30 MINUTES

PREP TIME: 5 minutes

COOK TIME: 10 minutes

ACCESSORIES: Grill Grate / Smart Thermometer

SUBSTITUTION TIP:
Watching your sugar consumption? Feel free to replace the brown sugar with an alternative sweetener made out of stevia, erythritol, or monkfruit. Or omit the brown sugar entirely and add 1 teaspoon ground cumin and 1 teaspoon coriander in its place.

¼ **cup finely ground coffee**

2 **tablespoons chili powder**

2 **tablespoons paprika**

1 **tablespoon sea salt**

1 **teaspoon freshly ground black pepper**

1 **teaspoon garlic powder**

1 **teaspoon onion powder**

¼ **cup light brown sugar, packed**

4 **(1-inch-thick) New York strip steaks**

Avocado oil

1. Plug the thermometer into the unit. Insert the Grill Grate and close the hood. Select GRILL, set the temperature to HI, then select PRESET. Use the arrows to the right to select BEEF, then choose MED (6) or desired doneness. Insert the Smart Thermometer into the thickest part of one of the steaks. Select START/STOP to begin preheating.

2. While the unit is preheating, in a small bowl, combine the coffee, chili powder, paprika, salt, pepper, garlic powder, onion powder, and brown sugar. Mix well.

3. On a large plate, drizzle the steaks with avocado oil on both sides, and generously rub and pat down the coffee mixture on both sides of the steaks.

4. When the unit beeps to signify it has preheated, place the steaks on the Grill Grate. Close the hood to begin cooking. The Foodi™ Grill will tell you when to flip the steak and when the desired internal temperature has been reached.

5. When cooking is complete, remove the steaks from the grill. Let them rest for about 5 minutes before slicing against the grain, then serve.

Filet Mignon with Blue Cheese Butter

Filet mignon is known for its tenderness and as a cut you might order at a restaurant on a special occasion. Filet mignon is only a small portion of the cow, making it a rare and pricey cut. When there isn't a lot of marbling on a steak, such as filet mignon, I like to pair it with butter to make it truly melt in your mouth. The combination of blue cheese and butter with a hint of garlic brings a sharp, salty, and creamy texture to these steaks.

5 INGREDIENTS / GLUTEN-FREE / NUT-FREE / UNDER 30 MINUTES

PREP TIME: 5 minutes

COOK TIME: 10 minutes

ACCESSORIES: Grill Grate / Smart Thermometer

DID YOU KNOW? If you love blue cheese, you could make a large blue cheese butter compound that you can easily put on breads, vegetables, or a baked potato. Add your favorite seasonings, like fresh parsley, rosemary, thyme, and garlic, and you'll have a flavorful butter that's ready for you anytime!

4 garlic cloves, minced

4 tablespoons (½ stick) unsalted butter

3 tablespoons blue cheese crumbles

4 (6-ounce) filet mignon steaks

Avocado oil

1. Plug the thermometer into the unit. Insert the Grill Grate and close the hood. Select GRILL, set the temperature to HI, then select PRESET. Use the arrows to the right to select BEEF, then choose MED (6) or desired doneness. Insert the Smart Thermometer into the thickest part of one of the steaks. Select START/STOP to begin preheating.

2. While the unit is preheating, in a small bowl, combine the garlic, butter, and blue cheese. Mix well to form a buttery paste.

3. Drizzle the steaks with avocado oil on both sides.

4. When the unit beeps to signify it has preheated, place the filets mignons on the Grill Grate. Close the hood to begin cooking.

5. When the Foodi™ Grill tells you to, flip the steaks, then add 1 tablespoon of the blue cheese butter on top of each steak. Close the hood and continue cooking until the Smart Thermometer indicates the desired internal temperature has been reached.

6. When cooking is complete, remove the steaks from the grill. Let them rest for about 5 minutes before serving.

Green Curry Beef

While Yellow Coconut Chicken Curry (page 103) is my favorite curry dish in this book, this green curry recipe is a close second. It is equally packed full of flavor. Green curry gets its color and flavor from green chiles, shallots, lemongrass, and lime, giving it a spicier and herbier flavor. Although green curry is spicier than yellow, adding coconut milk helps tone down the heat. The fish sauce helps bring this dish to life by adding salty and savory flavors, but if you can't find it or would rather leave it out, feel free to do so.

DAIRY-FREE / GLUTEN-FREE / NUT-FREE / UNDER 30 MINUTES

PREP TIME: 10 minutes

COOK TIME: 12 minutes

ACCESSORIES: Cooking Pot

VARIATION TIP: Replace the beef with eggplant, green beans and/or snow peas, and bamboo shoots to make this a hearty vegetarian dish.

1 yellow onion

1 red bell pepper

2 pounds sirloin steak

1 tablespoon minced garlic

1 tablespoon light brown sugar, packed

2 tablespoons green curry paste

1 teaspoon salt

½ teaspoon freshly ground black pepper

Juice of ½ lime

1 (13-ounce) can full-fat unsweetened coconut milk

2 tablespoons fish sauce (optional)

1 cup fresh Thai basil or sweet basil

1. Insert the Cooking Pot and close the hood. Select GRILL, set the temperature to MED, and set the time to 12 minutes. Select START/STOP to begin preheating.

2. While the unit is preheating, dice the onion, slice the red bell pepper, and thinly slice the steak into bite-size strips.

3. When the unit beeps to signify it has preheated, place the onion and garlic in the Cooking Pot. Then add the beef and stir with a wooden spoon. Close the hood and cook for 4 minutes.

4. After 4 minutes, open the hood and add the brown sugar, green curry paste, salt, pepper, lime juice, coconut milk, and fish sauce (if using). Close the hood and cook for 4 minutes. After 4 minutes, open the hood and stir the curry. Close the hood and cook for 4 minutes more.

5. When cooking is complete, open the hood, add the basil, and stir one more time. Close the hood and let the coconut curry sit for 5 minutes before serving.

Flank Steak Pinwheels

I like to call these pinwheels "meatwheels." They are versatile, as you can easily change the cheese and stuffing to your preferred ingredients or what you have in your refrigerator. No matter what combination you choose, these are always a hit. I love to prepare them on the Foodi™ Grill, as the cheese slowly oozes out, creating a nice cheese crust and a juicy center.

GLUTEN-FREE / NUT-FREE / UNDER 30 MINUTES

PREP TIME: 10 minutes

COOK TIME: 10 minutes

ACCESSORIES: Grill Grate

DID YOU KNOW? If you've never butterflied a steak before, it's simple to do. Cut the steak almost in half from one side (parallel to the cutting board), stopping just before you reach the other side. When you open the steak up, it'll be thinner and have two matching wings like a butterfly.

2 pounds flank steak

Salt

Freshly ground black pepper

4 ounces cream cheese, at room temperature

2 tablespoons minced garlic

½ cup shredded mozzarella cheese

4 tablespoons grated Parmesan cheese

2 cups fresh spinach

1. Insert the Grill Grate and close the hood. Select GRILL, set the temperature to HI, and set the time to 10 minutes. Select START/STOP to begin preheating.

2. While the unit is preheating, butterfly the steaks and season both sides with salt and pepper. Spread the cream cheese across the cut side of each steak and evenly distribute the garlic over the cream cheese. Layer the mozzarella, Parmesan cheese, and spinach on top. Starting from the bottom of each steak, roll the meat upward tightly over the filling. Use about 6 toothpicks, evenly spaced, to secure the seam. Then slice in between the toothpicks, creating 1½- to 2-inch-thick rolls.

3. When the unit beeps to signify it has preheated, place the pinwheels on the Grill Grate, cut-side down. Close the hood and grill for 5 minutes.

4. After 5 minutes, open the hood and flip the pinwheels. Close the hood and cook for 5 minutes more.

5. When cooking is complete, check the meat for doneness. If you prefer your beef more well done, continue cooking to your liking. Remove the pinwheels from the grill and serve.

Hamburger Steak with Mushroom Gravy

Similar to a Salisbury steak, you will never have to worry about this hamburger steak being too dry. Growing up, I frequently ate at a Filipino restaurant chain that had a similar dish served with white rice or mashed potatoes and gravy. Over time, it made sense to just make it at home and add my favorite toppings, like mushrooms or onions. Thus, this dish was born.

**FAMILY FAVORITE /
NUT-FREE / UNDER
30 MINUTES**

PREP TIME: 10 minutes

COOK TIME: 18 minutes

ACCESSORIES: Grill Grate

VARIATION TIP: Prepare a fifty-fifty mixture of ground pork and ground beef. The combination is unbelievably savory, juicy, and full of flavor from the pork fat.

For the hamburger steaks

1 cup plain bread crumbs

**2 tablespoons
Worcestershire sauce**

1 teaspoon onion powder

1 teaspoon garlic powder

1 large egg

1 teaspoon granulated sugar

1 teaspoon salt

**¼ teaspoon freshly
ground black pepper**

1 pound ground beef

For the mushroom gravy

2 cups beef broth

**4 tablespoons (½ stick)
unsalted butter**

**8 ounces white
mushrooms, sliced**

**1 tablespoon
Worcestershire sauce**

**4 tablespoons
all-purpose flour**

Salt

Freshly ground black pepper

To make the hamburger steaks

1. Insert the Grill Grate and close the hood. Select GRILL, set the temperature to HI, and set the time to 10 minutes. Select START/STOP to begin preheating.

2. While the unit is preheating, in a large bowl, combine the bread crumbs, Worcestershire sauce, onion powder, garlic powder, egg, sugar, salt, and pepper. Add the ground beef in chunks and loosely mix until just combined. Form the mixture into 4 equal-sized patties.

3. When the unit beeps to signify it has preheated, place the beef patties on the Grill Grate. Close the hood and grill for 5 minutes.

4. While the patties are cooking, gather and measure the ingredients for the gravy.

CONTINUED ▶

Hamburger Steak with Mushroom Gravy continued

5. After 5 minutes, open the hood and flip the burgers. Close the hood and cook for 5 minutes more.

6. When cooking is complete, use grill mitts to remove the Grill Grate and burgers from the unit.

To make the mushroom gravy

7. Add the beef broth, butter, mushrooms, and Worcestershire sauce to the Cooking Pot. Select GRILL, set the temperature to HI, and set the time to 8 minutes. Select START/STOP and then press the PREHEAT button to skip preheating. Close the hood and cook for 4 minutes.

8. After 4 minutes, open the hood and stir in the flour. Mix well. Close the hood and cook for 4 minutes more.

9. When cooking is complete, the sauce will be thickened and the butter will be completely melted. Season with salt and pepper. Pour the mushroom gravy over the hamburger steaks and serve.

Honey Barbecue Meat Loaf

I love meals that don't require much thought or effort, like meat loaf. One of the best things about meat loaf is that you can season it to your liking and add your favorite sauce to make it your own. This meat loaf is an easy meal that goes well with steamed vegetables, mashed potatoes, or Cheesy Garlic Bread (page 56). It is a simple and comforting dish everyone can enjoy.

DAIRY-FREE / FAMILY FAVORITE / NUT-FREE / UNDER 30 MINUTES

PREP TIME: 10 minutes

COOK TIME: 15 minutes

ACCESSORIES: Grill Grate / Smart Thermometer

HACK IT: Want your meat loaf to have a more uniform shape? Use a bread loaf pan and place it in the Cooking Pot. You can even wrap aluminum foil around it and pierce through the foil with the Smart Thermometer to get the correct temperature.

SUBSTITUTION TIP: Not into barbecue sauce? Coat the meat loaf with honey mustard or a sweet Dijon mustard sauce.

1 white onion, diced
1 cup plain bread crumbs
4 tablespoons minced garlic
2 tablespoons Worcestershire sauce
½ cup barbecue sauce, divided
2 tablespoons honey
2 large eggs
2 pounds ground beef

1. Plug the thermometer into the unit. Insert the Grill Grate and close the hood. Select GRILL, set the temperature to MED, then select PRESET. Use the arrows to the right to select BEEF. The unit will default to WELL to cook beef to a safe temperature. Select START/STOP to begin preheating.

2. While the unit is preheating, in a large bowl, combine the onion, bread crumbs, garlic, Worcestershire sauce, ¼ cup of barbecue sauce, honey, and eggs. Add the ground beef in chunks and loosely mix, then form the meat into a loaf about 3 inches high and 6 to 8 inches long. Insert the Smart Thermometer into the loaf.

3. When the unit beeps to signify it has preheated, place the meat loaf on the Grill Grate. Close the hood and grill until the Smart Thermometer indicates the internal temperature is 145°F.

4. When it does, open the hood and brush on the remaining ¼ cup of barbecue sauce. Close the hood and continue cooking until the Smart Thermometer indicates the meat loaf has reached 160°F.

5. When cooking is complete, remove the meat loaf from the grill and serve.

Lemongrass Beef Skewers

I really enjoy this sweet, savory, lemony combo. If you're new to lemongrass, this marinade is a must-try. It brings a citrusy aroma to grilled meats. Look for lemongrass paste in a tube or jar near the fresh herb/produce section at your local store, or order it online. This dish, one of my favorites, is inspired by Vietnamese cuisine, where it is served over vermicelli noodles or white rice.

DAIRY-FREE/ FAMILY FAVORITE / NUT-FREE / UNDER 30 MINUTES

PREP TIME: 10 minutes, plus 30 minutes to marinate

COOK TIME: 8 minutes

ACCESSORIES: Grill Grate / Ninja® Foodi™ Grill Kebab Skewers

VARIATION TIP: Use this marinade for grilled chicken, pork, shrimp, and even tofu.

3 tablespoons minced garlic

3 tablespoons light brown sugar, packed

3 tablespoons lemongrass paste

1 tablespoon soy sauce

1 tablespoon peeled minced fresh ginger

1 tablespoon avocado oil

½ small red onion, minced

2 pounds sirloin steak, cut into 1-inch cubes

Chopped fresh cilantro, for garnish

1. In a large bowl, combine the garlic, brown sugar, lemongrass paste, soy sauce, ginger, avocado oil, and onion until the sugar is dissolved. Add the steak cubes and massage them with the marinade. Place 5 or 6 cubes on each of 6 to 8 skewers, then place the skewers in a large rimmed baking sheet and coat with the remaining marinade. Set aside to marinate for at least 30 minutes. If marinating for longer, cover and refrigerate.

2. Insert the Grill Grate and close the hood. Select GRILL, set the temperature to HI, and set the time to 8 minutes. Select START/STOP to begin preheating.

3. When the unit beeps to signify it has preheated, place the skewers on the Grill Grate. Close the hood and grill for 4 minutes.

4. After 4 minutes, open the hood and flip the skewers. Close the hood and cook for 4 minutes more. If you prefer extra char, add 2 minutes to the cook time.

5. When cooking is complete, remove the skewers from the grill and serve, garnished with the cilantro.

Grilled Kalbi Beef Short Ribs

Korean barbecue has always been a favorite of mine. Similar to a teriyaki marinade, kalbi marinade has sweet and savory flavors. When I first got my Foodi™ Grill, this was one of the recipes that I knew I had to make at home. This dish is best served with white rice and some shredded cabbage, kimchi, or pickled veggies.

DAIRY-FREE / FAMILY FAVORITE / NUT-FREE

PREP TIME: 10 minutes, plus 30 minutes to marinate

COOK TIME: 10 minutes

ACCESSORIES: Grill Grate

VARIATION TIP: If you cannot find short ribs, you can use thinly sliced strip steak or rib eye to make bulgogi with this marinade. Partially freezing the steak before slicing it will help give you clean, thin cuts. If you have the time, marinate overnight and grill the next day to get even more flavor.

½ cup soy sauce

¼ cup water

½ cup light brown sugar, packed

¼ cup honey

2 tablespoons sesame oil

½ teaspoon onion powder

1 teaspoon garlic powder

1 teaspoon peeled minced fresh ginger

3 pounds short ribs

1 scallion, both white and green parts, sliced, for garnish

Sesame seeds, for garnish

1. In a large bowl, combine the soy sauce, water, brown sugar, honey, sesame oil, onion powder, garlic powder, and minced ginger until the sugar is dissolved. Place the short ribs in the bowl and massage the marinade into the meat. Set aside to marinate for at least 30 minutes. If marinating for longer, cover and refrigerate.

2. Insert the Grill Grate and close the hood. Select GRILL, set the temperature to HI, and set the time to 10 minutes. Select START/STOP to begin preheating.

3. When the unit beeps to signify it has preheated, place the short ribs on the Grill Grate. Close the hood and cook for 5 minutes.

4. After 5 minutes, open the hood and flip the short ribs. Close the hood and cook for 5 minutes more.

5. When cooking is complete, remove the short ribs from the grill and garnish with the scallions and sesame seeds. Serve.

One-Pot Chili

SERVES 4

A heartwarming and comforting bowl is what you will get with this chili. Everything is just thrown into the pot, making it an easy meal or side to cook up! This recipe is great with Maple Butter Corn Bread (page 65).

GLUTEN-FREE / NUT-FREE / UNDER 30 MINUTES

PREP TIME: 5 minutes

COOK TIME: 25 minutes

ACCESSORIES: Cooking Pot

HACK IT: Want to add some smoky flavor to your chili? Add 1 cup brewed coffee or stout beer (you'll just have to drink the rest!) to add some depth of flavor during the last 10 minutes of cooking.

1 small onion

1 pound ground beef

3 cloves garlic, minced

1 (14-ounce) can crushed tomatoes

1 (6-ounce) can tomato paste

1 cup beef broth

3 tablespoons chili powder

1 tablespoon ground cumin

1 teaspoon dried oregano

1 teaspoon paprika

1 (15-ounce) can beans (such as kidney, pinto, or black beans), drained and rinsed

1. Insert the Cooking Pot and close the hood. Select GRILL, set the temperature to LO, and set the time to 25 minutes. Select START/STOP to begin preheating.

2. While the unit is preheating, dice the onion.

3. When the unit beeps to signify it has preheated, put the ground beef, onion, and garlic in the Cooking Pot. Break apart the ground beef with a wooden spoon or spatula. Close the hood and cook for 5 minutes.

4. After 5 minutes, open the hood, stir, then stir in the crushed tomatoes, tomato paste, and beef broth. Add the chili powder, cumin, oregano, paprika, and beans and stir. Close the hood and cook for 10 minutes. After 10 minutes, open the hood and stir. Close the hood and cook for 10 minutes more.

5. When cooking is complete, serve the chili garnished with your favorite toppings, such as sour cream, shredded cheese, sliced scallions, and bacon bits.

Rib Eye Steak with Rosemary Butter

SERVES 4

No need to go to the steakhouse when you can make your own perfect rib eyes at home. Rib eyes are my favorite cut because of the beautiful marbling and fat content that brings in all the flavor. Add just a little bit of butter, salt, garlic, and rosemary for this simple, juicy, and delicious meal that you can serve with your favorite veggies or eat by itself.

5 INGREDIENTS / GLUTEN-FREE / NUT-FREE / UNDER 30 MINUTES

PREP TIME: 10 minutes

COOK TIME: 10 minutes

ACCESSORIES: Grill Grate / Smart Thermometer

HACK IT: If you want to save a little money yet enjoy eating rib eyes, buy a rib eye roast and cut it into steaks yourself.

VARIATION TIP: If rib eyes aren't in your budget, try chuck steak.

4 garlic cloves, minced

1 teaspoon salt

4 tablespoons (½ stick) unsalted butter, at room temperature

½ tablespoon chopped fresh rosemary (about 2 sprigs)

4 (1-pound) bone-in rib eye steaks

1. Plug the thermometer into the unit. Insert the Grill Grate and close the hood. Select GRILL, set the temperature to HI, then select PRESET. Use the arrows to the right to select BEEF, then choose MED (6) or desired doneness. Insert the Smart Thermometer into the thickest part of one of the steaks. Select START/STOP to begin preheating.

2. While the unit is preheating, in a small bowl, combine the garlic, salt, butter, and rosemary to form a butter paste.

3. When the unit beeps to signify it has preheated, place the steaks on the Grill Grate. Close the hood to begin cooking.

4. When the grill indicates it is time to flip, open the hood, flip the steaks, and add 1 tablespoon of the rosemary butter on top of each steak. Close the hood and cook until the Smart Thermometer indicates your desired internal temperature has been reached.

5. When cooking is complete, remove the steaks from the grill and let rest for 5 minutes before slicing against the grain. Serve.

Spicy Beef Lettuce Wraps

SERVES 4

When my husband and I got married, I was still new to the kitchen and made sure to stretch our dollar when it came to eating. I used ground beef in a lot of recipes because many times it was on sale and I could make a good warm meal within minutes. This is my husband's favorite for its simplicity and flavor. We never had a name for it, but he'd call it "sweet meat." Over the years, I revamped it to make it sweeter or spicier. For this recipe, I've made it spicy.

DAIRY-FREE / NUT-FREE / UNDER 30 MINUTES

PREP TIME: 10 minutes

COOK TIME: 10 minutes

ACCESSORIES: Cooking Pot

SUBSTITUTION TIP: You can also use ground chicken, ground pork, or ground turkey for this recipe.

VARIATION TIP: Don't want it spicy? Omit the chile and sriracha.

1 pound ground beef

1 tablespoon sesame oil

1 tablespoon minced garlic

1 teaspoon peeled minced fresh ginger

3 tablespoons light brown sugar, packed

¼ cup soy sauce

1 teaspoon salt

½ teaspoon freshly ground black pepper

2 teaspoons sriracha

1 red chile, thinly sliced, or ¼ teaspoon red pepper flakes

½ cup sliced scallions, both white and green parts

12 butter lettuce leaves

1. Insert the Cooking Pot and close the hood. Select GRILL, set the temperature to HI, and set the time to 10 minutes. Select START/STOP to begin preheating.

2. When the unit beeps to signify it has preheated, place the ground beef in the Cooking Pot. Carefully break the ground beef apart with a wooden spoon or spatula. Stir in the sesame oil, garlic, and ginger. Close the hood and cook for 5 minutes.

3. After 5 minutes, open the hood and stir the ground beef. Stir in the brown sugar, soy sauce, salt, pepper, and sriracha. Close the hood and cook for 5 minutes more.

4. When cooking is complete, open the hood and stir in the chile and scallions. Close the hood and let sit for about 3 minutes for the mixture to set.

5. Scoop the ground beef mixture into the lettuce leaves and serve.

Peppercorn Beef Tenderloin

I used to be intimated by beef tenderloin because of its cost and the pressure to make sure it is cooked just right. If you are entertaining a crowd or want to make a special meal, this beef tenderloin dish is a great, easy starting point. A beautiful, charred crust of crushed peppercorns adorns this tender, flavorful cut.

5 INGREDIENTS / DAIRY-FREE / GLUTEN-FREE / NUT-FREE

PREP TIME: 15 minutes

COOK TIME: 30 minutes

ACCESSORIES: Grill Grate / Smart Thermometer

DID YOU KNOW?
Tenderloin is often not a uniform size, so the cook time will not be even from the thickest to the thinnest part of the meat. You will want to tuck the thin (tail) end under the center and tie it with kitchen twine or butcher's twine every 2 inches to make a uniform size to get the perfect level of doneness throughout. You can also ask your butcher to tie it for you.

¾ cup tricolored peppercorns or black peppercorns, crushed

2 garlic cloves, minced

2 tablespoons avocado oil

1 tablespoon kosher salt

¼ cup yellow mustard or horseradish

1 (3-pound) beef tenderloin, trimmed

1. In a small bowl, combine the crushed peppercorns, garlic, avocado oil, salt, and mustard. Using a basting brush, coat the tenderloin all over with the mustard mixture. Then press the mixture into the meat with your hands.

2. Plug the thermometer into the unit. Insert the Grill Grate and close the hood. Select ROAST, set the temperature to 400°F, then select PRESET. Use the arrows to the right to select BEEF. The unit will default to WELL to cook to a safe temperature. Insert the Smart Thermometer into the thickest part of the loin. Select START/STOP to begin preheating.

3. When the unit beeps to signify it has preheated, place the tenderloin on the Grill Grate. (If the Splatter Shield is touching the tenderloin when you close the hood, use grill mitts to remove the Grill Grate and place the tenderloin in the Cooking Pot instead.) Close the hood and cook until the Smart Thermometer indicates your desired internal temperature has been reached.

4. When cooking is complete, remove the tenderloin and let rest for 10 minutes before slicing and serving.

Stuffed-Onion Burgers

SERVES 6

In this dish, I've combined my love of onions with my love of thick, juicy, homemade burgers. This recipe makes six ⅓-pound burgers on your Foodi™ Grill. Here, I use red onions for their color and to give the burgers a slightly sweeter taste. When red onions are cooked, they lose the spicy and pungent flavor that you get when eaten raw, and they will bring your burger to a whole new sweeter level.

5 INGREDIENTS / DAIRY-FREE / GLUTEN-FREE / FAMILY FAVORITE / NUT-FREE / UNDER 30 MINUTES

PREP TIME: 10 minutes

COOK TIME: 15 minutes

ACCESSORIES: Grill Grate

DID YOU KNOW? Making an indentation in the middle of your patty will prevent the burger from puffing up and breaking out of the onion wrap.

VARIATION TIP: For even more flavor, during the last 5 minutes of cooking, brush some sweet barbecue sauce over the onion rings and on top of the burgers.

2 large red onions

1 teaspoon onion powder

1 teaspoon garlic powder

2 teaspoons sea salt

2 teaspoons freshly ground black pepper

4 tablespoons gluten-free Worcestershire sauce

2 pounds ground beef

1. Cut both ends off the onions. Slice each onion crosswise into thirds and peel off the papery outer skin. Separate the outer two rings (keeping the pair together) from each third for a stable and firm onion ring wrapper.

2. Insert the Grill Grate and close the hood. Select GRILL, set the temperature to HI, and set the time to 15 minutes. Select START/STOP to begin preheating.

3. In a large bowl, combine the onion powder, garlic powder, salt, pepper, and Worcestershire sauce. Add the ground beef in chunks and loosely mix. Form the mixture into 6 equal-size patties. Stuff the burger patties into the onion rings and make a small indentation in the middle of each patty with your thumb.

4. When the unit beeps to signify it has preheated, place the patties on the Grill Grate. Close the hood and grill for 7 minutes, 30 seconds.

5. After 7 minutes, 30 seconds, open the hood and flip the burgers. Close the hood and cook for 7 minutes, 30 seconds more for medium-well burgers. If you prefer your burgers more well-done, continue cooking to your liking.

6. When cooking is complete, remove the burgers from the grill and serve.

Sweet and Tangy Beef

SERVES 4

Sweet onion, red bell pepper, and a tangy sauce make this dish a restaurant-quality meal you can make at home. Feel free to add more veggies of your choice to turn this into more of a stir-fry, but I prefer this dish with white rice or ramen noodles. This is another easy weeknight meal to bring to your table in under 30 minutes.

DAIRY-FREE / NUT-FREE / UNDER 30 MINUTES

PREP TIME: 10 minutes

COOK TIME: 12 minutes

ACCESSORIES: Cooking Pot

SUBSTITUTION TIP: Try this with rib eye, hanger, or flank steak. You can also switch the beef out for tofu or chicken.

For the beef

- 2 pounds top sirloin steak, thinly sliced
- 1 tablespoon cornstarch
- 3 tablespoons avocado oil
- 3 tablespoons soy sauce
- 2 tablespoons oyster sauce
- 1 tablespoon peeled minced fresh ginger
- 1 tablespoon sesame oil
- ½ teaspoon salt
- 1 onion, coarsely chopped
- 1 red bell pepper, coarsely chopped

For the sweet and tangy sauce

- ½ cup water
- 2 tablespoons ketchup
- 2 tablespoons oyster sauce
- 2 tablespoons light brown sugar, packed
- 1 teaspoon salt
- 1 teaspoon sesame oil
- 1 tablespoon white vinegar
- 1 tablespoon Worcestershire sauce

To make the beef

1. Insert the Cooking Pot and close the hood. Select GRILL, set the temperature to HI, and set the time to 12 minutes. Select START/STOP to begin preheating.

2. In a large bowl, combine the beef, cornstarch, avocado oil, soy sauce, oyster sauce, ginger, sesame oil, and salt. Mix well so the beef slices are fully coated.

3. When the unit beeps to signify it has preheated, transfer the beef to the Cooking Pot. Close the hood and cook for 6 minutes.

CONTINUED ▶

To make the sweet and tangy sauce

4. While the beef is cooking, in a small bowl, combine the water, ketchup, oyster sauce, brown sugar, salt, sesame oil, vinegar, and Worcestershire sauce. Stir until the sugar is dissolved.

5. After 6 minutes, open the hood and stir the beef. Add the onion and red bell pepper to the Cooking Pot. Close the hood and cook for 2 minutes. After 2 minutes, open the hood and add the sauce to the pot. Close the hood and cook for 4 minutes more.

6. When cooking is complete, spoon the beef and sauce over white rice, if desired. Serve.

Uncle's Famous Tri-Tip

My uncle is known for serving up tri-tip that he has smoked on the grill. I've adapted his "famous tri-tip," as it's something I look forward to seeing on my family's table. What normally takes hours to smoke can now be cooked in less than 30 minutes. If you wish to double the recipe, the Foodi™ Grill conveniently fits two 3-pound tri-tips, which can cook at the same time!

DAIRY-FREE / GLUTEN-FREE / NUT-FREE

PREP TIME: 10 minutes, plus overnight to marinate

COOK TIME: 20 minutes

ACCESSORIES: Grill Grate / Smart Thermometer

HACK IT: Don't have time to marinate overnight? Prepare the same recipe but omit the red wine vinegar. Oil up the tri-tip, then combine all the dry seasonings with the honey mustard for a rub and let marinate for 15 to 30 minutes.

¼ **cup avocado oil**

½ **cup red wine vinegar**

¼ **cup light brown sugar, packed**

4 **tablespoons honey mustard**

1 **tablespoon garlic powder**

1 **tablespoon onion powder**

1 **tablespoon paprika**

1 **tablespoon salt**

1 **tablespoon freshly ground black pepper**

3 **pounds tri-tip**

1. In a large resealable bag, combine the avocado oil, red wine vinegar, brown sugar, honey mustard, garlic powder, onion powder, paprika, salt, and pepper. Add the tri-tip, seal, and massage the mixture into the meat. Refrigerate overnight.

2. About 20 minutes before grilling, remove the bag from the refrigerator so the marinade becomes liquid again at room temperature.

3. Plug the thermometer into the unit. Insert the Grill Grate and close the hood. Select GRILL, set the temperature to MED, and select PRESET. Use the arrows to the right to select BEEF, then choose desired doneness. Insert the Smart Thermometer into the thickest part of the meat. Select START/STOP to begin preheating.

4. When the unit beeps to signify it has preheated, place the tri-tip on the Grill Grate, fat-side up. Close the hood to begin cooking.

5. When the Foodi™ Grill indicates it is time to flip, open the hood and flip the tri-tip. Close the hood and continue cooking until the Smart Thermometer indicates your desired internal temperature has been reached.

6. When cooking is complete, remove the tri-tip from the grill. Let rest for 10 minutes before slicing against the grain. Serve.

Pork Spareribs with Peanut Sauce, *page 158*

7

Pork & Lamb

Bacon-Wrapped Stuffed Sausage

SERVES 4

Bacon lovers unite! Surprise your guests with this fun, bacon-wrapped sausage. I have made this in an oven a few times, and no matter what I've stuffed it with, it's been a hit! Once you get the rolling, stuffing, and weaving down, the possibilities are endless. Doing this on the Foodi™ Grill has made it 100 times better because of the easy cleanup and not having to worry about grease spills and splatters.

5 INGREDIENTS / GLUTEN-FREE / NUT-FREE / UNDER 30 MINUTES

PREP TIME: 15 minutes

COOK TIME: 15 minutes

ACCESSORIES: Grill Grate

VARIATION TIP: Use maple sausage for some sweetness or hot Italian for a kick. Change up your breakfast by using breakfast sausage and stuffing it with your favorite breakfast items, like hash browns and eggs.

1 pound ground Italian sausage (not links)

1 cup fresh spinach leaves

⅓ cup sun-dried tomatoes, drained

½ cup shredded provolone cheese

14 slices thin-sliced bacon

1. Cut off the two corners (small cuts) of a gallon-size resealable plastic bag. (This makes the next part easier.) Place the sausage in the bag, then press the meat until it is evenly flat and fills the entire bag. Using scissors, cut the side seams of the bag, then peel back the top and flip the flattened sausage onto a sheet of parchment paper. Gently pull back and remove the plastic bag.

2. Layer the spinach leaves, sun-dried tomatoes, and provolone cheese evenly across the bottom half of the sausage. Lift up the end of the wax paper, rolling the sausage over the stuffing, and slowly peel back the wax paper as you continue rolling, leaving the sausage roll on the last bit of wax paper.

3. Insert the Grill Grate and close the hood. Select GRILL, set the temperature to HI, and set the time to 15 minutes. Select START/STOP to begin preheating.

4. While the unit is preheating, on a new piece of wax paper, place 7 bacon slices side by side but not touching each other. Place another bacon slice across the 7 slices, weaving it over and under them, creating a basket-weave pattern. Repeat this with the remaining 6 bacon slices. Once the bacon is woven together, carefully place the sausage roll on the bottom portion of the bacon weave. Then, lifting the end of the wax paper under the bacon, roll it up tightly, until the bacon is wrapped around the stuffed sausage.

5. When the unit beeps to signify it has preheated, place the bacon-wrapped sausage roll on the Grill Grate. Close the hood and grill for 8 minutes.

6. After 8 minutes, open the hood and flip the sausage roll. Close the hood and cook for 7 minutes more.

7. When cooking is complete, open the hood and check the sausage roll. If you prefer your bacon crispier, continue cooking to your liking. Remove the sausage from the grill and serve.

Brown-Sugared Ham

This brown-sugared ham is an easy way to feed the family (or guests) any time of year. It's a great holiday dish, as well, and making sandwiches is a sure way to level up those leftovers. By using a fully cooked ham, the hard part is done. All that's left is adding a delicious and flavorful brown sugar glaze.

DAIRY-FREE / GLUTEN-FREE / NUT-FREE

PREP TIME: 10 minutes

COOK TIME: 30 minutes

ACCESSORIES: Cooking Pot / Smart Thermometer

HACK IT: Use half of the brown sugar glaze at the beginning of the cooking and the remaining half during the last 10 minutes of cooking to get a beautiful golden glaze.

1 (3-pound) bone-in, fully cooked ham quarter

3 tablespoons Dijon mustard

¼ cup pineapple juice

¼ cup apple cider vinegar

1 cup light brown sugar, packed

1 teaspoon cinnamon

½ teaspoon ground ginger

1. Plug the thermometer into the unit. Insert the Cooking Pot and close the hood. Select ROAST, set the temperature to 350ºF, then select PRESET. Use the arrows to the right to select PORK. The unit will default to WELL to cook pork to a safe temperature. Insert the Smart Thermometer into the thickest part of the ham. Select START/STOP to begin preheating.

2. While the unit is preheating, score the ham using a sharp knife, creating a diamond pattern on top. Brush on the Dijon mustard.

3. In a small bowl, combine the pineapple juice, vinegar, brown sugar, cinnamon, and ginger.

4. When the unit beeps to signify it has preheated, place the ham in the Cooking Pot. Brush some of the glaze over the entire ham, then pour the rest on top so the glaze can seep into the scores. Close the hood to begin cooking.

5. When cooking is complete, the Smart Thermometer will indicate that the desired temperature has been reached. Remove the ham from the pot and let rest for at least 10 minutes before slicing. Serve.

Burnt Ends

With these burnt ends, you can bring the outdoor grilling technique indoors. Burnt ends are often made with beef brisket, but my family loves all things pork, so I opted for a pork butt here. I've used a similar technique for making these outside so that we could enjoy the sticky, sweet, and caramelized flavor at home year-round.

GLUTEN-FREE / NUT-FREE

PREP TIME: 10 minutes

COOK TIME: 40 minutes

ACCESSORIES: Cooking Pot

VARIATION TIP: You can also use pork belly for this recipe.

1 tablespoon garlic powder

1 tablespoon sea salt

1 tablespoon paprika

¼ teaspoon freshly ground black pepper

2 pounds pork butt, cut into 1-inch cubes

½ cup barbecue sauce

¼ cup light brown sugar, packed

¼ cup honey

4 tablespoons (½ stick) unsalted butter, sliced

1. Insert the Cooking Pot and close the hood. Select ROAST, set the temperature to 300°F, and set the time to 20 minutes. Select START/STOP to begin preheating.

2. While the unit is preheating, in a large bowl, combine the garlic powder, salt, paprika, and pepper. Add the pork and toss until generously coated on all sides.

3. When the unit beeps to signify it has preheated, place the pork in the Cooking Pot in a single layer. Close the hood and roast for 10 minutes.

4. After 10 minutes, open the hood and flip the pork cubes. Close the hood and cook for 10 minutes more.

5. At this point, the pork should have a nice char. Place the pork cubes in the center of a large piece of aluminum foil. Add the barbecue sauce, brown sugar, and honey and massage them into the roasted pork. Add the butter, then seal the foil. Place the packet back in the Cooking Pot.

6. Select ROAST, set the temperature to 350ºF, and set the time to 20 minutes. Select START/STOP and then press PREHEAT to skip preheating. Close the hood and cook for 20 minutes.

7. When cooking is complete, remove the foil packet. Be careful opening the foil, because the steam will be very hot. The pork should be nicely coated with sauce that has thickened. If you want more char and caramelization of the burnt ends, carefully place the open foil packet back in the Cooking Pot. Select GRILL, set the temperature to HI, and set the time to 10 minutes. Select START/STOP and then press PREHEAT to skip preheating. Close the hood and cook for 10 minutes or until charred to your liking.

Crackling Pork Roast

By far, this is my favorite way to eat pork. The most enjoyable part to eat and marvel over is the golden top layer, full of crunch, so make sure you keep that rind on. The rind is what brings all the flavor and oils that help the whole roast cook itself. If you've ever tried chicharrones, you'll enjoy this even more by making it at home.

5 INGREDIENTS / GLUTEN-FREE / NUT-FREE

PREP TIME: 10 minutes, plus overnight to brine

COOK TIME: 1 hour 30 minutes

ACCESSORIES: Cooking Pot / Smart Thermometer

HACK IT: If you are pressed for time and do not want to wait for the roast to dry-brine overnight, you can boil the roast. Fully submerge the roast in a pot of water, bring to a boil, and boil for 20 to 30 minutes. As the pork boils, foam and pork residue float to the top; discard it using a spoon. The pork will turn a white-grayish hue, and the skin will look rubbery. After removing it from the boiling water, let the pork rest and cool for 5 to 10 minutes. Pat the skin dry with a paper towel and season the skin generously with salt. Then, AIR CRISP it at 400°F for 30 to 40 minutes, or until you've achieved the perfect golden crackling crust.

1 (3- to 4-pound) boneless pork shoulder, rind on

Kosher salt

1. Pat the roast dry with a paper towel. Using a sharp knife, score the rind, creating a diamond pattern on top. Season generously with salt. Place it in the refrigerator, uncovered, overnight to brine.

2. Plug the thermometer into the unit. Insert the Cooking Pot and close the hood. Select ROAST, set the temperature to 350°F, then select PRESET. Use the arrows to the right to select PORK. The unit will default to WELL to cook pork to a safe temperature. Insert the Smart Thermometer into the thickest part of the meat. Select START/STOP to begin preheating.

3. When the unit beeps to signify it has preheated, place the roast in the Cooking Pot. Close the hood to begin cooking.

4. When cooking is complete, the Smart Thermometer will indicate that the desired temperature has been reached. Remove the pork and let it rest for 10 minutes before slicing.

Crispy Pork Belly Bites

SERVES 6

If you love bacon, you are going to love this pork belly recipe. Don't be intimidated by the fatty pieces—they're full of flavor and help cook the meat to perfection. One of my favorite things to do with pork belly is to make it into super crispy, bite-size little squares I can dip in my favorite sauces. With crispy and charred edges all around and a tender, juicy center, these will leave you craving more.

5 INGREDIENTS / DAIRY-FREE / FAMILY FAVORITE / GLUTEN-FREE / NUT-FREE / UNDER 30 MINUTES

PREP TIME: 10 minutes

COOK TIME: 20 minutes

ACCESSORIES: Grill Grate

VARIATION TIP: If you are cooking pork belly with a thick layer of skin, I recommend using a sharp knife to score it—but do not cut into the meat itself. If you prefer your pork belly skin crackling instead of chargrilled, use the slower cooking process of Crackling Pork Roast (page 142).

1 tablespoon garlic powder

1 tablespoon sea salt

1 tablespoon paprika

¼ teaspoon freshly ground black pepper

2 pounds pork belly (3 to 4 slabs)

1. Insert the Grill Grate and close the hood. Select GRILL, set the temperature to HI, and set the time to 20 minutes. Select START/STOP to begin preheating.

2. While the unit is preheating, in a large bowl, combine the garlic powder, salt, paprika, and pepper.

3. Pat the pork belly dry with a paper towel. Place it in the seasoning and toss to generously coat the pork belly on all sides.

4. When the unit beeps to signify it has preheated, place the pork belly on the Grill Grate, skin-side up. Close the hood and grill for 10 minutes.

5. After 10 minutes, open the hood and flip the pork. Close the hood and cook for 10 minutes more.

6. When cooking is complete, remove the pork belly from the grill and serve.

Crusted Pork Chops with Honey-Maple Jalapeño Glaze

This glaze offers the perfect sweet and spicy combo for these crispy and crunchy pork chops. I have always been intimidated by cooking pork chops because they can become too dry too quickly. Not anymore! These will be cooked to perfection, and you'll get an unbelievable crust and a juicy inside with a sweet sauce that gives some kick.

DAIRY-FREE / NUT-FREE / UNDER 30 MINUTES

PREP TIME: 10 minutes

COOK TIME: 15 minutes

ACCESSORIES: Grill Grate

DID YOU KNOW? Adding a pinch of cornstarch to the glaze mix will make it thicker.

2 large eggs

2 cups panko bread crumbs

1 teaspoon Italian seasoning

1 teaspoon garlic powder

6 (6-ounce) boneless pork chops

¼ cup honey

¼ cup maple syrup

¼ cup soy sauce

1 jalapeño, sliced (seeds optional)

1. Insert the Grill Grate and close the hood. Select GRILL, set the temperature to MED, and set the time to 15 minutes. Select START/STOP to begin preheating.

2. While the unit is preheating, create an assembly line with 2 large bowls. In one bowl, whisk the eggs. In the other bowl, combine the panko bread crumbs, Italian seasoning, and garlic powder. One at a time, dip the pork chops in the egg and then in the panko mixture until fully coated and set aside.

3. In a small bowl, combine the honey, maple syrup, soy sauce, and jalapeño slices.

4. When the unit beeps to signify it has preheated, place the pork chops on the Grill Grate. Close the hood and grill for 7 minutes, 30 seconds.

5. After 7 minutes, 30 seconds, open the hood and flip the pork chops. Spoon half of the honey glaze over the chops. Close the hood and cook for 7 minutes, 30 seconds more.

6. When cooking is complete, remove the pork chops from the grill and drizzle with the remaining glaze. Let the pork chops rest for a few minutes before serving.

Herb and Pesto Stuffed Pork Loin

SERVES 8

Juicy, flavorful, and simple, this pork loin is stuffed with a fresh homemade pesto sauce. One of the benefits of making your own sauce is that you get the full-on flavor from the fresh herbs without having to worry about nut allergies or unwanted additives. Plus, there's no food processor needed for this one.

GLUTEN-FREE / NUT-FREE / UNDER 30 MINUTES

PREP TIME: 10 minutes

COOK TIME: 15 minutes

ACCESSORIES: Grill Grate / Smart Thermometer

VARIATION TIP: Want some crunch? Add pine nuts to your homemade pesto sauce. Not into pesto? Switch it up for the sauce in Pork Chops with Creamy Mushroom Sauce (page 152).

1 (4-pound) boneless center-cut pork loin

½ cup avocado oil

½ cup grated Parmesan cheese

2 tablespoons finely chopped fresh basil

1 tablespoon finely chopped fresh parsley

1 tablespoon chopped fresh chives

½ teaspoon finely chopped fresh rosemary

5 garlic cloves, minced

1. Butterfly the pork loin. You can use the same method as you would for a chicken breast or steak (see page 118), but because a pork loin is thicker, you can perform this double butterfly technique: Place the boneless, trimmed loin on a cutting board. One-third from the bottom of the loin, slice horizontally from the side (parallel to the cutting board), stopping about ½ inch from the opposite side, and open the flap like a book. Make another horizontal cut from the thicker side of the loin to match the thickness of the first cut, stopping again ½ inch from the edge. Open up the flap to create a rectangular piece of flat meat.

2. Plug the thermometer into the unit. Insert the Grill Grate and close the hood. Select GRILL, set the temperature to MED, and select PRESET. Use the arrows to the right to select PORK. The unit will default to WELL to cook pork to a safe temperature. Select START/STOP to begin preheating.

3. While the unit is preheating, in a small bowl, combine the avocado oil, Parmesan cheese, basil, parsley, chives, rosemary, and garlic. Spread the pesto sauce evenly over the cut side of each tenderloin. Starting from a longer side, roll up the pork tightly over the filling. Use toothpicks to secure the ends. Insert the Smart Thermometer into the thickest part of the meat.

4. When the unit beeps to signify it has preheated, place the loin on the Grill Grate. Close the hood to begin cooking.

5. When the Foodi™ Grill indicates it's time to flip, open the hood and flip the loin. Close the hood to continue cooking.

6. When cooking is complete, the Smart Thermometer will indicate that the internal temperature has been reached. Open the hood and remove the loin. Let the meat rest for 10 minutes before slicing in between the toothpicks. Serve.

Honey-Garlic Ribs

SERVES 6

Baby back ribs are smaller, leaner, and meatier compared to beef ribs. I still want these to fall off the bone as well as get every bite full of honey-garlic flavor. The key to making these ribs is to cook them slowly at a fairly low temperature and then grill them at a high temperature at the end to get a nice char.

DAIRY-FREE / NUT-FREE

PREP TIME: 10 minutes

COOK TIME: 1 hour 10 minutes

ACCESSORIES: Grill Grate

SUBSTITUTION TIP: Feel free to replace the minced garlic with garlic powder, but remember, 1 garlic clove is equal to ⅛ teaspoon garlic powder.

2 (2- to 3-pound) racks baby back ribs

Sea salt

½ cup soy sauce

1 cup honey

4 garlic cloves, minced

1 teaspoon paprika

3 tablespoons light brown sugar, packed

1. Insert the Grill Grate and close the hood. Select BAKE, set the temperature to 300°F, and set the time to 1 hour. Select START/STOP to begin preheating.

2. While the unit is preheating, generously season each rack with salt, then wrap each in aluminum foil.

3. When the unit beeps to signify it has preheated, place the foil-wrapped ribs on the Grill Grate. Close the hood and cook for 1 hour.

4. While the ribs are cooking, in a small bowl, combine the soy sauce, honey, garlic, paprika, and brown sugar until the sugar is dissolved.

5. When cooking is complete, remove the ribs from the grill. Slowly open the foil (but don't remove it) and brush the sauce over the ribs. Pour the remaining sauce over both racks.

6. Place the slightly opened packets of racks back onto the Grill Grate. Select GRILL, set the temperature to HI, and set the time to 10 minutes. Select START/STOP and then press the PREHEAT button to skip preheating. Close the hood and cook for 5 minutes.

7. After 5 minutes, open the hood, flip the rib racks, and place them back in the foil. Close the hood and cook for 5 minutes more or until you achieve your desired level of char.

8. When cooking is complete, remove the racks from the grill and serve.

Italian Sausage and Peppers

I am all for simple and easy meals, and this is one of them. I came across the concept for this recipe while searching for food ideas after I accidentally bought some spicy Italian sausage. The hubby can't handle the heat, so to tame it, I added some white wine vinegar. The combo of spice and vinegar soon became a new favorite, and we enjoy this meal weekly.

5 INGREDIENTS / GLUTEN-FREE / NUT-FREE / UNDER 30 MINUTES

PREP TIME: 5 minutes

COOK TIME: 10 minutes

ACCESSORIES: Cooking Pot

VARIATION TIP: Serve this as a sub sandwich. Add some Dijon or honey mustard, shredded lettuce, or any or your favorite toppings.

1 green bell pepper

1 large red onion

1 pound ground Italian sausage (not links)

1 tablespoon garlic, minced

2 tablespoons white wine vinegar

1. Insert the Cooking Pot and close the hood. Select GRILL, set the temperature to HI, and set the time to 10 minutes. Select START/STOP to begin preheating.

2. While the unit is preheating, cut the bell pepper into strips and slice the red onion.

3. When the unit beeps to signify it has preheated, place the sausage, garlic, and vinegar in the Cooking Pot. Slowly break apart the sausage using a wooden spoon or a spatula. Close the hood and cook for 5 minutes.

4. After 5 minutes, open the hood and stir the sausage. Add the bell pepper and onion. Close the hood and cook for 5 minutes more.

5. When cooking is complete, stir the sausage, pepper, and onion again. Serve.

Grilled Pork Banh Mi

This light and flavorful sandwich is inspired by the popular Vietnamese street food and is easy to put together with perfectly grilled, caramelized pork. The flavoring is similar to Lemongrass Beef Skewers (page 123) but focuses more on the sweet caramelization instead of the lemony taste. I love having everything ready for guests to assemble so they can create their own pork banh mi sandwiches with all the toppings and dressings.

DAIRY-FREE / NUT-FREE

PREP TIME: 10 minutes, plus 30 minutes to marinate

COOK TIME: 15 minutes

ACCESSORIES: Cooking Pot

SUBSTITUTION TIP: If you are not into crunchy baguette bread, use a brioche roll for a softer texture. If you want a spicier mayo, combine ¼ cup mayonnaise with 1 teaspoon sriracha.

3 tablespoons light brown sugar, packed

1 tablespoon soy sauce

3 tablespoons minced garlic

Juice of 2 limes

1 shallot, finely minced

2 pounds pork tenderloin, cut into 1-inch-thick slices

1 daikon radish, cut into thin strips

1 large carrot, cut into thin strips

3 tablespoons rice vinegar

½ teaspoon kosher salt

1 teaspoon granulated sugar

6 sandwich-size baguettes

Mayonnaise

1 cucumber, thinly sliced

Fresh cilantro

1 jalapeño, sliced

1. In a large bowl, combine the brown sugar, soy sauce, garlic, lime juice, shallot, and pork tenderloin slices. Marinate for at least 30 minutes. If marinating for longer, cover and refrigerate.

2. Insert the Cooking Pot and close the hood. Select GRILL, set the temperature to HI, and set the time to 15 minutes. Select START/STOP to begin preheating.

3. While the unit is preheating, in a medium bowl, combine the daikon, carrot, rice vinegar, salt, and sugar.

4. When the unit beeps to signify it has preheated, place the pork in the Cooking Pot. Feel free to add a little bit of the marinade to the pot. Close the hood and cook for 8 minutes.

5. After 8 minutes, open the hood and stir the pork. Close the hood and cook for 7 minutes more.

6. When cooking is complete, slice open each baguette and spread mayonnaise on both sides. Add a layer each of pork, pickled daikon and carrot, cucumber, cilantro, and jalapeño slices and serve.

Pork Chops with Creamy Mushroom Sauce

SERVES 6

Dress up pork chops with this delicious creamy mushroom sauce. The Foodi™ Grill cooks these chops to perfection, and the easy, flavorful sauce brings the whole dish to life. This is the ultimate fast, simple-yet-satisfying dinner—ideal as either an easy weeknight meal or weekend dinner party fare.

GLUTEN-FREE / NUT-FREE / UNDER 30 MINUTES

PREP TIME: 5 minutes

COOK TIME: 10 minutes

ACCESSORIES: Grill Grate / Cooking Pot

VARIATION TIP: Feel free to add some sliced onions to the creamy mushroom sauce or any additional herbs for more flavor.

1 cup heavy (whipping) cream
½ cup chicken broth
1 tablespoon cornstarch
1 teaspoon garlic powder

6 (6-ounce) boneless pork chops
8 ounces mushrooms, sliced

1. Insert the Grill Grate and close the hood. Select GRILL, set the temperature to HI, and set the time to 10 minutes. Select START/STOP to begin preheating.

2. While the unit is preheating, in a medium bowl, whisk together the heavy cream, chicken broth, cornstarch, and garlic powder.

3. When the unit beeps to signify it has preheated, place the pork chops on the Grill Grate. Close the hood and grill for 5 minutes.

4. After 5 minutes, open the hood and use grill mitts to remove the Grill Grate and the chops. Pour the cream mixture into the Cooking Pot. Put the Grill Grate back into the unit and flip the pork chops. Close the hood and cook for 5 minutes more.

5. When cooking is complete, remove the pork chops from the grill. Use grill mitts to remove the Grill Grate from the unit and stir the cream mixture. Add the sliced mushrooms, close the hood, and let sit for 5 minutes. Pour the creamy mushroom sauce over the pork chops and serve.

Pulled Pork Sandwiches

SERVES 6 TO 8

Pulled pork can take well over 3 to 4 hours on an outdoor grill. You don't have to wait that long to enjoy barbecued pulled-pork taste anymore. By cutting your pork shoulder into smaller pieces, you will be able to cut that time by half! You can now have tender, pull-apart meat by mimicking traditional outdoor grilling techniques.

NUT-FREE

PREP TIME: 15 minutes, plus 30 minutes to rest

COOK TIME: 1 hour 30 minutes

ACCESSORIES: Grill Grate / Cooking Pot / Smart Thermometer

HACK IT: Use your favorite barbecue rub to season the pork in place of the seasoning mix in this recipe.

1 tablespoon onion powder

1 tablespoon garlic powder

1 tablespoon salt

1 teaspoon freshly ground black pepper

1 teaspoon ground cumin

1 teaspoon ground cayenne pepper

3 tablespoons light brown sugar, packed

1 tablespoon granulated sugar

3 to 4 pounds pork shoulder, cut into 3 or 4 equal pieces

3 tablespoons unsalted butter, sliced

3 tablespoons honey

4 tablespoons barbecue sauce

Hamburger buns or sandwich bread

1. Plug the thermometer into the unit. Insert the Grill Grate and close the hood. Select ROAST, set the temperature to 350ºF, and set the time to 90 minutes. Select START/STOP to begin preheating.

2. While the unit is preheating, in a small bowl, combine the onion powder, garlic powder, salt, black pepper, cumin, cayenne pepper, brown sugar, and granulated sugar. Rub the mixture on all sides of the pork pieces. Insert the Smart Thermometer into the thickest part of the meat.

3. When the unit beeps to signify it has preheated, place the pork on the Grill Grate. Manually select the temperature setting to reach 165ºF. Close the hood and cook for 45 minutes or until the Smart Thermometer indicates the temperature has been reached.

4. When cooking is complete, open the hood and remove the Smart Thermometer. Use grill mitts to remove the Grill Grate and pork shoulder. Place the pork pieces on top of a large piece of aluminum foil. Top with the butter slices and drizzle with the honey and barbecue sauce. Close the foil over the pork and

CONTINUED ▶

crimp it to seal.

5. Place the foil-wrapped pork in the Cooking Pot. Carefully pierce the foil to reinsert the Smart Thermometer in the thickest part of the meat. Manually select the temperature setting to reach 200ºF. Close the hood and cook for 45 minutes.

6. When cooking is complete, the Smart Thermometer will indicate that the desired temperature has been reached. Open the hood and use grill mitts to remove the foil-wrapped pork. Let the meat rest in the foil for 30 minutes. Once it has rested, shred the pork using two forks and place some meat on top of a bun, topped with more barbecue sauce, if desired. Serve.

Ranch and Cheddar Pork Chops

I used to worry that my pork chops would turn out dry, but not anymore, thanks to the Foodi™ Grill! Topping your pork chops with this easy ranch and cheddar topping makes them extra creamy and juicy. This is an easy, delicious meal with little prep that will have you ready to eat in 15 minutes.

5 INGREDIENTS / GLUTEN-FREE / NUT-FREE / UNDER 30 MINUTES

PREP TIME: 5 minutes

COOK TIME: 10 minutes

ACCESSORIES: Grill Grate

SUBSTITUTION TIP: If you can't find ranch seasoning, use 3 tablespoons ranch dressing and reduce the cream cheese to 4 ounces.

VARIATION TIP: Add bacon crumbles on top for bacon, ranch, and cheddar pork chops. Not into pork chops? Use the same ranch and cheddar mix on top of chicken breast.

8 ounces cream cheese, at room temperature

1 tablespoon ranch seasoning mix

½ cup shredded cheddar cheese

6 (6-ounce) boneless pork chops

1. Insert the Grill Grate and close the hood. Select GRILL, set the temperature to HI, and set the time to 10 minutes. Select START/STOP to begin preheating.

2. While the unit is preheating, in a small bowl, combine the cream cheese, ranch seasoning, and cheddar cheese.

3. When the unit beeps to signify it has preheated, place the pork chops on the Grill Grate. Close the hood and grill for 5 minutes.

4. After 5 minutes, open the hood and flip the chops. Then top each with the ranch-cheese mixture. Close the hood and cook for 5 minutes more.

5. When cooking is complete, remove the chops from the grill and serve.

Sizzling Pork Sisig

SERVES 6 TO 8

Pork sisig is a tasty Filipino dish that gets its name from the word sisigan, *which means "to make it sour." It was used as a cure for hangovers or to relieve nausea in pregnant women. Now, we think of it as a crispy, meaty dish that brings out the spice from chiles as well as savory and tangy flavors from the soy sauce, citrus, and vinegar. I knew I had to make this recipe on the Foodi™ Grill because it's best served sizzling.*

DAIRY-FREE / NUT-FREE

PREP TIME: 20 minutes

COOK TIME: 50 minutes

ACCESSORIES: Cooking Pot

SUBSTITUTION TIP: If you do not have red Thai chiles available, you can supply the heat with a jalapeño or by using 1 teaspoon red pepper flakes.

3 pounds pork shoulder or pork belly, cut into 1-inch-thick slices

2 tablespoons soy sauce

2 tablespoons rice vinegar

2 tablespoons fish sauce

Juice of 1 lemon, divided

1 tablespoon garlic powder

¼ teaspoon peeled minced fresh ginger

1 small red onion, diced

2 red Thai chiles, sliced

1. Insert the Cooking Pot and close the hood. Select ROAST, set the temperature to 350ºF, and set the time to 30 minutes. Select START/STOP to begin preheating.

2. When the unit beeps to signify it has preheated, place the pork in the Cooking Pot. Close the hood and cook for 15 minutes.

3. After 15 minutes, open the hood and flip the pork. Close the hood and cook for 15 minutes more.

4. When cooking is complete, remove the pork and set aside to cool.

5. While the pork is cooling, prepare the sauce. In a small bowl, combine the soy sauce, vinegar, fish sauce, juice of ½ lemon, garlic powder, and ginger. Place the diced onion and sliced chiles in a separate small bowl and set aside. Once the pork has cooled down enough to handle, cut the pork into ½-inch cubes.

6. Wash and dry the Cooking Pot. Then insert the Cooking Pot and close the hood. Select GRILL, set the temperature to HI, and set the time to 20 minutes. Select START/STOP to begin preheating.

7. When the unit beeps to signify it has preheated, place the pork in the Cooking Pot. Close the hood and cook for 10 minutes.

8. After 10 minutes, open the hood, stir the pork, and pour in the sauce. Close the hood and cook for 10 minutes more.

9. When cooking is complete, transfer the pork and sauce to a bowl. Add the onion and chiles on top and squeeze the juice of the remaining ½ lemon over the top. Serve.

Pork Spareribs with Peanut Sauce

Change it up from the typical barbecue sauce by trying out this peanut butter sauce with your ribs. I like pouring it over the ribs when they are done or just placing it in a bowl to dip the ribs in. Similar to a dipping sauce for spring rolls, this peanut sauce gives some extra crunch and creaminess to the chargrilled ribs.

DAIRY-FREE

PREP TIME: 10 minutes

COOK TIME: 30 minutes

ACCESSORIES: Grill Grate / Smart Thermometer

VARIATION TIP: You can brush this peanut butter sauce on the ribs during the last 5 minutes of grilling so the flavors cook on as a beautiful glaze. If doing so, I suggest replacing the crunchy peanut butter with a creamy peanut butter.

2 (2- to 3-pound) racks St. Louis–style spareribs

Sea salt

½ cup crunchy peanut butter

1 tablespoon rice vinegar

2 tablespoons hoisin sauce

1 tablespoon honey

2 tablespoons soy sauce

1 teaspoon garlic powder

1. Plug the thermometer into the unit. Insert the Grill Grate and close the hood. Select GRILL, set the temperature to MED, and select PRESET. Use the arrows to the right to select PORK. The unit will default to WELL to cook the pork to a safe temperature. Insert the Smart Thermometer into the thickest part of the meat between two bones, making sure it does not touch bone. Select START/STOP to begin preheating.

2. When the unit beeps to signify it has preheated, place the racks of ribs on the Grill Grate. Close the hood to begin cooking.

3. When the Foodi™ Grill indicates it's time to flip, open the hood and flip the racks. Then close the hood to continue cooking.

4. While the ribs are cooking, in a small bowl, combine the peanut butter, vinegar, hoisin sauce, honey, soy sauce, and garlic powder and mix until well blended.

5. When cooking is complete, the Smart Thermometer will indicate that the desired internal temperature has been reached. Open the hood and remove the ribs. Either pour the sauce over the ribs or divide the sauce between individual bowls for dipping. Serve.

Balsamic Honey Mustard Lamb Chops

Every once in a while, I crave these lamb chops. It's usually around the holidays or when I see a good sale at the grocery store. Some people find lamb to have a gamey flavor, but when you marinate the meat in balsamic vinegar and dress it with honey and rosemary, the gaminess is minimal. Every time I have made this dish, the sliced rack of lamb looks like it came from a five-star restaurant.

DAIRY-FREE / GLUTEN-FREE / NUT-FREE

PREP TIME: 10 minutes, plus 1 hour to marinate

COOK TIME: 45 minutes to 1 hour

ACCESSORIES: Cooking Pot / Smart Thermometer

VARIATION TIP: Want some added spice without a lot of heat? Switch out the yellow mustard for Dijon mustard to give these lamb chops some kick.

¼ **cup avocado oil**
½ **cup balsamic vinegar**
2 **garlic cloves, minced**
1 **teaspoon salt**
½ **teaspoon freshly ground black pepper**

2 **tablespoons honey**
1 **tablespoon yellow mustard**
1 **tablespoon fresh rosemary**
1 **(2- to 3-pound) rack of lamb**

1. In a large bowl, whisk together the avocado oil, vinegar, garlic, salt, pepper, honey, mustard, and rosemary. Add the lamb and massage and coat all sides of the meat with the marinade. Cover and refrigerate for at least 1 hour.

2. Plug the thermometer into the unit. Insert the Cooking Pot and close the hood. Select ROAST, set the temperature to 350°F, and select PRESET. Use the arrows to the right to select BEEF/LAMB. The unit will default to WELL to cook lamb to a safe temperature. Insert the Smart Thermometer in the thickest part of the lamb without touching bone. Select START/STOP to begin preheating.

3. When the unit beeps to signify it has preheated, place the rack of lamb in the Cooking Pot. Close the hood to begin cooking.

4. When cooking is complete, the Smart Thermometer will indicate that the specified internal temperature has been reached. Remove the lamb from the pot and serve.

Garlic Herb Crusted Lamb

SERVES 6

A beautiful charred crust of herbs and garlic cover this leg of lamb. The aromas linger as you grill this up. Be patient, as it will be worth the wait. You'll be able to taste each herb in the seasoning in every bite.

GLUTEN-FREE / NUT-FREE

PREP TIME: 10 minutes, plus 30 minutes to marinate

COOK TIME: 1 hour

ACCESSORIES: Grill Grate / Smart Thermometer

VARIATION TIP: Try a balsamic honey mustard glaze. Instead of using the garlic-herb mixture, marinate the lamb in 1 cup balsamic vinegar, then coat it with ½ cup yellow mustard and 1 cup honey as your "crust."

¼ cup red wine vinegar

3 garlic cloves, minced

1 tablespoon garlic powder

1 tablespoon paprika

1 tablespoon ground cumin

1 tablespoon dried parsley

1 tablespoon dried thyme

1 tablespoon dried oregano

1 teaspoon salt

½ teaspoon freshly ground black pepper

Juice of ½ lemon

1 (3-pound) boneless leg of lamb

1. In a large bowl, mix together the vinegar, garlic, garlic powder, paprika, cumin, parsley, thyme, oregano, salt, pepper, and lemon juice until well combined—the marinade will turn into a thick paste. Add the leg of lamb and massage the marinade into the meat. Coat the lamb with the marinade and let sit for at least 30 minutes. If marinating for longer, cover and refrigerate.

2. Plug the thermometer into the unit. Insert the Grill Grate and close the hood. Select GRILL, set the temperature to LO, and set the time to 30 minutes. Insert the Smart Thermometer into the thickest part of the meat. Select START/STOP to begin preheating.

3. When the unit beeps to signify it has preheated, place the lamb on the Grill Grate. Select the BEEF/LAMB preset and choose MEDIUM-WELL or according to your desired doneness. Close the hood and cook for 30 minutes.

4. After 30 minutes, which is the maximum time for the LO setting, select GRILL again, set the temperature to LO, and set the time to 30 minutes. Select START/STOP and press PREHEAT to skip preheating. Cook until the Smart Thermometer indicates that the desired internal temperature has been reached.

5. When cooking is complete, remove the lamb from the grill and serve.

Lamb Kefta Kebabs

SERVES 4 TO 6

The first time I made lamb kefta kebabs was on a charcoal barbecue grill—outdoors, of course. The meat was definitely tasty, but I was new to grilling, and the wooden skewers burned because I didn't properly soak them first, and that resulted in losing some of the meat to the grill. With the Foodi™ Grill, I can make these kebabs without having to worry about sacrificing any precious meat. Serve these with an easy cucumber, tomato, and feta cheese salad.

DAIRY-FREE / GLUTEN-FREE / NUT-FREE / UNDER 30 MINUTES

PREP TIME: 5 minutes

COOK TIME: 10 minutes

ACCESSORIES: Grill Grate / Ninja® Foodi™ Grill Kebab Skewers

VARIATION TIP: You can use ground beef in place of ground lamb. Also, if you cannot find ground lamb, cut lamb into 1-inch cubes for the kebabs.

1 small red onion, minced

4 garlic cloves, minced

2 teaspoons dried parsley

2 teaspoons dried oregano

2 teaspoons ground cumin

2 teaspoons salt

2 pounds ground lamb

1. In a large bowl, combine the onion, garlic, parsley, oregano, cumin, and salt. Add the ground lamb in chunks and loosely mix. Form the mixture into 2-inch-long cylinders about 1 inch thick.

2. Insert the Grill Grate and close the hood. Select GRILL, set the temperature to MED, and set the time to 10 minutes. Select START/STOP to begin preheating.

3. While the unit is preheating, thread 2 or 3 lamb cylinders each onto skewers.

4. When the unit beeps to signify it has preheated, place the skewers on the Grill Grate. Close the hood and cook for 5 minutes.

5. After 5 minutes, open the hood and flip the skewers. Close the hood and cook for 5 minutes more.

6. When cooking is complete, remove the kebabs from the grill. Serve with store-bought or homemade tzatziki sauce (see page 163).

Rosemary and Garlic Lamb Pitas

When my husband tried these lamb pitas, he declared, "These taste just like our favorite gyro place!" As much as I would love to own one of those machines that magically cuts off meat from a vertical spinning spit, I've managed to recreate our favorite dish at home by seasoning the lamb with a blend common to the Mediterranean. The thinly sliced lamb, inside a warm pita, along with the homemade tzatziki sauce is a combo you won't forget.

NUT-FREE / UNDER 30 MINUTES

PREP TIME: 10 minutes, plus 30 minutes to marinate

COOK TIME: 12 minutes

ACCESSORIES: Grill Grate

HACK IT: Don't have time to make your own tzatziki sauce? Buy an already-made sauce instead.

For the lamb

¼ cup extra-virgin olive oil

1 tablespoon garlic powder

2 garlic cloves, minced

2 teaspoons onion powder

Juice of ½ lemon

¼ teaspoon nutmeg

2 tablespoons fresh rosemary

1 teaspoon salt

2 pounds boneless lamb, thinly sliced

6 pitas

For the tzatziki sauce

2 cups Greek yogurt

1 tablespoon garlic powder

¼ teaspoon onion powder

2 teaspoons salt

2 tablespoons fresh dill

2 tablespoons freshly squeezed lemon juice

⅛ teaspoon freshly ground black pepper

1 tablespoon extra-virgin olive oil

1 cucumber, seeded and diced

To make the lamb

1. In a large bowl, whisk together the olive oil, garlic powder, minced garlic, onion powder, lemon juice, nutmeg, rosemary, and salt. Add the lamb and massage the mixture into the meat. Cover and marinate for 30 minutes.

2. Insert the Grill Grate and close the hood. Select GRILL, set the temperature to HI, and set the time to 12 minutes. Select START/STOP to begin preheating.

3. When the unit beeps to signify it has preheated, place the lamb slices on the Grill Grate in a single layer. Close the hood and cook for 6 minutes.

4. After 6 minutes, open the hood and flip the meat. Close the hood and cook for 6 minutes more.

CONTINUED ▶

Rosemary and Garlic Lamb Pitas <small>continued</small>

To make the tzatziki sauce

5. While the lamb is cooking, in a medium bowl, combine the yogurt, garlic powder, onion powder, salt, dill, lemon juice, pepper, and olive oil. Add the cucumber and mix well.

6. Serve the lamb inside warm pita pockets and top with tzatziki sauce.

Tomato and Lamb Stew

SERVES 6

When it's rainy or cold weather, I crave a good hearty stew. Although this recipe is often made with goat, I've adapted it to use lamb, as it is more accessible. My mom and dad have cooked this dish many times, using many different ingredients, from liver pâté to chickpeas, green peas, and pineapple. No matter how it's made, it's a comforting meal and is best served as is or over white rice.

GLUTEN-FREE / NUT-FREE

PREP TIME: 15 minutes

COOK TIME: 1 hour

ACCESSORIES: Cooking Pot

VARIATION TIP: For more texture, throw in a 15-ounce can of chickpeas (drained and rinsed) or 2 cups of green peas when adding the bell peppers. Frozen peas work well, because they will help bring moisture to the stew as they cook.

2 tablespoons unsalted butter

1 yellow onion, diced

4 garlic cloves, minced

2 pounds lamb shoulder roast, cut into 1-inch cubes

3 cups beef broth

1 large potato, cubed

1 medium carrot, sliced

3 bay leaves

Salt

Freshly ground black pepper

1 (8-ounce) can tomato sauce

1 red bell pepper, chopped

1 green bell pepper, chopped

1. Insert the Cooking Pot and close the hood. Select ROAST, set the temperature to 350°F, and set the time to 1 hour. Select START/STOP to begin preheating.

2. When the unit beeps to signify it has preheated, place the butter, onion, and garlic in the Cooking Pot. Then add the lamb and stir with a wooden spoon. Close the hood and cook for 10 minutes.

3. After 10 minutes, open the hood and add the beef broth, potato, carrot, and bay leaves, and then season with salt and pepper. Stir to combine. Close the hood and cook for 20 minutes.

4. After 20 minutes, open the hood and stir in the tomato sauce. Close the hood and cook for 10 minutes. After 10 minutes, open the hood and stir. Close the hood and cook for 10 minutes. After 10 minutes, open the hood and add the bell peppers. Close the hood and cook for 10 minutes more.

5. When cooking is complete, open the hood, stir the stew, and remove the bay leaves. Transfer to bowls and serve.

Flatbread Pizza, *page 182*

8
Meatless

Black-Pepper Garlic Tofu

SERVES 4

Using freshly crushed peppercorns is the key to getting all the flavor in this dish. I have always been the person who adds loads of black pepper to my ketchup for dipping French fries. I like to think that this black pepper sauce is similar to that but leveled up with tofu and some vegetables for a perfect sweet, spicy, and savory meal.

NUT-FREE / UNDER 30 MINUTES / VEGETARIAN

PREP TIME: 10 minutes

COOK TIME: 9 minutes

ACCESSORIES: Cooking Pot

VARIATION TIP: Want to add more veggies to make this dish a stir-fry? Add sliced mushrooms and a sliced green bell pepper for more color and pop. Serve it over white rice for a heartier meal.

1 (14-ounce) package firm tofu, cut into 1-inch cubes

1½ teaspoons cornstarch, divided

2 tablespoons avocado oil

1 medium white onion, diced

1 red bell pepper, cut into thin strips

1 teaspoon peeled minced fresh ginger

2 garlic cloves, minced

2 tablespoons black peppercorns, crushed

2 tablespoons soy sauce

1 tablespoon light brown sugar, packed

¼ cup ketchup

1 tablespoon unsalted butter, melted

1. Insert the Cooking Pot and close the hood. Select GRILL, set the temperature to MED, and set the time to 9 minutes. Select START/STOP to begin preheating.

2. While the unit is preheating, on a large plate, coat the tofu cubes with 1 teaspoon of cornstarch.

3. When the unit beeps to signify it has preheated, add the avocado oil to the Cooking Pot. Then add the tofu and stir with a wooden spoon. Close the hood and cook for 3 minutes.

4. After 3 minutes, open the hood and flip and mix the tofu around. Add the onion, red bell pepper, ginger, and garlic. Stir to mix well. Close the hood and cook for 3 minutes.

5. While the tofu is cooking, in a small bowl, mix together the black peppercorns, soy sauce, brown sugar, ketchup, butter, and remaining ½ teaspoon of cornstarch until the sugar and cornstarch are dissolved.

6. After 3 minutes, open the hood. Pour in the sauce and stir. Close the hood and cook for 3 minutes more.

7. When cooking is complete, open the hood and stir the mixture one more time. Serve.

Broccoli and Tofu Teriyaki

SERVES 4

Tofu is packed with protein and has a well-balanced amino acid profile. It was one of the first types of proteins I fed my children. This recipe calls for the broccoli and tofu to be grilled and then tossed and coated in a sweet teriyaki sauce. If you want to make it gluten-free, use coconut or liquid aminos in place of the soy sauce.

DAIRY-FREE / NUT-FREE / UNDER 30 MINUTES / VEGAN

PREP TIME: 10 minutes

COOK TIME: 8 minutes

ACCESSORIES: Grill Grate / Cooking Pot

VARIATION TIP: Want to change up the veggie? Use asparagus, green beans, bell peppers, snap peas, mushrooms, or a combo of them all!

1 (14-ounce) package firm tofu, cut into ½-inch cubes

1 medium head broccoli, chopped into florets (3 to 4 cups)

Extra-virgin olive oil

1 cup water

⅓ cup soy sauce

3 tablespoons light brown sugar, packed

1 tablespoon peeled minced fresh ginger

¼ teaspoon garlic powder

1 teaspoon cornstarch

1. Insert the Grill Grate and close the hood. Select GRILL, set the temperature to HI, and set the time to 8 minutes. Select START/STOP to begin preheating.

2. While the unit is preheating, on a large plate, lightly coat the tofu and broccoli florets with extra-virgin olive oil.

3. When the unit beeps to signify it has preheated, place the broccoli and tofu pieces on the Grill Grate. Close the hood and grill for 4 minutes.

4. While the tofu and broccoli are cooking, in a small bowl, mix together the water, soy sauce, brown sugar, ginger, garlic powder, and cornstarch until the sugar and cornstarch are dissolved.

5. After 4 minutes, open the hood and use grill mitts to remove the Grill Grate and the broccoli and tofu. Carefully pour the soy sauce mix into the Cooking Pot and add the broccoli and tofu. Close the hood and cook for 4 minutes more.

6. When cooking is complete, open the hood and stir. Serve.

Buffalo Cauliflower Bites

A healthy alternative to chicken wings that is gluten-free and vegetarian, this recipe uses cauliflower that is grilled to be tender on the inside and crispy on the outside. You can serve these up on game day for everyone who can appreciate that they are lower in fat, higher in fiber, and not fried. To make this vegan, use vegan butter.

5 INGREDIENTS / GLUTEN-FREE / NUT-FREE / UNDER 30 MINUTES / VEGETARIAN

PREP TIME: 10 minutes

COOK TIME: 15 minutes

ACCESSORIES: Grill Grate

HACK IT: Instead of making your own Buffalo sauce, you can use an already-made Buffalo sauce from the grocery store. There are even creamy Buffalo sauces you can buy.

2 heads cauliflower, cut into florets

Extra-virgin olive oil

⅛ teaspoon garlic powder

1 teaspoon salt

Freshly ground black pepper

4 tablespoons (½ stick) unsalted butter, sliced

1 cup hot sauce

1. Insert the Grill Grate and close the hood. Select GRILL, set the temperature to LO, and set the time to 15 minutes. Select START/STOP to begin preheating.

2. While the unit is preheating, put the cauliflower in a large bowl and drizzle with olive oil. Toss to coat, then season with the garlic powder, salt, and pepper. Toss to mix.

3. When the unit beeps to signify it has preheated, place the florets on the Grill Grate. Close the hood and cook for 7 minutes.

4. After 7 minutes, open the hood and flip and mix the florets. Close the hood and cook for 5 minutes.

5. After 5 minutes, open the hood and use grill mitts to remove the Grill Grate and cauliflower. Add the butter and hot sauce to the Cooking Pot. If you want the cauliflower a little more grilled, place the Grill Grate back in the unit. Either way, close the hood and cook for 3 minutes more.

6. When cooking is complete, transfer the cauliflower to a large bowl. Pour the Buffalo sauce over the florets and toss. Serve alone or with ranch dressing, carrots, and celery sticks.

Cheese and Spinach Stuffed Portobellos

Simple and delicious, these stuffed portobellos are the perfect grilled mushrooms filled with spinach and a creamy, crispy cheese topping. Portobello mushrooms are a great alternative to meat and a good source of B vitamins, potassium, and antioxidants.

GLUTEN-FREE / NUT-FREE / UNDER 30 MINUTES / VEGETARIAN

PREP TIME: 10 minutes

COOK TIME: 8 minutes

ACCESSORIES: Grill Grate

VARIATION TIP: If you want to add crunch, garnish with some sliced almonds or pine nuts.

- 4 large portobello mushrooms, rinsed, stemmed, and gills removed
- 4 ounces cream cheese, at room temperature
- ½ cup mayonnaise
- ½ cup sour cream
- 1 teaspoon onion powder
- ¼ teaspoon garlic powder
- ¼ cup grated Parmesan cheese
- ½ cup shredded mozzarella cheese
- 2 cups fresh spinach

1. Insert the Grill Grate and close the hood. Select GRILL, set the temperature to HI, and set the time to 8 minutes. Select START/STOP to begin preheating.

2. When the unit beeps to signify it has preheated, place the mushrooms on the Grill Grate, cap-side up. Close the hood and cook for 4 minutes.

3. While the mushrooms are grilling, in a large bowl, combine the cream cheese, mayonnaise, sour cream, onion powder, garlic powder, Parmesan cheese, mozzarella cheese, and spinach. Mix well.

4. After 4 minutes, open the hood and flip the mushrooms. Evenly distribute the filling inside the caps. Close the hood and cook for 4 minutes more.

5. When cooking is complete, remove the stuffed mushrooms from the grill and serve.

Crispy Noodle Vegetable Stir-Fry

SERVES 4

Growing up, this was an all-time favorite dish to order at our local Chinese restaurant. It also made me eat my veggies because the sauce they were drenched in was delicious. The noodles come out crispy, but once you pour the sauce over, they soften and resemble chow mein. If you'd like to swap out the ramen noodles, check the international aisle at your local grocery store for chow mein, lo mein, wonton noodles, or soba.

DAIRY-FREE / NUT-FREE / UNDER 30 MINUTES / VEGETARIAN

PREP TIME: 10 minutes

COOK TIME: 20 minutes

ACCESSORIES: Cooking Pot

HACK IT: Use a bag of frozen mixed vegetables. Add them to the Cooking Pot and cook for 5 to 7 minutes before adding the sauce.

4 cups water

3 (5-ounce) packages instant ramen noodles (flavor packets removed) or 1 (12-ounce) package chow mein noodles

Extra-virgin olive oil, for drizzling, plus 3 tablespoons

3 garlic cloves, minced

3 teaspoons peeled minced fresh ginger

1 red bell pepper, cut into thin strips

4 ounces white mushrooms, sliced

1 (8-ounce) can sweet baby corn, drained

2 cups snap peas

2 cups broccoli florets

1 small carrot, diagonally sliced

1 cup vegetable broth

1 cup soy sauce

¼ cup rice vinegar

1 tablespoon sesame oil

3 tablespoons sugar

1 tablespoon cornstarch

1. Insert the Cooking Pot and close the hood. Select GRILL, set the temperature to HI, and set the time to 20 minutes. Select START/STOP to begin preheating.

2. When the unit beeps to signify it has preheated, pour the water into the Cooking Pot and add the ramen noodles. Close the hood and cook for 5 minutes.

3. After 5 minutes, open the hood and remove the Cooking Pot. Drain the noodles and set aside. Insert the Grill Grate (along with the Cooking Pot). Make a large bed of noodles on the Grill Grate and drizzle olive oil over them. Close the hood and cook for 5 minutes. (If using chow mein noodles, flip them halfway through.)

4. After 5 minutes, the ramen noodles should be crispy and golden brown. Transfer the crispy noodles to a large serving plate.

CONTINUED ▶

5. Use grill mitts to remove the Grill Grate. To the Cooking Pot, add the remaining 3 tablespoons of olive oil and the garlic and ginger. Close the hood and cook for 2 minutes.

6. After 2 minutes, open the hood and add the red bell pepper, mushrooms, baby corn, snap peas, broccoli, and carrot. Close the hood and cook for 5 minutes.

7. While the vegetables are cooking, in a small bowl, combine the vegetable broth, soy sauce, vinegar, sesame oil, sugar, and cornstarch and mix until the sugar and cornstarch are dissolved.

8. After 5 minutes, open the hood, stir the vegetables, and add the broth mixture. Close the hood and cook for 3 minutes more.

9. When cooking is complete, open the hood and stir once more. Close the hood and let the vegetables sit in the pot for 3 minutes. Then, pour the vegetables and sauce on top of the crispy noodle bed and serve.

Double "Egg" Plant (Eggplant Omelets)

SERVES 4

I call this recipe Double "Egg" Plant because it uses both eggplant and eggs to make eggplant omelets. Known as tortang talong *in Tagalog, this is a very popular dish that my parents, aunts, uncles, and elders all made while we were growing up. It is inexpensive, simple, meatless, and easily feeds the whole family. Although typically fried, it's just as tasty on the Foodi™ Grill. A filling meal that can be eaten by itself, these omelets can be dipped in ketchup (try spicy ketchup!) or served with white rice.*

5 INGREDIENTS / DAIRY-FREE / GLUTEN-FREE / NUT-FREE / UNDER 30 MINUTES / VEGETARIAN

PREP TIME: 10 minutes

COOK TIME: 16 minutes

ACCESSORIES: Grill Grate

SUBSTITUTION TIP: If you like it spicy, you can mix the ketchup with ⅛ teaspoon red pepper flakes or 1 tablespoon sriracha instead of hot sauce.

4 Chinese eggplants

2 large eggs

Garlic powder

Salt

Freshly ground black pepper

¼ cup ketchup

1 tablespoon hot sauce (optional)

1. Insert the Grill Grate. Select GRILL, set the temperature to HI, and set the time to 10 minutes. Select START/STOP to begin preheating.

2. When the unit beeps to signify it has preheated, place the whole eggplants on the Grill Grate. Close the hood and cook for 5 minutes.

3. After 5 minutes, open the hood and flip the eggplants. Close the hood and cook for 5 minutes more.

4. When cooking is complete, the eggplant skin will be charred and cracked and the flesh will be soft. Remove the eggplants from the grill and set aside to cool.

5. Once the eggplants have cooled down, peel the skin. Then, using a fork, flatten the eggplants with a brushing motion until they become pear shaped and about the thickness of a pancake.

6. Select GRILL, set the temperature to HI, and set the time to 6 minutes. Select START/STOP to begin preheating.

7. While the unit is preheating, in a large bowl, whisk the eggs. Dip each eggplant into the egg mixture to coat both sides, then season both sides with garlic powder, salt, and pepper.

CONTINUED ▶

Double "Egg" Plant (Eggplant Omelets) continued

8. When the grill beeps to signify it has preheated, place the coated eggplants on the Grill Grate. Close the hood and grill for 3 minutes.

9. After 3 minutes, open the hood and flip the eggplants. Close the hood and cook for 3 minutes more. Add more time if needed until you get your desired crispiness of the omelets.

10. When cooking is complete, remove the eggplant omelets from the grill. In a small bowl, combine the ketchup and hot sauce (if using), or just use ketchup if you do not like spice, and serve alongside the omelets for dipping.

Eggplant Parmigiana

This is a vegetarian alternative to the popular chicken Parmesan dish. For this recipe, I have omitted the bread crumbs to keep it super light, but feel free to use them if you want a crispy texture. Enjoy this quick and light weeknight meal by dipping it into your favorite marinara sauce or serving it just like this.

GLUTEN-FREE / NUT-FREE / UNDER 30 MINUTES / VEGETARIAN

PREP TIME: 10 minutes

COOK TIME: 12 minutes

ACCESSORIES: Cooking Pot / Grill Grate

VARIATION TIP: Omit the ricotta cheese and use fresh mozzarella instead.

2 large eggs

½ cup grated Parmesan cheese, plus more for garnish

1 tablespoon Italian seasoning

1 teaspoon garlic powder

2 Italian eggplants, cut into ¾-inch-thick discs

½ cup ricotta cheese

1 cup prepared marinara sauce

½ cup shredded mozzarella cheese

Fresh basil, for garnish

1. Insert the Grill Grate and close the hood. Select GRILL, set the temperature to HI, and set the time to 12 minutes. Select START/STOP to begin preheating.

2. While the unit is preheating, create an assembly line with 2 large bowls. In one bowl, whisk the eggs. In the other bowl, combine the Parmesan cheese, Italian seasoning, and garlic powder. Dip the eggplant discs in the egg wash and then into the Parmesan crumbs until fully coated.

3. When the unit beeps to signify it has preheated, place the eggplant on the Grill Grate in a single layer. Close the hood and grill for 4 minutes.

4. After 4 minutes, open the hood and flip the eggplant. Close the hood and cook for 4 minutes.

5. After 4 minutes, open the hood and use grill mitts to remove the Grill Grate and eggplant.

CONTINUED ▶

6. Place an eggplant disc in the Cooking Pot. Spoon about 1 teaspoon of ricotta cheese across the disc and then top with another eggplant disc, forming a sandwich. Add a teaspoon of marinara sauce on top, followed by shredded mozzarella cheese. Repeat with the remaining eggplant discs, ricotta cheese, marinara sauce, and mozzarella cheese. Close the hood and cook for 4 minutes more.

7. When cooking is complete, remove the eggplant. Garnish with fresh basil leaves and top with more grated Parmesan, and serve.

Zucchini and Onions au Gratin

SERVES 4

You won't miss the traditional potatoes in this creamy and cheesy dish. This zucchini au gratin makes the perfect side or a great casserole to serve to crowds. The creamy cheese sauce reminds me of a sour cream and onion dip. I like to think of this as a healthier version of baked chips.

NUT-FREE / UNDER 30 MINUTES / VEGETARIAN

PREP TIME: 10 minutes

COOK TIME: 15 minutes

ACCESSORIES: Cooking Pot

VARIATION TIP: Switch out the grated Parmesan cheese for grated Gruyère cheese or pepper Jack to change up the flavor.

1 cup panko bread crumbs

1 cup grated Parmesan cheese

1 large white onion, sliced

3 zucchini, cut into thin discs

1 teaspoon sea salt

1 teaspoon freshly ground black pepper

1 teaspoon onion powder

1 cup heavy (whipping) cream

1 tablespoon unsalted butter, at room temperature

1 teaspoon cornstarch

1. Insert the Cooking Pot and close the hood. Select GRILL, set the temperature to MED, and set the time to 15 minutes. Select START/STOP to begin preheating.

2. While the unit is preheating, in a large bowl, combine the panko bread crumbs and Parmesan cheese.

3. When the unit beeps to signify it has preheated, add the onion to the Cooking Pot. Close the hood and cook for 2 minutes.

4. After 2 minutes, open the hood and add the zucchini, salt, pepper, and onion powder. Stir to mix. Close the hood and cook for 2 minutes.

5. After 2 minutes, open the hood and stir in the heavy cream, butter, and cornstarch. Close the hood and cook for 3 minutes.

6. After 3 minutes, the vegetable mixture should be creamy and thick. Evenly spread the bread crumb mixture over the top. Close the hood and cook for 8 minutes more.

7. When cooking is complete, the top will be golden brown and crunchy. Remove from the grill and serve.

Green Beans with Sun-Dried Tomatoes and Feta

Green bean casserole reminds me of the holidays. Now you can enjoy it as a hearty meal year-round. This green bean dish is lighter than the typical casserole, almost like a warm salad. You'll enjoy the combination of sweet tomatoes, tangy feta cheese crumbles, and crunchy green beans.

5 INGREDIENTS / GLUTEN-FREE / NUT-FREE / UNDER 30 MINUTES / VEGETARIAN

PREP TIME: 10 minutes

COOK TIME: 8 minutes

ACCESSORIES: Grill Grate

VARIATION TIP: Add pine nuts or walnuts to this salad for some more crunch, or squeeze fresh lime juice over the top.

2 pounds green beans, ends trimmed

2 tablespoons extra-virgin olive oil

1 teaspoon salt

½ teaspoon freshly ground black pepper

1 cup sun-dried tomatoes packed in oil, undrained, sliced

6 ounces feta cheese, crumbled

1. Insert the Grill Grate and close the hood. Select GRILL, set the temperature to HI, and set the time to 8 minutes. Select START/STOP to begin preheating.

2. While the unit is preheating, in a large bowl, toss the green beans with the olive oil, salt, and pepper.

3. When the unit beeps to signify it has preheated, place the green beans on the Grill Grate. Close the hood and grill for 4 minutes.

4. After 4 minutes, open the hood and flip the green beans. Close the hood and cook for 4 minutes more.

5. When cooking is complete, transfer the green beans to a large bowl. Add the sun-dried tomatoes and mix together. Top with the feta cheese and serve.

Flatbread Pizza

Pizza is an all-time favorite for a reason. And it's easy to add your favorite vegetables as toppings. This recipe is a good way to use up any vegetables before they go bad. When making a vegetable flatbread, I like to use a creamy white sauce, like Alfredo. If you want to make mini bite-size pizzas, be sure to check out Mini Caprese Pizzas (page 44).

NUT-FREE / UNDER
30 MINUTES / VEGETARIAN

PREP TIME: 10 minutes

COOK TIME: 10 minutes

ACCESSORIES: Grill Grate

SUBSTITUTION TIP: Don't have Alfredo sauce? Use ranch dressing or pesto as your sauce base. You can also make your own Alfredo sauce by combining 1 cup heavy (whipping) cream; 1 tablespoon unsalted butter; a pinch each of garlic powder, Italian seasoning, salt, and pepper; and 1 cup grated Parmesan cheese in a medium saucepan over low heat.

1 (14-ounce) package refrigerated pizza dough

2 tablespoons extra-virgin olive oil

½ cup prepared Alfredo sauce

1 medium zucchini, cut into ⅛-inch-thick discs

½ cup fresh spinach

½ red onion, sliced

4 cherry tomatoes, sliced

1. Insert the Grill Grate and close the hood. Select GRILL, set the temperature to MED, and set the time to 10 minutes. Select START/STOP to begin preheating.

2. While the unit is preheating, roll out the dough into a rectangle slightly smaller than the Grill Grate (8 by 11 inches). Brush the olive oil on both sides of the dough.

3. When the unit beeps to signify it has preheated, place the dough on the Grill Grate. Close the hood and grill for 5 minutes.

4. After 5 minutes, open the hood and flip the dough. (Or skip flipping, if you'd rather.) Spread the Alfredo sauce across the dough, leaving a 1-inch border. Layer the zucchini, spinach, red onion, and cherry tomatoes across the dough. Close the hood and cook for 5 minutes more.

5. When cooking is complete, remove the pizza from the grill. Slice and serve.

Grilled Mozzarella and Tomatoes

This is a simple, tasty dish that doesn't require much effort or thought. It can be a perfect side dish, an appetizer, or even a light meal. The tomato acts as a great base for the shredded mozzarella (or you can use fresh), and the herby dressing makes it all pop. Adjust the seasoning to your liking. This dish cooks quickly—you'll be eating in no time.

5 INGREDIENTS / GLUTEN-FREE / NUT-FREE / UNDER 30 MINUTES / VEGETARIAN

PREP TIME: 5 minutes

COOK TIME: 5 minutes

ACCESSORIES: Grill Grate

VARIATION TIP: Not into Italian dressing? Use your favorite vinaigrette instead.

4 large, round, firm tomatoes

½ cup Italian dressing

1 cup shredded mozzarella

½ cup chopped fresh basil, for garnish

1. Insert the Grill Grate and close the hood. Select GRILL, set the temperature to HI, and set the time to 5 minutes. Select START/STOP to begin preheating.

2. While the unit is preheating, cut the tomatoes in half crosswise. Pour about 1 tablespoon of Italian dressing on each tomato half.

3. When the unit beeps to signify it has preheated, place the tomatoes on the Grill Grate, cut-side up. If the tomatoes won't stand upright, slice a small piece from the bottom to level them out. Close the hood and grill for 2 minutes.

4. After 2 minutes, open the hood and evenly distribute the mozzarella cheese on top of the tomatoes. Close the hood and cook for 3 minutes more, or until the cheese is melted.

5. When cooking is complete, remove the tomatoes from the grill. Garnish with the basil and serve.

Grilled Artichokes with Garlic Aioli

SERVES 4

Don't be intimidated by the artichoke's spiky leaves and furry center. I'll give you a couple of tips and tricks to grill this delicious veggie. Most artichoke recipes require that you boil them. But grilling artichokes gives them a great char and means fewer steps—and fewer dishes!

FAMILY FAVORITE / GLUTEN-FREE / NUT-FREE / VEGETARIAN

PREP TIME: 15 minutes

COOK TIME: 33 minutes

ACCESSORIES: Grill Grate

HACK IT: Cut a lemon in half and, with each cut you make on the artichoke, rub the lemon on the artichoke to prevent oxidation (slow down the browning) while you cut and prepare the other artichokes. It also adds a hint of lemon flavor.

For the artichokes

4 artichokes

8 tablespoons avocado oil

8 tablespoons minced garlic

Salt

Freshly ground black pepper

For the garlic aioli

½ cup mayonnaise

1 garlic clove, minced

1 tablespoon apple cider vinegar

⅛ teaspoon paprika

To make the artichokes

1. Pull off the tough outer leaves near the stem of the artichoke and trim the bottom of the stem. Cut off the top third (½ to 1 inch) of the artichoke. Trim the tips of the leaves that surround the artichoke, as they can be sharp and thorny. Then cut the artichoke in half lengthwise. This exposes the artichoke heart. Use a spoon to remove the fuzzy choke, scraping to make sure it is cleaned away, then rinse the artichoke.

2. Insert the Grill Grate and close the hood. Select GRILL, set the temperature to LO, and set the time to 25 minutes. Select START/STOP to begin preheating.

3. While the unit is preheating, prepare 8 large pieces of aluminum foil for wrapping. Place an artichoke half, cut-side up, in the center of a foil piece. Drizzle 1 tablespoon of avocado oil into the center of the artichoke half and add 1 tablespoon of minced garlic. Season with salt and pepper. Seal the foil packet, making sure all sides are closed. Repeat for each artichoke half.

4. When the unit beeps to signify it has preheated, place the foil-wrapped artichokes on the Grill Grate. Close the hood and grill for 25 minutes.

CONTINUED ▶

5. When cooking is complete, the stem and heart will be soft, about the consistency of a cooked potato. Remove the artichokes from the foil.

6. Select GRILL, set the temperature to MAX, and set the time to 8 minutes. Place the artichokes on the Grill Grate, cut-side down. Select START/STOP and then press the PREHEAT button to skip preheating. Close the hood and cook for 4 minutes.

7. After 4 minutes, open the hood and flip the artichokes. Season with additional salt and pepper, if desired. Close the hood and cook for 4 minutes more.

8. When cooking is complete, remove the artichokes from the grill.

To make the garlic aioli

9. In a small bowl, combine the mayonnaise, garlic, vinegar, and paprika. Serve alongside the artichokes for dipping.

Grilled Vegetable Quesadillas

My family loves quesadillas. Who doesn't love a tortilla loaded with cheese? This is also a great way to sneak in some vegetables. If you want to be adventurous, you can try flavored tortillas, like wheat, spinach, sun-dried tomato, or cilantro, to make regular flour tortillas more colorful!

NUT-FREE / UNDER 30 MINUTES / VEGETARIAN

PREP TIME: 10 minutes

COOK TIME: 8 minutes

ACCESSORIES: Grill Grate

HACK IT: If you do not care about your veggies being grilled first, you can prepare your quesadilla with the cheese and raw vegetables and grill it all at once. If you want to achieve grill marks on your tortilla, brush melted butter on both sides of the quesadilla, facedown first.

1 medium onion, chopped

1 medium summer squash, halved lengthwise and thinly sliced into half-moons

1 medium zucchini, halved lengthwise and thinly sliced into half-moons

Extra-virgin olive oil

4 (10-inch) flour tortillas

1 cup shredded mozzarella cheese

¼ cup chopped fresh cilantro (optional)

1. Insert the Grill Grate and close the hood. Select GRILL, set the temperature to HI, and set the time to 8 minutes. Select START/STOP to begin preheating.

2. In a large bowl, combine the onion, summer squash, and zucchini and lightly coat with olive oil.

3. When the unit beeps to signify it has preheated, place the vegetables on the Grill Grate in a single layer. Close the hood and cook for 4 minutes.

4. While the vegetables are grilling, place the tortillas on a large tray and cover half of each with about ¼ cup of mozzarella.

5. After 4 minutes, open the hood and transfer the vegetables to the tortillas, evenly spreading on top of the cheese. Top the vegetables with the cilantro (if using). Fold the other half of each tortilla over to close. Place the quesadillas on the Grill Grate. Close the hood and cook for 2 minutes.

6. After 2 minutes, open the hood and flip the quesadillas. Close the hood and cook for 2 minutes more.

7. When cooking is complete, the cheese will be melted and the tortillas will be crispy. Remove the quesadillas from the grill and serve.

Honey-Sriracha Brussels Sprouts

If you're not already a fan of Brussels sprouts, you need to try this sweet, spicy, and tangy version. It's an easy recipe that makes a perfect side dish for dinner or to bring to a get-together. When seasoned well, Brussels sprouts might just become a healthy addiction.

5 INGREDIENTS / DAIRY-FREE / GLUTEN-FREE / UNDER 30 MINUTES / VEGETARIAN

PREP TIME: 5 minutes

COOK TIME: 20 minutes

ACCESSORIES: Crisper Basket

HACK IT: To save time, buy a bag of Brussels sprouts that have already been trimmed and halved.

SUBSTITUTION TIP: Don't have honey? Use maple syrup instead.

2 pounds Brussels sprouts, halved lengthwise, ends trimmed

2 tablespoons avocado oil

4 tablespoons honey or coconut palm sugar

2 teaspoons sriracha

Juice of 1 lemon

1. Insert the Crisper Basket and close the hood. Select AIR CRISP, set the temperature to 390°F, and set the time to 20 minutes. Select START/STOP to begin preheating.

2. While the unit is preheating, in a large bowl, toss the Brussels sprouts with the avocado oil.

3. When the unit beeps to signify it has preheated, place the Brussels sprouts in the Crisper Basket. Close the hood and cook for 10 minutes.

4. After 10 minutes, open the hood and toss the Brussels sprouts. Close the hood and cook for 10 minutes more. If you choose, before the last 5 minutes, open the hood and toss the Brussels sprouts one more time.

5. When cooking is complete, open the hood and transfer the Brussels sprouts to a large bowl. Or if you like more crisping and browning of your sprouts, continue cooking to your liking.

6. In a small bowl, whisk together the honey, sriracha, and lemon juice. Drizzle this over the Brussels sprouts and toss to coat. Serve.

Loaded Zucchini Boats

SERVES 4

Loaded zucchini boats were one of the first foods I made when I started a low-carb lifestyle. Since then I have been hooked, because I can fill them up with practically anything and I don't miss starchier foods. Plus, these boats are easy to prepare and make an awesome side dish or a light meal.

NUT-FREE / UNDER
30 MINUTES / VEGETARIAN

PREP TIME: 10 minutes

COOK TIME: 10 minutes

ACCESSORIES: Grill Grate

VARIATION TIP: Fill the zucchini boats with marinara sauce and top with mozzarella cheese for a pasta-inspired dish.

4 medium zucchini

1 cup panko bread crumbs

2 garlic cloves, minced

½ small white onion, diced

½ cup grated Parmesan cheese

1 tablespoon Italian seasoning

1. Insert the Grill Grate and close the hood. Select GRILL, set the temperature to HI, and set the time to 10 minutes. Select START/STOP to begin preheating.

2. While the unit is preheating, cut the zucchini in half lengthwise. Carefully scoop out the flesh and put it in a medium bowl. Set the boats aside.

3. Add the panko bread crumbs, garlic, onion, Parmesan cheese, and Italian seasoning to the bowl and mix well. Spoon the filling into each zucchini half.

4. When the unit beeps to signify it has preheated, place the zucchini boats on the Grill Grate, cut-side up. Close the hood and grill for 10 minutes.

5. When cooking is complete, the cheese will be melted and the tops will be crispy and golden brown. Remove the zucchini boats from the grill and serve.

Perfect Grilled Asparagus

SERVES 4

Asparagus is one of the easiest vegetables to cook and doesn't require any peeling or special cutting techniques. I love asparagus plain and simple as much as I like to spruce it up by adding some fresh lemon juice, a drizzle of balsamic vinegar, or even grated Parmesan cheese. The possibilities are endless.

5 INGREDIENTS / DAIRY-FREE / GLUTEN-FREE / NUT-FREE / UNDER 30 MINUTES / VEGAN

PREP TIME: 5 minutes

COOK TIME: 6 minutes

ACCESSORIES: Grill Grate

VARIATION TIP: Season the asparagus with ⅛ teaspoon garlic powder along with the salt and pepper to give the asparagus a hint of garlic flavor.

24 asparagus spears, woody ends trimmed

Extra-virgin olive oil, for drizzling

Sea salt

Freshly ground black pepper

1. Insert the Grill Grate and close the hood. Select GRILL, set the temperature to HI, and set the time to 6 minutes. Select START/STOP to begin preheating.

2. While the unit is preheating, place the asparagus in a large bowl and drizzle with the olive oil. Toss to coat, then season with salt and pepper.

3. When the unit beeps to signify it has preheated, place the spears evenly spread out on the Grill Grate. Close the hood and grill for 3 minutes.

4. After 3 minutes, open the hood and flip and move the spears around. Close the hood and cook for 3 minutes more.

5. When cooking is complete, remove the asparagus from the grill and serve.

Roasted Butternut Squash

Butternut squash reminds me of all things fall and winter. The hardest part about butternut squash is cutting and prepping it. But don't worry, I'll walk you through it. Once you know how to cook butternut squash, you'll be able to make delicious soups, side dishes, or an easy mash that goes great with grilled meats.

5 INGREDIENTS / DAIRY-FREE / GLUTEN-FREE / NUT-FREE / VEGAN

PREP TIME: 10 minutes

COOK TIME: 40 minutes

ACCESSORIES: Cooking Pot

HACK IT: You can also buy frozen peeled and diced butternut squash that is ready to roast. Drizzle with extra-virgin olive oil, season, and roast for 15 minutes.

2 butternut squash	**Salt**
Avocado oil, for drizzling	**Freshly ground black pepper**

1. Cut off the stem end of each squash, then cut the squash in half lengthwise. To do this, carefully rock the knife back and forth to cut through the tough skin and flesh. Use a spoon to scrape out the seeds from each half.

2. Insert the Cooking Pot and close the hood. Select ROAST, set the temperature to 400°F, and set the time to 40 minutes. Select START/STOP to begin preheating.

3. While the unit is preheating, drizzle the avocado oil over the butternut squash flesh. I also like to rub it in with my hands. Season with salt and pepper.

4. When the unit beeps to signify it has preheated, place the butternut squash in the Cooking Pot, cut-side down. Close the hood and cook for 40 minutes.

5. When cooking is complete, the flesh will be soft and easy to scoop out with a spoon. Remove from the grill and serve.

Sweet and Spicy Corn on the Cob

I've taken a popular sweet chili sauce and added some spice to bring corn to a whole new level. I figured if sweet chili sauce can be used as a dipping sauce for meats and egg rolls, then it'd be great added to corn. Turns out I was right. A simple adjustment to the sweet and spicy glaze to make it creamy helps this sauce stick to your corn.

NUT-FREE / UNDER
30 MINUTES / VEGETARIAN

PREP TIME: 10 minutes

COOK TIME: 12 minutes

ACCESSORIES: Grill Grate

VARIATION TIP: Want it spicier? Add more sriracha. Don't like spice? Omit the sriracha. The addition of mayonnaise and sour cream tones down the kick in the sweet chili sauce.

6 ears corn, shucked

Avocado oil, for drizzling

Salt

Freshly ground black pepper

½ cup sweet chili sauce

¼ cup sour cream

¼ cup mayonnaise

2 tablespoons sriracha

Juice of 1 lime

¼ cup chopped cilantro, for garnish

1. Insert the Grill Grate and close the hood. Select GRILL, set the temperature to MAX, and set the time to 12 minutes. Select START/STOP to begin preheating.

2. While the unit is preheating, drizzle the corn with avocado oil, rubbing it in to coat. Season with salt and pepper all over.

3. When the unit beeps to signify it has preheated, place the corn on the Grill Grate. Close the hood and grill for 6 minutes.

4. After 6 minutes, open the hood and flip the corn. Close the hood and cook 6 minutes more.

5. While the corn is cooking, in a small bowl, combine the sweet chili sauce, sour cream, mayonnaise, sriracha, and lime juice.

6. When cooking is complete, remove the corn from the grill. Coat the ears with the sweet chili sauce mixture. Garnish with the cilantro and serve.

Sweet Pepper Poppers

SERVES 4

My first time trying out these bright red, yellow, and orange peppers, I was immediately hooked by their crunch and sweetness. Although they are small, they make an ideal snack that you can eat fresh, or they can help bulk up your salads. I found myself eating them just with cream cheese. For this recipe, I use a pimiento cheese spread with cheddar cheese and mayonnaise for that perfect tangy and sweet combo.

5 INGREDIENTS / GLUTEN-FREE / NUT-FREE / UNDER 30 MINUTES / VEGETARIAN

PREP TIME: 10 minutes

COOK TIME: 7 minutes

ACCESSORIES: Grill Grate

VARIATION TIP: Use an already-made hummus dip to make hummus-stuffed sweet peppers.

10 mini sweet peppers
½ cup mayonnaise
1 cup shredded sharp cheddar cheese
½ teaspoon onion powder
⅛ teaspoon cayenne powder (optional)

1. Insert the Grill Grate and close the hood. Select GRILL, set the temperature to HI, and set the time to 7 minutes. Select START/STOP to begin preheating.

2. While the unit is preheating, cut the peppers in half lengthwise and scoop out the seeds and membranes. In a small bowl, combine the mayonnaise, cheddar cheese, onion powder, and cayenne powder (if using). Spoon the cheese mixture into each sweet pepper half.

3. When the unit beeps to signify it has preheated, place the sweet peppers on the Grill Grate, cut-side up. Close the hood and grill for 7 minutes.

4. When cooking is complete, remove the peppers from the grill and serve. Or if you prefer your peppers more charred, continue cooking to your liking.

Veggie Taco Pie

SERVES 4

On busy nights, cook this easy taco pie. This recipe doesn't call for you to stand around worrying about flipping or making sure it's cooked properly—that's the beauty of the Foodi™ Grill. Assemble all the ingredients, heat, and then it's ready to eat. To make this vegan, swap the sour cream and cheddar cheese for vegan versions.

NUT-FREE / UNDER 30 MINUTES / VEGETARIAN

PREP TIME: 10 minutes

COOK TIME: 15 minutes

ACCESSORIES: Cooking Pot

VARIATION TIP: Want more of a pie texture? Use store-bought refrigerated dough to make an actual piecrust, and layer on the toppings.

HACK IT: Instead of making your own, use a packet of taco seasoning—about 3 tablespoons or more.

1 (15-ounce) can pinto beans, drained and rinsed

1 tablespoon chili powder

2 teaspoons ground cumin

2 teaspoons sea salt

1 teaspoon paprika

½ teaspoon garlic powder

½ teaspoon onion powder

½ teaspoon dried oregano

4 small flour tortillas

1 cup sour cream

1 (14-ounce) can diced tomatoes, drained

1 (15-ounce) can black beans, drained and rinsed

2 cups shredded cheddar cheese

1. Insert the Cooking Pot and close the hood. Select BAKE, set the temperature to 350ºF, and set the time to 15 minutes. Select START/STOP to begin preheating.

2. While the unit is preheating, in a large bowl, mash the pinto beans with a fork. Add the chili powder, cumin, salt, paprika, garlic powder, onion powder, and oregano and mix until well combined. Place a tortilla in the bottom of a 6-inch springform pan. Spread a quarter of the mashed pinto beans on the tortilla in an even layer, then layer on a quarter each of the sour cream, tomatoes, black beans, and cheddar cheese in that order. Repeat the layers three more times, ending with cheese.

3. When the unit beeps to signify it has preheated, place the pan in the Cooking Pot. Close the hood and cook for 15 minutes.

4. When cooking is complete, the cheese will be melted. Remove the pan from the grill and serve.

Shrimp Boil, *page 219*

9

Seafood

Blackened Salmon

If you love Blackened Chicken (page 91), be sure to try this blackened salmon. Adding bold spices on top of melted butter results in a flavorful dark crust that is achieved with no flipping. You will easily appreciate the flavors in this dish that you can serve over steamed broccoli, Alfredo pasta, or a fresh spinach salad.

GLUTEN-FREE / NUT-FREE / UNDER 30 MINUTES

PREP TIME: 5 minutes

COOK TIME: 5 minutes

ACCESSORIES: Grill Grate

VARIATION TIP: Use skin-on salmon and make crispy salmon skins. Grill the fillets skin-side down, and when cooking is complete, slide a spatula in between each fillet and its skin, remove the flesh, and continue grilling just the skins for an additional 2 minutes until crispy. You can use them as garnish for added crunch or eat them as chips!

2 tablespoons unsalted butter, at room temperature

1 tablespoon paprika

1 teaspoon garlic powder

1 teaspoon dried oregano

1 teaspoon light brown sugar, packed

¼ teaspoon sea salt

⅛ teaspoon freshly ground black pepper

⅛ teaspoon cayenne pepper

6 (4- to 5-ounce) skinless salmon fillets

1. Insert the Grill Grate. Place the butter in a small heat-safe bowl, place the bowl on the Grill Grate, and close the hood. Select GRILL, set the temperature to HI, and set the time to 5 minutes. Select START/STOP to begin preheating. After 1 minute of preheating (set a separate timer), remove the bowl with the butter. Close the hood to continue preheating.

2. While the unit is preheating, in a small bowl, mix together the paprika, garlic powder, oregano, brown sugar, salt, black pepper, and cayenne pepper. Brush the melted butter on top of each salmon fillet. Evenly and generously coat the top with the seasoning mix.

3. When the unit beeps to signify it has preheated, place the salmon fillets on the Grill Grate. Close the hood and grill for 5 minutes.

4. When cooking is complete, the salmon will be opaque and should flake easily with a fork. (If you want, you can also use the Smart Thermometer at the end of cooking to check that the internal temperature of the salmon has reached 145°F.) Remove the salmon from the grill and serve.

Buttered Lobster Tails

Don't be intimated by grilling your own lobster tails at home—it isn't as hard as it seems. Add this lobster to a steak dinner, like Rib Eye Steak with Rosemary Butter (page 126), for a surf-and-turf meal, or make this for your sweetheart for a romantic dinner or to impress a crowd. Cooking lobster at home costs half as much as what you'd pay at a restaurant, if not way less—and is just as delicious.

**5 INGREDIENTS /
GLUTEN-FREE / NUT-FREE /
UNDER 30 MINUTES**

PREP TIME: 15 minutes

COOK TIME: 7 minutes

ACCESSORIES: Grill Grate

VARIATION TIP: Squeeze some lemon juice on top of the lobster tail meat before grilling. If you have a favorite pesto sauce, you can add that on top, too. There is no wrong way to season your lobster, but simple is best.

6 (4-ounce) lobster tails

Paprika

Salt

Freshly ground black pepper

4 tablespoons (½ stick) unsalted butter, melted

3 garlic cloves, minced

1. Place the lobster tails shell-side up on a cutting board. Using kitchen shears, cut each shell down the center, stopping at the base of the tail. Carefully crack open the shell by sliding your thumbs between the shell and meat and delicately pulling apart. Wiggle, pull, and lift the meat out of the shell. Remove the vein and digestive tract, if present. Rest the meat on top of the shell for a beautiful display.

2. Insert the Grill Grate and close the hood. Select GRILL, set the temperature to HI, and set the time to 7 minutes. Select START/STOP to begin preheating.

3. While the unit is preheating, season the lobster meat with paprika, salt, and pepper.

4. In a small bowl, combine the melted butter and garlic.

5. When the unit beeps to signify it has preheated, place the lobster tails on their shells on the Grill Grate. Close the hood and grill for 4 minutes.

6. After 4 minutes, open the hood and brush the garlic butter on the lobster meat. Close the hood and cook for 3 minutes more.

7. When cooking is complete, the lobster meat will be opaque and the shell will be orangey red. Serve with more melted butter or a sauce of your choice.

Chili-Lime Shrimp Skewers

When you want something light and refreshing, chili-lime shrimp is the answer. Simple ingredients give this dish some kick, tang, and sweetness from a honey glaze. Add a salad to give yourself a complete meal.

DAIRY-FREE / GLUTEN-FREE / NUT-FREE / UNDER 30 MINUTES

PREP TIME: 15 minutes

COOK TIME: 10 minutes

ACCESSORIES: Grill Grate / Ninja® Foodi™ Grill Kebab Skewers

VARIATION TIP: For even more flavor, pair these skewers with cilantro-lime rice. Make instant rice as directed on the package and add 1 teaspoon garlic powder, 1 cup chopped fresh cilantro, and the juice of 1 lime.

2 pounds jumbo shrimp, peeled
1 tablespoon chili powder
¼ teaspoon ground cumin
¼ teaspoon dried oregano
¼ teaspoon garlic powder
2 tablespoons honey
Juice of 2 limes, divided
Instant rice, prepared as directed

1. Insert the Grill Grate and close the hood. Select GRILL, set the temperature to HI, and set the time to 5 minutes. Select START/STOP to begin preheating.

2. While the unit is preheating, thread 4 or 5 shrimp onto each of 8 skewers, leaving about an inch of space at the bottom. Place the skewers on a large plate.

3. In a small bowl, combine the chili powder, cumin, oregano, and garlic powder. Lightly coat the shrimp with the dry rub. In the same bowl, add the honey and the juice of ½ lime to any remaining seasoning. Mix together.

4. When the unit beeps to signify it has preheated, place 4 shrimp skewers on the Grill Grate. Brush the shrimp with some of the honey mixture. Close the hood and grill for 2 minutes, 30 seconds.

5. After 2 minutes, 30 seconds, open the hood and squeeze the juice of another ½ lime over the skewers and flip. Brush on more honey mixture. Close the hood and cook for 2 minutes, 30 seconds.

6. When cooking is complete, the shrimp should be opaque and pink. Remove the skewers from the grill. Select GRILL, set the temperature to HI, and set the time to 5 minutes. Select START/STOP to begin and press PREHEAT to skip preheating. Repeat steps 4 and 5 for the remaining 4 skewers. When all of the skewers are cooked, serve with the rice.

Coconut Shrimp with Orange Chili Sauce

In the past, I've often fried coconut shrimp. Now I let the Foodi™ Grill do all the work, and I no longer have to stand near the stove worrying about oil spills and splatters. This popular, family-favorite restaurant dish can now be made at home in a matter of minutes. If orange chili sauce isn't your jam, serve these coconut shrimp with sweet chili sauce.

DAIRY-FREE / FAMILY FAVORITE / UNDER 30 MINUTES

PREP TIME: 10 minutes

COOK TIME: 16 minutes

ACCESSORIES: Cooking Pot

HACK IT: Instead of individually coating the shrimp, add all of the peeled shrimp to the egg wash, then transfer the shrimp into the coconut panko bread crumbs to coat them all together.

For the coconut shrimp

2 large eggs

1 cup sweetened coconut flakes

1 cup panko bread crumbs

½ teaspoon salt

¼ teaspoon freshly ground black pepper

2 pounds jumbo shrimp, peeled

For the orange chili sauce

½ cup orange marmalade

1 teaspoon sriracha or ¼ teaspoon red pepper flakes

To make the coconut shrimp

1. Insert the Grill Grate and close the hood. Select GRILL, set the temperature to HI, and set the time to 16 minutes. Select START/STOP to begin preheating.

2. While the unit is preheating, create an assembly line with 2 large bowls. In one bowl, whisk the eggs. In the other bowl, combine the coconut flakes, panko bread crumbs, salt, and pepper. One at a time, dip the shrimp in the egg and then into the coconut flakes until fully coated.

3. When the unit beeps to signify it has preheated, place half the shrimp on the Grill Grate in a single layer. Close the hood and cook for 4 minutes.

CONTINUED ▶

4. After 4 minutes, open the hood and flip the shrimp. Close the hood and cook for 4 minutes more. After 4 minutes, open the hood and remove the shrimp from the grill.

5. Repeat steps 3 and 4 for the remaining shrimp.

To make the orange chili sauce

6. In a small bowl, combine the orange marmalade and sriracha. Serve as a dipping sauce alongside the coconut shrimp.

Crab Cakes with Lemon-Garlic Aioli

Typically fried in oil, crab cakes are just as crunchy and tasty when grilled—and healthier to boot. Don't pay for overpriced crab cakes when you can easily make them at home. Serve these fresh off the Foodi™ Grill or add them to a sandwich or salad.

NUT-FREE

PREP TIME: 10 minutes, plus 30 minutes to set

COOK TIME: 16 minutes

ACCESSORIES: Grill Grate

HACK IT: You can find crabmeat at your local grocery store in a plastic container by the seafood counter or in the refrigerated area with other seafood. This saves a lot of time from having to cook and remove crabmeat from its shell!

VARIATION TIP: You can use canned solid white albacore tuna instead to make tuna cakes.

For the crab cakes
1 large egg
1 tablespoon Old Bay seasoning
1 tablespoon dried parsley
1 tablespoon soy sauce
1 tablespoon minced garlic
¼ cup grated Parmesan cheese
½ cup mayonnaise
½ cup panko bread crumbs
1 pound lump crabmeat
Avocado oil cooking spray

For the lemon-garlic aioli
½ cup mayonnaise
1 teaspoon garlic powder
Juice of 1 lemon
¼ teaspoon paprika

To make the crab cakes

1. In a large bowl, whisk the egg, then add the Old Bay seasoning, parsley, soy sauce, garlic, Parmesan cheese, mayonnaise, and panko bread crumbs and mix well. Add the crabmeat and fold it in gently so the crabmeat does not fall apart. Form the mixture into 12 equal-size patties. Place the patties on a large baking sheet and refrigerate for at least 30 minutes.

2. Insert the Grill Grate and close the hood. Select Grill, set the temperature to HI, and set the time to 8 minutes. Select START/STOP to begin preheating.

3. When the unit beeps to signify it has preheated, spray avocado oil on both sides of 6 crab cakes and place them on the Grill Grate. Close the hood and cook for 4 minutes.

4. After 4 minutes, open the hood and flip the crab cakes. Close the hood and cook for 4 minutes more.

CONTINUED ▶

5. When cooking is complete, remove the crab cakes from the grill. Select GRILL, set the temperature to HI, and set the time to 8 minutes. Select START/STOP to begin and press PREHEAT to skip preheating. Repeat steps 3 and 4 for the remaining 6 crab cakes.

To make the lemon-garlic aioli

6. While the crab cakes are cooking, in a small bowl, combine the mayonnaise, garlic powder, lemon juice, and paprika. Feel free to add more lemon or a few dashes of hot sauce to adjust the taste to your liking.

7. When all of the crab cakes are cooked, serve with the sauce.

Crab Rangoons

This is an easier-than-you-think recipe for a popular Chinese takeout appetizer. I've revamped it to include more crab, for an equal crab-to-cream-cheese ratio. There have been times when I ordered these and could taste only the cream cheese. Making these at home, you can control the flavors and the price.

FAMILY FAVORITE / NUT-FREE / UNDER 30 MINUTES

PREP TIME: 15 minutes

COOK TIME: 10 minutes

ACCESSORIES: Grill Grate

HACK IT: While you're filling and sealing each wonton wrapper, place a moistened paper towel on top of the package so the other wrappers do not dry out. If you want to follow the traditional wonton-wrapping technique, you can fold them into triangular pockets instead.

SUBSTITUTION TIP: Lump crabmeat can be used in place of imitation crabmeat.

- 8 ounces cream cheese, at room temperature
- 1 (8-ounce) package imitation crabmeat, diced
- 2 tablespoons chopped scallions, both white and green parts
- 1 teaspoon garlic powder
- 1 teaspoon soy sauce
- 1 teaspoon Worcestershire sauce
- 1 package wonton wrappers (40 to 50 wrappers)
- ¼ cup water
- 4 tablespoons avocado oil

1. In a large bowl, combine the cream cheese, imitation crabmeat, scallions, garlic powder, soy sauce, and Worcestershire sauce.

2. Insert the Grill Grate and close the hood. Select GRILL, set the temperature to LO, and set the time to 5 minutes. Select START/STOP to begin preheating.

3. While the unit is preheating, place a wonton wrapper on a flat surface. Moisten the edges with water and place a heaping teaspoon of the crab mixture in the center. Bring the 4 sides together and then pinch the top, forming a cross. Make sure all the edges are sealed. Repeat with the remaining wrappers and crab mixture.

4. When the unit beeps to signify it has preheated, brush half the rangoons with avocado oil and place them on the Grill Grate. Close the hood and cook for 5 minutes.

5. When cooking is complete, the rangoons will be crispy and golden brown. Remove the rangoons from the grill. Select GRILL, set the temperature to HI, and set the time to 5 minutes. Select START/STOP to begin and press PREHEAT to skip preheating. Repeat step 4 for the remaining rangoons.

6. Serve the rangoons with sweet chili sauce or Orange Chili Sauce (page 201).

Crusted Codfish

With this recipe, you no longer have to resort to frozen fish sticks. Crispy, crunchy, and tender, these crusted cod fillets make a quick weeknight meal. I like to keep cod fillets in the freezer, but using fresh works, too, and the dish comes together in a snap.

5 INGREDIENTS / UNDER 30 MINUTES

PREP TIME: 10 minutes

COOK TIME: 8 minutes

ACCESSORIES: Grill Grate

VARIATION TIP: Don't have pistachios? Use pine nuts, almonds, or walnuts to give your fish some added crunch.

1 cup panko bread crumbs

2 tablespoons grated Parmesan cheese

¼ cup chopped pistachios

4 (4-ounce) frozen cod fillets, thawed

4 tablespoons Dijon mustard

Cooking spray

1. Insert the Grill Grate and close the hood. Select GRILL, set the temperature to HI, and set the time to 8 minutes. Select START/STOP to begin preheating.

2. While the unit is preheating, on a large plate, mix together the panko bread crumbs, Parmesan cheese, and pistachios. Evenly coat both sides of the cod fillets with the mustard, then press the fillets on the panko mixture on both sides to create a crust.

3. When the unit beeps to signify it has preheated, spray the crusted fillets with cooking spray and place them on the Grill Grate. Close the hood and grill for 4 minutes.

4. After 4 minutes, open the hood and flip the fillets. Close the hood and cook for 4 minutes more.

5. When cooking is complete, remove the fillets from the grill and serve.

Striped Bass with Sesame-Ginger Scallions

Striped bass has a unique and rich flavor. It's a large fish, and, when cooked well, it melts in your mouth. If striped bass is not available, this recipe can work with any whitefish, like cod, flounder, or sole. Using fresh ginger brings out all the flavors in this dish.

DAIRY-FREE / NUT-FREE / UNDER 30 MINUTES

PREP TIME: 10 minutes

COOK TIME: 8 minutes

ACCESSORIES: Cooking Pot

SUBSTITUTION TIP: If you don't have rice wine, use ½ cup rice wine vinegar and 4 teaspoons granulated sugar.

VARIATION TIP: If you don't like the texture of sliced ginger, you can use 1 tablespoon jarred or bottled ginger paste. Add it to the soy sauce mixture instead of putting it on top of the fish.

4 (8-ounce) striped bass fillets
Extra-virgin olive oil
2 (1-inch) pieces fresh ginger, peeled and thinly sliced
½ cup soy sauce
½ cup rice wine (mirin)
2 tablespoons sesame oil
¼ cup light brown sugar, packed
¼ cup water
¼ cup sliced scallions, both white and green parts, for garnish

1. Insert the Cooking Pot and close the hood. Select GRILL, set the temperature to HI, and set the time to 8 minutes. Select START/STOP to begin preheating.

2. While the unit is preheating, drizzle the fish fillets with olive oil.

3. When the unit beeps to signify it has preheated, place the fillets in the Cooking Pot in a single layer. Place the ginger slices on top of the fillets. Close the hood and cook for 6 minutes.

4. While the fish is cooking, in a small bowl, whisk together the soy sauce, rice wine, sesame oil, brown sugar, and water until the sugar dissolves.

5. After 6 minutes, open the hood and pour the soy sauce mixture over the fish. Close the hood and cook for 2 minutes more.

6. When cooking is complete, open the hood and remove the fillets from the grill. Garnish with the scallions and serve.

Grilled Mahi-Mahi Tacos with Spicy Coleslaw

Mahi-mahi is a fish that holds up well on the grill, and its meat has a slightly sweet taste. It pairs well with fresh citrus flavors, like lime or lemon, and some spice to balance it all out. If you aren't into spice, feel free to switch out the spicy mayo with Creamy Cilantro Sauce (page 111).

DAIRY-FREE / GLUTEN-FREE / NUT-FREE / UNDER 30 MINUTES

PREP TIME: 10 minutes

COOK TIME: 10 minutes

ACCESSORIES: Grill Grate

HACK IT: Use a prepackaged bag of coleslaw that includes shredded green and red cabbage and carrots to save you prep time.

1 teaspoon garlic powder

1 teaspoon onion powder

1 tablespoon paprika

¼ teaspoon salt

4 (8-ounce) mahi-mahi fillets

Avocado oil

Juice of 2 limes, divided

1 cup mayonnaise

1 tablespoon sriracha

⅛ teaspoon cayenne pepper

½ head red cabbage, shredded

8 (6-inch) corn tortillas

1. Insert the Grill Grate and close the hood. Select GRILL, set the temperature to MED, and set the time to 10 minutes. Select START/STOP to begin preheating.

2. While the unit is preheating, in a small bowl, combine the garlic powder, onion powder, paprika, and salt. Place the mahi-mahi fillets on a large plate and rub avocado oil on both sides. Then squeeze the juice of 1 lime on top and generously coat the fillets with the seasoning mix.

3. When the unit beeps to signify it has preheated, place the fillets on the Grill Grate. Close the hood and grill for 8 minutes.

4. While the mahi-mahi is cooking, in a large bowl, combine the mayonnaise, sriracha, cayenne pepper, and the juice of the remaining lime. Add the shredded cabbage to the bowl and stir until combined.

5. After 8 minutes, open the hood and remove the fillets from the grill. Place the tortillas on the Grill Grate. Close the hood to warm them for 2 minutes. Feel free to flip after 1 minute, if desired.

6. Cut the mahi-mahi into ½-inch to 1-inch strips. To assemble the tacos, place the mahi-mahi pieces on the tortillas and dress with the spicy coleslaw mix. Serve.

Garlic Butter Shrimp Kebabs

Shrimp on the Foodi™ Grill cooks up quickly. This dish is similar to shrimp scampi in that the shrimp is bathed in butter and garlic. But I've changed things up by bringing these to the grill on skewers. Use fresh garlic if you can, because it's bolder, with a better aroma, especially as it infuses the butter.

GLUTEN-FREE / NUT-FREE / UNDER 30 MINUTES

PREP TIME: 15 minutes

COOK TIME: 10 minutes

ACCESSORIES: Grill Grate / Ninja® Foodi™ Grill Kebab Skewers

HACK IT: In a pinch, you can use jarred minced garlic or 1 teaspoon garlic powder instead of mincing fresh garlic.

2 tablespoons unsalted butter, at room temperature

4 garlic cloves, minced

2 pounds jumbo shrimp, peeled

1 tablespoon garlic salt

1 teaspoon dried parsley

1. Insert the Grill Grate. Place the butter and minced garlic in a heat-safe bowl, place the bowl on the Grill Grate, and close the hood. Select GRILL, set the temperature to HI, and set the time to 5 minutes. Select START/STOP to begin preheating. After 1 minute of preheating (set a separate timer), remove the bowl with the butter. Close the hood to continue preheating.

2. While the unit is preheating, place 4 or 5 shrimp on each of 8 skewers, with at least 1 inch left at the bottom. Place the skewers on a large plate. Lightly coat them with the garlic salt and parsley.

3. When the unit beeps to signify it has preheated, place 4 skewers on the Grill Grate. Brush some of the melted garlic butter on the shrimp. Close the hood and grill for 2 minutes, 30 seconds.

4. After 2 minutes, 30 seconds, open the hood and brush the shrimp with garlic butter again, then flip the skewers. Brush on more garlic butter. Close the hood and cook for 2 minutes, 30 seconds more.

5. When cooking is complete, the shrimp will be opaque and pink. Remove the skewers from the grill. Select GRILL, set the temperature to HI, and set the time to 5 minutes. Select START/STOP to begin and press PREHEAT to skip preheating. Repeat steps 3 and 4 for the remaining skewers. When all the skewers are cooked, serve.

Honey-Walnut Shrimp

SERVES 4

Creamy, crunchy, and sweet, this shrimp recipe is adapted from the dish most requested by my family when we want Chinese takeout. It's also the most expensive item on the menu. But making it at home is much more budget-friendly. And it comes together even faster than ordering takeout!

FAMILY FAVORITE / UNDER 30 MINUTES

PREP TIME: 10 minutes

COOK TIME: 8 minutes

ACCESSORIES: Grill Grate

SUBSTITUTION TIP:
Powdered sugar dissolves easier into the mayonnaise, but if you don't have any, substitute it with granulated sugar. If you don't have heavy cream, replace it and the sugar with 3 tablespoons sweetened condensed milk.

2 ounces walnuts

2 tablespoons honey

1 egg

1 cup panko bread crumbs

1 pound shrimp, peeled

½ cup mayonnaise

1 teaspoon powdered sugar

2 tablespoons heavy (whipping) cream

Scallions, both white and green parts, sliced, for garnish

1. Insert the Grill Grate. In a small heat-safe bowl, combine the walnuts and honey, then place the bowl on the Grill Grate and close the hood. Select GRILL, set the temperature to HI, and set the time to 8 minutes. Select START/STOP to begin preheating. After 2 minutes of preheating (set a separate timer), remove the bowl. Close the hood to continue preheating.

2. While the unit is preheating, create an assembly line with 2 large bowls. In the first bowl, whisk the egg. Put the panko bread crumbs in the other bowl. One at a time, dip the shrimp in the egg and then into the panko bread crumbs until well coated. Place the breaded shrimp on a plate.

3. When the unit beeps to signify it has preheated, place the shrimp on the Grill Grate in a single layer. Close the hood and cook for 4 minutes.

4. After 4 minutes, open the hood and flip the shrimp. Close the hood and cook for 4 minutes more.

5. While the shrimp are cooking, in a large bowl, combine the mayonnaise, powdered sugar, and heavy cream and mix until the sugar has dissolved.

6. When cooking is complete, remove the shrimp from the grill. Add the cooked shrimp and honey walnuts to the mayonnaise mixture and gently fold them together. Garnish with scallions and serve.

Lemon-Garlic Butter Scallops

SERVES 6

The meat of a scallop is part of the muscle of the shellfish, and if it is overcooked, it becomes rubbery and tough. Thankfully, cooking scallops is fast and easy, and when cooked to perfection, they practically melt in your mouth. These lemony, garlicky, and buttery scallops are seared in the Cooking Pot. The dish is ready to serve in less than 15 minutes.

5 INGREDIENTS / GLUTEN-FREE / NUT-FREE / UNDER 30 MINUTES

PREP TIME: 10 minutes

COOK TIME: 4 minutes

ACCESSORIES: Cooking Pot

VARIATION TIP: Want a creamier texture to the garlic butter? Add ¼ cup heavy cream to the garlic-butter mixture and stir together. Add additional lemon slices to the Cooking Pot for a more lemony vibe.

2 pounds large sea scallops

Salt

Freshly ground black pepper

3 tablespoons avocado oil

3 garlic cloves, minced

8 tablespoons (1 stick) unsalted butter, sliced

Juice of 1 lemon

Chopped fresh parsley, for garnish

1. Insert the Cooking Pot and close the hood. Select GRILL, set the temperature to HI, and set the time to 4 minutes. Select START/STOP to begin preheating.

2. While the unit is preheating, pat the scallops dry with a paper towel and season them with salt and pepper. After 5 minutes of preheating (set a separate timer), open the hood and add the avocado oil and garlic to the Cooking Pot, then close the hood to continue preheating.

3. When the unit beeps to signify it has preheated, use a spatula to spread the oil and garlic around the bottom of the Cooking Pot. Place the scallops in the pot in a single layer. Close the hood and cook for 2 minutes.

4. After 2 minutes, open the hood and flip the scallops. Add the butter to the pot and drizzle some lemon juice over each scallop. Close the hood and cook for 2 minutes more.

5. When cooking is complete, open the hood and flip the scallops again. Spoon melted garlic butter on top of each. The scallops should be slightly firm and opaque. Remove the scallops from the grill and serve, garnished with the parsley.

Lobster Rolls

The first time I had a lobster roll, I was hooked! I've used lobster tails and even langos-tinos (Spanish for "little lobsters") for these sandwiches—both versions are delicious. Whatever type you use, you are in for a treat. When using frozen lobster, as I do here, be sure that it is completely thawed before cooking. If you are using fresh lobster tails, I suggest preparing it by following the recipe for Buttered Lobster Tails (page 199). I like these simple, meaty rolls on buttered bread with just a touch of mayo, but add any top-pings you'd like.

NUT-FREE / UNDER 30 MINUTES

PREP TIME: 5 minutes

COOK TIME: 7 minutes

ACCESSORIES: Grill Grate

VARIATION TIP: Want some added crunch? Dice a celery rib and add it to the mayonnaise mixture.

¼ **cup mayonnaise**

Juice of ½ lemon

¼ **teaspoon sea salt**

⅛ **teaspoon freshly ground black pepper**

1 teaspoon dried parsley

Dash paprika

1 pound frozen lobster meat, thawed, cut into 1-inch pieces

Unsalted butter, at room temperature

4 sandwich rolls, such as French rolls, hoagie rolls, or large hot dog buns

1 lemon, cut into wedges

1. Insert the Grill Grate and close the hood. Select GRILL, set the temperature to MED, and set the time to 7 minutes. Select START/STOP to begin preheating.

2. While the unit is preheating, in a large bowl, combine the mayonnaise, lemon juice, salt, pepper, parsley, and paprika.

3. When the unit beeps to signify it has preheated, place the lobster meat on the Grill Grate. Close the hood and grill for 4 minutes.

4. While the lobster is cooking, spread the butter on the sandwich rolls.

5. After 4 minutes, open the hood and remove the lobster meat. Set aside on a plate. Place the sandwich rolls on the grill, buttered-side down. Close the hood and grill for 2 minutes.

6. After 2 minutes, open the hood and flip the rolls. Close the hood and cook for 1 minute more.

7. When the bread is toasted and golden brown, remove it from the grill. Add the lobster meat to the mayonnaise mixture and gently fold in until well combined. Spoon the lobster meat into the sandwich rolls. Serve with the lemon wedges.

Orange-Ginger Soy Salmon

SERVES 4

This sweet and tangy salmon recipe makes a quick, easy, and delicious weeknight meal for the family or when entertaining. Let the Foodi™ Grill do the work on this one. No need to worry about flipping the fillets. You'll get perfectly charred edges with soft, moist flesh. Serve this over rice with your favorite vegetables for a healthy, family-friendly meal.

FAMILY FAVORITE /
NUT-FREE / UNDER
30 MINUTES

PREP TIME: 5 minutes

COOK TIME: 12 minutes

ACCESSORIES: Cooking Pot

HACK IT: If you don't have fresh ginger or garlic, you can use jarred. You can also substitute ¼ cup freshly squeezed orange juice for the orange marmalade. I like using marmalade because it has orange pulp in it, so I suggest using high-pulp orange juice.

½ **cup low-sodium soy sauce**

¼ **cup orange marmalade**

3 **tablespoons light brown sugar, packed**

1 **tablespoon peeled minced fresh ginger**

1 **garlic clove, minced**

4 **(8-ounce) skin-on salmon fillets**

1. In a large bowl, whisk together the soy sauce, orange marmalade, brown sugar, ginger, and garlic until the sugar is dissolved. Set aside one-quarter of the marinade in a small bowl. Place the salmon fillets skin-side down in the marinade in the large bowl.

2. Insert the Grill Grate and close the hood. Select GRILL, set the temperature to MED, and set the time to 12 minutes. Select START/STOP to begin preheating.

3. When the unit beeps to signify it has preheated, place the salmon fillets on the Grill Grate, skin-side down. Spoon the remaining marinade in the large bowl over the fillets. Close the hood and cook for 10 minutes.

4. After 10 minutes, open the hood and brush the reserved marinade in the small bowl over the fillets. Close the hood and cook for 2 minutes more.

5. When cooking is complete, the salmon will be opaque and should flake easily with a fork. (If you want, you can also use the Smart Thermometer at the end of cooking to check that the internal temperature of the salmon has reached 145°F.) Remove the fillets from the grill and serve.

Seared Tuna with Citrus Ponzu Sauce

SERVES 4

This has to be one of the easiest and fastest recipes out there. Can you imagine dinner ready in less than 15 minutes? No marinating is required for this perfectly grilled tuna that is crispy and salty on the outside and moist and tender on the inside. If you're a sushi lover like me, this dish is hard not to love. Serve these seared tuna steaks with a salad or over white rice.

DAIRY-FREE / NUT-FREE / UNDER 30 MINUTES

PREP TIME: 5 minutes

COOK TIME: 6 minutes

ACCESSORIES: Grill Grate

SUBSTITUTION TIP: Rice wine should be available at most grocery stores, but if not, you can use ⅓ cup rice wine vinegar and increase the granulated sugar to 4 teaspoons. To make this recipe gluten-free, use coconut aminos or tamari in place of the soy sauce.

VARIATION TIP: If you are not into raw fish, you can cook your tuna steaks well-done. Just add 4 minutes to the cook time.

Extra-virgin olive oil

4 (4- to 5-ounce) ahi tuna steaks (at least 1 inch thick)

Salt

Freshly ground black pepper

¼ cup soy sauce

⅓ cup rice wine (mirin)

1 teaspoon granulated sugar

Juice of 2 limes

Juice of 2 lemons

1 tablespoon sesame seeds, for garnish (optional)

Scallions, both white and green parts, sliced, for garnish

1. Insert the Grill Grate and close the hood. Select GRILL, set the temperature to MAX, and set the time to 6 minutes. Select START/STOP to begin preheating.

2. While the unit is preheating, drizzle the olive oil over the tuna steaks and rub it in for a nice coat. Season both sides with salt and pepper.

3. When the unit beeps to signify it has preheated, place the tuna steaks on the Grill Grate. Close the hood and cook for 3 minutes.

4. After 3 minutes, open the hood and flip the steak. Close the hood and cook for 3 minutes more.

5. While the tuna steaks are cooking, in a small bowl, whisk together the soy sauce, rice wine, sugar, lime juice, and lemon juice until the sugar is dissolved.

6. When cooking is complete, open the hood and remove the tuna steaks from the grill. Garnish with sesame seeds (if using) and scallions. Serve with the citrus ponzu sauce for dipping.

Mom's Lemon-Pepper Salmon

My mom always knew how to feed a crowd. If it was just us, we'd eat this salmon with white rice and some vegetables. If it was a party, she'd make a big batch and it'd be the first dish to vanish. As I started making my own dishes, this was one I'd always fall back on because there's no marinating, no special preparation, just simple ingredients—and it is always so good.

5 INGREDIENTS / DAIRY-FREE / GLUTEN-FREE / NUT-FREE / UNDER 30 MINUTES

PREP TIME: 5 minutes

COOK TIME: 8 minutes

ACCESSORIES: Grill Grate

VARIATION TIP: If you are not into lemon pepper, feel free to add other seasonings, like salt, pepper, paprika, dried parsley, or garlic and onion powder, to the mayonnaise base in its place.

¼ **cup mayonnaise**

4 **(4- to 5-ounce) skin-on salmon fillets**

1 **tablespoon lemon-pepper seasoning**

1. Insert the Grill Grate and close the hood. Select GRILL, set the temperature to MED, and set the time to 8 minutes. Select START/STOP to begin preheating.

2. While the unit is preheating, spread the mayonnaise evenly on the flesh of each salmon fillet. Season with the lemon pepper.

3. When the unit beeps to signify it has preheated, place the fillets on the Grill Grate, skin-side down. Close the hood and cook for 8 minutes.

4. When cooking is complete, the salmon will be opaque and should flake easily with a fork. (If you want, you can also use the Smart Thermometer at the end of cooking to check that the internal temperature of the salmon has reached 145°F.) Remove the salmon from the grill and serve.

Shrimp Boil

Now you can have a shrimp boil at home! Adjust the seasonings to make this as spicy or mild as you like. I've made this recipe to be on the milder side so everyone can enjoy it. Leaving just the tails on the shrimp makes for easier eating without any peeling, but you can use head-on shrimp, too, as my family does. Slurp away!

GLUTEN-FREE / NUT-FREE / UNDER 30 MINUTES

PREP TIME: 10 minutes

COOK TIME: 10 minutes

ACCESSORIES: Cooking Pot / Grill Grate

VARIATION TIP: Feel free to add some ears of corn, spicy sausage, and potatoes to your shrimp boil. I suggest cooking the potatoes on the Grill Grate first. Then grill the corn and sausage. You may need to adjust the cooking time to make sure the potatoes are cooked until tender. Then put the corn, sausage, potatoes, and shrimp in the Cooking Pot with the butter in step 4. Want more spice? Add more cayenne pepper or even a few teaspoons of your favorite hot sauce to the mixture.

- 2 tablespoons lemon-pepper seasoning
- 2 tablespoons light brown sugar, packed
- 2 tablespoons minced garlic
- 2 tablespoons Old Bay seasoning
- ¼ teaspoon Cajun seasoning
- ¼ teaspoon paprika
- ¼ teaspoon cayenne pepper
- 1 teaspoon garlic powder
- 1½ cups (3 sticks) unsalted butter, cut into quarters
- 2 pounds shrimp

1. Insert the Cooking Pot and close the hood. Select GRILL, set the temperature to MED, and set the time to 10 minutes. Select START/STOP to begin preheating.

2. While the unit is preheating, in a small bowl, combine the lemon pepper, brown sugar, minced garlic, Old Bay seasoning, Cajun seasoning, paprika, cayenne pepper, and garlic powder.

3. When the unit beeps to signify it has preheated, place the butter and the lemon-pepper mixture in the Cooking Pot. Insert the Grill Grate and place the shrimp on it in a single layer. Close the hood and grill for 5 minutes.

4. After 5 minutes, open the hood and use grill mitts to remove the Grill Grate. Place the shrimp in the Cooking Pot. Stir to combine. Close the hood and cook for 5 minutes more.

5. When cooking is complete, open the hood and stir once more. Then close the hood and let the butter set with the shrimp for 5 minutes. Serve.

Tomato-Stuffed Grilled Sole

Jazz up your fish by stuffing it. Sole fillets can be found both frozen and fresh and tend to be more on the affordable side than other fish. Because the fillet is quite thin, it makes for easy rolling. This recipe creates a crunchy crust on the outside and a creamy center.

5 INGREDIENTS / DAIRY-FREE / NUT-FREE / UNDER 30 MINUTES

PREP TIME: 10 minutes

COOK TIME: 7 minutes

ACCESSORIES: Grill Grate

VARIATION TIP: Stuff your sole fillets with asparagus instead of tomatoes to get some added crunch.

6 tablespoons mayonnaise

1 teaspoon garlic powder

1 (14-ounce) can diced tomatoes, drained

6 (4-ounce) sole fillets

Cooking spray

6 tablespoons panko bread crumbs

1. Insert the Grill Grate and close the hood. Select GRILL, set the temperature to HI, and set the time to 7 minutes. Select START/STOP to begin preheating.

2. While the unit is preheating, in a small bowl, combine the mayonnaise and garlic powder. Slowly fold in the tomatoes, making sure to be gentle so they don't turn to mush. Place the sole fillets on a large, flat surface and spread the mayonnaise across the top of each. Roll up the fillets, creating pinwheels. Spray the top of each roll with cooking spray, then press 1 tablespoon of panko bread crumbs on top of each.

3. When the unit beeps to signify it has preheated, place the fillets on the Grill Grate, seam-side down. Close the hood and grill for 7 minutes.

4. When cooking is complete, the panko bread crumbs will be crisp, and the fish will have turned opaque. Remove the fish from the grill and serve.

Tilapia with Cilantro and Ginger

Sweet, tangy, salty, and spicy flavors all infuse this fish dish. When I was growing up, my dad would often bring home a whole fried tilapia fish—sometimes two—for us to eat. Tilapia is sometimes described as being flavorless, but it was the different sauces that we would dip it into that made it so enjoyable. For this recipe, I've mixed my two favorite flavors, cilantro and ginger, into this yummy sauce.

DAIRY-FREE / GLUTEN-FREE / NUT-FREE / UNDER 30 MINUTES

PREP TIME: 10 minutes

COOK TIME: 8 minutes

ACCESSORIES: Cooking Pot

SUBSTITUTION TIP: Can't find tilapia? Use catfish, red snapper, or trout. Don't have time to make your own sauce? Buy an already-made dipping sauce.

Extra-virgin olive oil

4 (8-ounce) tilapia fillets

2 tablespoons soy sauce

1 teaspoon sesame oil

1 tablespoon honey

1 tablespoon peeled minced fresh ginger

½ cup chopped fresh cilantro

1. Insert the Cooking Pot and close the hood. Select GRILL, set the temperature to HI, and set the time to 8 minutes. Select START/STOP to begin preheating.

2. While the unit is preheating, drizzle the fish fillets with olive oil.

3. When the unit beeps to signify it has preheated, place the fillets in the Cooking Pot in a single layer. Close the hood and cook for 6 minutes.

4. While the fish is cooking, in a small bowl, whisk together the soy sauce, sesame oil, honey, ginger, and cilantro.

5. After 6 minutes, open the hood and pour the sauce over the fillets. Close the hood and cook for 2 minutes more.

6. When cooking is complete, remove the fillets from the grill and serve.

Halibut with Lemon and Capers

Capers add an extra bit of tanginess that goes great with fish dishes, as they provide a tasty salty flavor. For this recipe, capers and a fresh slice of lemon on top of the fish while cooking give you all the tanginess that you need.

GLUTEN-FREE / NUT-FREE / UNDER 30 MINUTES

PREP TIME: 5 minutes

COOK TIME: 8 minutes

ACCESSORIES: Cooking Pot

SUBSTITUTION TIP: If you don't have capers, squeeze the juice of 2 lemons on top of the fillets while cooking. Add a little extra lemon juice and 1 teaspoon salt to the buttery sauce.

4 halibut steaks (at least 1 inch thick)

Extra-virgin olive oil

1 lemon

1 cup white wine

3 garlic cloves, minced

4 tablespoons capers

4 tablespoons (½ stick) unsalted butter, sliced

1. Insert the Cooking Pot and close the hood. Select GRILL, set the temperature to HI, and set the time to 8 minutes. Select START/STOP to begin preheating.

2. While the unit is preheating, drizzle the fish fillets with olive oil. Cut half the lemon into thin slices and place them on top of the fillets.

3. When the unit beeps to signify it has preheated, place the fillets in the Cooking Pot. Close the hood and cook for 4 minutes.

4. After 4 minutes, open the hood and add the white wine. Close the hood and cook for 2 minutes. After 2 minutes, open the hood and add the garlic, capers, and butter. Squeeze the juice of the remaining ½ lemon over the fish. Close the hood and cook for 2 minutes more.

5. When cooking is complete, open the hood and spoon the sauce over the fish. If the capers have not popped, give about half of them a tap with the spoon to pop them. Stir the sauce and serve with the fillets.

Peaches-and-Cake Skewers, *page 242*

10
Desserts

Apple Pie Crumble

Nothing beats a fresh-baked apple pie. This apple pie crumble uses fresh apples and simple ingredients likely already in your pantry. No need to worry about special dough or perfecting that crust. Here the warm apple filling is topped with a crisp, crunchy, and buttery topping. The only regret you may have is that you didn't make more!

NUT-FREE / UNDER 30 MINUTES / VEGETARIAN

PREP TIME: 10 minutes

COOK TIME: 20 minutes

ACCESSORIES: Cooking Pot

SUBSTITUTION TIP: Make this into a peach cobbler by using peaches instead of apples. You can even use a 16-ounce can of unsweetened peaches (drained) instead of fresh peaches if they are out of season.

- **3 small apples, such as Honeycrisp, Gala, Pink Lady, or Granny Smith, peeled, cored, and cut into ⅛-inch-thick slices**
- **¼ cup granulated sugar**
- **½ teaspoon cinnamon**
- **½ cup quick-cooking oatmeal**
- **4 tablespoons (½ stick) unsalted butter, at room temperature**
- **½ cup all-purpose flour**
- **½ cup light brown sugar, packed**

1. Insert the Cooking Pot and close the hood. Select GRILL, set the temperature to LO, and set the time to 20 minutes. Select START/STOP to begin preheating.

2. While the unit is preheating, put the apples in a large bowl and coat with the granulated sugar and cinnamon. In a medium bowl, combine the oatmeal, butter, flour, and brown sugar, stirring to make clumps for the top layer.

3. Place the apples in a 6-inch springform pan in an even layer. Spread the oatmeal topping over the apples.

4. When the unit beeps to signify it has preheated, place the pan in the Cooking Pot. Close the hood and cook for 20 minutes.

5. After 20 minutes, open the hood and remove the pan from the unit. The apples should be soft and the topping golden brown. Serve.

Biscuit Raisin Bread

SERVES 6 TO 8

This easy, pull-apart bread with a melted brown sugar coating and raisins on top resembles what some call "monkey bread." To change it up, I stuff each biscuit with cream cheese, which gives a creamy surprise in each bite. Your family and guests will love it whether enjoyed for breakfast or as an after-dinner treat with coffee, and you'll appreciate the simplicity and ease of this treat.

5 INGREDIENTS / NUT-FREE / UNDER 30 MINUTES / VEGETARIAN

PREP TIME: 10 minutes

COOK TIME: 20 minutes

ACCESSORIES: Cooking Pot

VARIATION TIP: Roll the raisins inside the balls along with the cream cheese, skip the bread loaf pan, and place the balls directly in the Cooking Pot for 8 to 10 minutes. The sugar glaze is optional.

1 (12-ounce) package refrigerated buttermilk biscuits (10 biscuits)

8 ounces cream cheese, cut into 40 cubes

¼ cup light brown sugar, packed

4 tablespoons (½ stick) unsalted butter, melted

½ cup raisins

1. Insert the Cooking Pot and close the hood. Select GRILL, set the temperature to LO, and set the time to 20 minutes. Select START/STOP to begin preheating.

2. While the unit is preheating, separate the biscuits and cut each into quarters. Flatten each quarter biscuit with your palm and place 1 cream cheese cube on the center. Wrap the dough around the cream cheese and press to seal, forming a ball. Place the biscuit balls in a 9-by-5-inch bread loaf pan. They will be layered over each other.

3. In a small bowl, combine the brown sugar and melted butter. Pour this over the biscuit balls evenly.

4. When the unit beeps to signify it has preheated, place the loaf pan in the Cooking Pot. Close the hood and grill for 10 minutes.

5. After 10 minutes, open the hood and evenly scatter the raisins on the top layer. Close the hood and cook for 10 minutes more.

6. When cooking is complete, remove the loaf pan from the pot. Remove the bread from the pan, slice, and serve.

Everyday Cheesecake

SERVES 4

When I first learned how to make cheesecake, I was blown away by how much cream cheese was called for in most recipes. My recipe uses only one package instead of the typical four. This cheesecake is something my whole family craves. We use different-flavored cookie crusts each week to mix things up. I call this Everyday Cheesecake because it's light, it can cater to everyone's taste buds, and it always hits that sweet spot.

NUT-FREE / VEGETARIAN

PREP TIME: 15 minutes, plus 4 hours to cool

COOK TIME: 35 minutes

ACCESSORIES: Cooking Pot

HACK IT: Use an electric mixer to combine the cheesecake filling. Use the bottom or side of a measuring cup to press down and crush the cookies. You can also use a heavy-bottomed glass to press down the crumbs and butter when forming the crust.

1 large egg

8 ounces cream cheese, at room temperature

¼ cup heavy (whipping) cream

¼ cup sour cream

¼ cup powdered sugar

1 teaspoon vanilla extract

5 ounces cookies, such as chocolate, vanilla, cinnamon, or your favorite

4 tablespoons (½ stick) unsalted butter, melted

1. In a large bowl, whisk the egg. Then add the cream cheese, heavy cream, and sour cream and whisk until smooth. Slowly add the powdered sugar and vanilla, whisking until fully mixed.

2. Insert the Cooking Pot and close the hood. Select BAKE, set the temperature to 350°F, and set the time to 35 minutes. Select START/STOP to begin preheating.

3. While the unit is preheating, crush the cookies into fine crumbs. Place them in a 6-inch springform pan and drizzle evenly with the melted butter. Using your fingers, press down on the crumbs to form a crust on the bottom of the pan. Pour the cream cheese mixture on top of the crust. Cover the pan with aluminum foil, making sure the foil fully covers the sides of the pan and tucks under the bottom so it does not lift up and block the Splatter Shield as the air flows while baking.

4. When the unit beeps to signify it has preheated, place the springform pan in the Cooking Pot. Close the hood and cook for 25 minutes.

5. After 25 minutes, open the hood and remove the foil. Close the hood and cook for 10 minutes more.

6. When cooking is complete, remove the pan from the Cooking Pot and let the cheesecake cool for 1 hour, then place the cheesecake in the refrigerator for at least 3 hours. Slice and serve.

Candied Pecans

Candied pecans make for a great snack. They add the perfect crunch as a topping for salad, yogurt, or vanilla ice cream and are also a great way to dress up trail mix. You can switch out the sugar for a sugar substitute, such as stevia, monk fruit, or erythritol, if you want to make these diabetic-friendly or for those following a keto or low-carb diet.

DAIRY-FREE / GLUTEN-FREE / UNDER 30 MINUTES / VEGETARIAN

PREP TIME: 10 minutes

COOK TIME: 20 minutes

ACCESSORIES: Cooking Pot

VARIATION TIP: Feel free to use different nuts or a mixture of nuts, like almonds, cashews, or walnuts. If you want to add some heat, add 1 teaspoon cayenne pepper to give these a spicy kick.

1 large egg white

1 teaspoon vanilla extract

1 tablespoon water

¼ cup granulated sugar

¼ cup light brown sugar, packed

1 teaspoon ground cinnamon

1 teaspoon salt

1 pound pecan halves

1. Insert the Cooking Pot and close the hood. Select GRILL, set the temperature to MED, and set the time to 20 minutes. Select START/STOP to begin preheating.

2. While the unit is preheating, in a large bowl, whisk together the egg white, vanilla, and water until it becomes frothy.

3. In a small bowl, combine the granulated sugar, brown sugar, cinnamon, and salt. Add the pecans to the egg mixture, coating them well. Then add the sugar mixture and stir to coat the pecans evenly.

4. When the unit beeps to signify it has preheated, evenly spread the pecans in the Cooking Pot. Close the hood and grill for 5 minutes.

5. After 5 minutes, open the hood and stir the pecans. Close the hood and cook for 5 minutes. Repeat until the pecans have cooked for 20 minutes total.

6. When cooking is complete, remove the pecans from the Cooking Pot and spread them on a baking sheet to cool to room temperature. Store in a resealable bag or airtight container.

Grilled Apple Fries with Caramel Cream Cheese Dip

SERVES 4

I've always loved candied caramel apples, but they hurt my teeth trying to bite into them. Plus, I can never wait for the caramel to set on the apple before taking that first bite. These grilled apple fries help solve that problem, and it's a fun dessert the whole family can enjoy. Enjoy these crispy and warm apples dipped in a sweet, creamy caramel sauce.

NUT-FREE / UNDER 30 MINUTES / VEGETARIAN

PREP TIME: 10 minutes

COOK TIME: 5 minutes

ACCESSORIES: Grill Grate

VARIATION TIP: Instead of apples, try grilling pineapples or peaches. You can also crush walnuts or pecans and press your fruit of choice into the crushed nuts instead of flour for a gluten-free version.

- **4 apples, such as Honeycrisp, Gala, Pink Lady, or Granny Smith, peeled, cored, and sliced**
- **¼ cup heavy (whipping) cream**
- **1 tablespoon granulated sugar**
- **¼ teaspoon cinnamon**
- **¼ cup all-purpose flour**
- **4 ounces cream cheese, at room temperature**
- **1 tablespoon caramel sauce**
- **1 tablespoon light brown sugar, packed**

1. Insert the Grill Grate and close the hood. Select GRILL, set the temperature to MAX, and set the time to 5 minutes. Select START/STOP to begin preheating.

2. In a large bowl, toss the apple slices with the heavy cream, granulated sugar, and cinnamon to coat. Slowly shake in the flour and continue mixing to coat.

3. In a small bowl, mix together the cream cheese, caramel sauce, and brown sugar until smooth. Set aside.

4. When the unit beeps to signify it has preheated, place the apples on the Grill Grate in a single layer. Close the hood and grill for 2 minutes, 30 seconds.

5. After 2 minutes, 30 seconds, open the hood and flip and toss the apples around. Close the hood and cook for 2 minutes, 30 seconds more.

6. When cooking is complete, open the hood and remove the apple chips from the grill. Serve with the sauce.

Cinnamon-Sugar Dessert Chips

During my childhood, this was a dessert I would make at home in the microwave. I simply spread butter, cinnamon, and sugar on a tortilla and rolled it up like a cinnamon roll. This dessert is a revamp of that childhood dish, but I turn the tortillas into chips rather then rolling them up.

5 INGREDIENTS / NUT-FREE / UNDER 30 MINUTES / VEGETARIAN

PREP TIME: 10 minutes

COOK TIME: 10 minutes

ACCESSORIES: Grill Grate

VARIATION TIP: Turn these into dessert nachos and dress them up with your favorite fresh fruits, caramel sauce, and whipped cream.

10 (6-inch) flour tortillas

8 tablespoons (1 stick) unsalted butter, melted

1 tablespoon cinnamon

¼ cup granulated sugar

½ cup chocolate syrup, for dipping

1. Insert the Grill Grate and close the hood. Select GRILL, set the temperature to HI, and set the time to 10 minutes. Select START/STOP to begin preheating.

2. While the unit is preheating, cut the tortillas into 6 equal wedges. In a large resealable bag, combine the tortillas, butter, cinnamon, and sugar and shake vigorously to coat the tortillas.

3. When the unit beeps to signify it has preheated, add half the tortillas to the Grill Grate. Close the hood and cook for 2 minutes, 30 seconds.

4. After 2 minutes, 30 seconds, open the hood and use a spatula to quickly flip the chips or move them around. Close the hood and cook for 2 minutes, 30 seconds more.

5. After 2 minutes, 30 seconds, open the hood and remove the grilled chips and repeat the process with the remaining tortillas.

6. Serve with the chocolate syrup for dipping.

Grilled Banana S'mores

This recipe combines the crunchiness of s'mores with the tastiness of a banana split. S'mores can be messy, and grilling a banana on an outdoor grill is next to impossible. But grilling them on the Foodi™ Grill creates less of a mess, and it's an easier way to hold the s'mores together. Do you eat this with a fork or spoon? Use whatever gets it from the plate to your mouth fastest!

5 INGREDIENTS / NUT-FREE / UNDER 30 MINUTES / VEGETARIAN

PREP TIME: 10 minutes

COOK TIME: 6 minutes

ACCESSORIES: Cooking Pot

SUBSTITUTION TIP: Don't have chocolate chips? Use chocolate syrup, peanut butter, or a chocolate-hazelnut spread.

VARIATION TIP: Use white chocolate, caramel, or butterscotch-flavored chips instead of milk chocolate. If you want a different kind of crunch, use crushed peanuts or slivered almonds in place of the graham crackers.

4 large bananas

1 cup milk chocolate chips

1 cup mini marshmallows

4 graham crackers, crushed

1. Insert the Cooking Pot and close the hood. Select GRILL, set the temperature to HI, and set the time to 6 minutes. Select START/STOP to begin preheating.

2. While the unit is preheating, prepare the banana boats. Starting at the bottom of a banana, slice the peel lengthwise up one side and then the opposite side. Pull the top half of the peel back, revealing the fruit underneath, but keeping the bottom of the banana peel intact. With a spoon, carefully scoop out some of the banana. (Eat it or set it aside.) Repeat with each banana. Equally divide the chocolate chips and marshmallows between the banana boats.

3. When the unit beeps to signify it has preheated, place the bananas in the Cooking Pot. Close the hood and cook for 6 minutes.

4. When cooking is complete, remove the bananas from the grill and sprinkle the crushed graham crackers on top. Serve.

Grilled Strawberry Pound Cake

This dessert classic can be made on the Foodi™ Grill. Ready-made pound cake can be found at your local grocery store in the bakery or freezer section. The beauty of making these on the grill is that the sugar caramelizes in a way it cannot with typical baking and reheating. You'll be left with impressive grill marks on your pound cake.

5 INGREDIENTS / NUT-FREE / UNDER 30 MINUTES / VEGETARIAN

PREP TIME: 10 minutes

COOK TIME: 8 minutes

ACCESSORIES: Grill Grate

VARIATION TIP:
Strawberries not in season? Use another fruit that is in season or use frozen fruit. If using frozen, thaw it first by leaving it in a bowl at room temperature. You do not want to add frozen fruit to your pound cake as it may make the cake become watery.

1 loaf pound cake, cut into ¼-inch-thick slices (8 slices)

4 tablespoons (½ stick) unsalted butter, melted

2 cups strawberries, sliced

1 tablespoon granulated sugar

Juice of ¼ lemon

1. Insert the Grill Grate and close the hood. Select GRILL, set the temperature to HI, and set the time to 8 minutes. Select START/STOP to begin preheating.

2. While the unit is preheating, brush both sides of the pound cake slices with the melted butter. In a small bowl, combine the strawberries, sugar, and lemon juice.

3. When the unit beeps to signify it has preheated, place 4 slices of pound cake on the Grill Grate. Close the hood and grill for 2 minutes.

4. After 2 minutes, open the hood and flip the pound cake slices. Top each with ¼ cup of strawberries. Close the hood and cook for 2 minutes.

5. After 2 minutes, open the hood and carefully remove the grilled pound cake. Repeat steps 3 and 4 with the remaining pound cake and strawberries. Serve.

Lemon Squares

I love the tartness of these lemon squares. They have the perfect tart-and-sweet combination. These lemon squares always yell out summer to me as they're refreshing, tangy, and light. But they can—and should—be enjoyed year-round. They're great for an after-lunch treat, as a dessert, or with tea or coffee.

NUT-FREE / VEGETARIAN

PREP TIME: 10 minutes, plus 2 hours to cool

COOK TIME: 35 minutes

ACCESSORIES: Cooking Pot

HACK IT: Once you have set the crust in the pan, use a fork to pierce it so it remains level and does not rise and puff up while it bakes.

1 cup all-purpose flour

8 tablespoons (1 stick) unsalted butter, at room temperature

⅓ cup powdered sugar, plus additional for dusting

2 large eggs

⅔ cup granulated sugar

½ teaspoon baking powder

¼ teaspoon salt

Juice of 1 lemon

1. Insert the Cooking Pot and close the hood. Select BAKE, set the temperature to 325°F, and set the time to 35 minutes. Select START/STOP to begin preheating.

2. While the unit is preheating, in a large bowl, combine the flour, butter, and powdered sugar. Use your hands to smash and mix until the mixture has a crumbly texture. Transfer the mixture to a 6-inch square pan, using your fingers to press the dough into the bottom of the pan to form a crust.

3. When the unit beeps to signify it has preheated, place the pan in the Cooking Pot. Close the hood and cook for 5 minutes.

4. While the crust is baking, in a small bowl, beat the eggs, then add the sugar, baking powder, salt, and lemon juice and mix until well combined.

5. After 5 minutes, open the hood and pour the lemon filling over the crust. Cover the pan with aluminum foil (use grill mitts), making sure the foil tucks under the bottom of the pan so it does not lift up and block the Splatter Shield as the air flows while baking. Close the hood and cook for 20 minutes.

6. After 20 minutes, open the hood and remove the foil. Close the hood and bake uncovered for 10 minutes more.

7. When cooking is complete, remove the pan and let cool for at least 1 to 2 hours. Dust with additional powdered sugar and serve.

Mini Brownie Cakes

MAKES 4

Move over, boxed brownies! I'm always for easy and simple recipes, and this is one of my favorites. These brownie cakes are crispy on the outside and ooey-gooey and fudgy on the inside. Having these set up in their own ramekins makes them easy to serve and ensures everyone gets a fair share. Don't forget the vanilla ice cream, which complements these warm brownies perfectly.

NUT-FREE / UNDER 30 MINUTES / VEGETARIAN

PREP TIME: 10 minutes

COOK TIME: 15 minutes

ACCESSORIES: Cooking Pot

HACK IT: You can microwave your butter to melt it instead of using the Foodi™ Grill during the preheat step. Either way, be sure that the melted butter cools slightly before adding it to the eggs. Otherwise you will end up with cooked egg pieces in your brownie mixture.

8 tablespoons (1 stick) unsalted butter

2 large eggs

¼ cup unsweetened cocoa powder

½ cup granulated sugar

½ teaspoon vanilla extract

⅛ teaspoon salt

½ cup all-purpose flour

1. Cut the butter into quarters and divide them between 2 (6-ounce) ramekins. Insert the Cooking Pot, place the ramekins in the pot, and close the hood. Select GRILL, set the temperature to LO, and set the time to 15 minutes. Select START/STOP to begin preheating. After 3 minutes of preheating (set a separate timer), use grill mitts to remove the ramekins and set aside. Close the hood to continue preheating.

2. While the unit is preheating, in a large bowl, whisk the eggs together, then add the cocoa powder, sugar, vanilla, and salt. Sift or gradually shake the flour into the bowl as you continue mixing. Then stir in the melted butter to form a smooth batter. Divide the batter evenly among 4 (6-ounce) ramekins, filling them no more than three-quarters full.

3. When the unit beeps to signify it has preheated, place the ramekins in the Cooking Pot. Close the hood and cook for 15 minutes.

4. When cooking is complete, open the hood and remove the ramekins. The brownies are done when a toothpick inserted in the center comes out clean. (Cooking them for 15 minutes usually gives the brownies a crispy crust with a fudgy center. Add another 3 to 5 minutes if you wish to cook the center all the way through.)

Pecan Pie

This was my mom's go-to dessert, and it was always popular during the holidays. It brings back many memories of my sister and me in the kitchen shaping what my mom would call "pecan tassies"—miniature pecan pies. It was common for her to make 100 of these at a time! I've decided to turn Mom's recipe into a pie because it makes for less prep.

FAMILY FAVORITE / UNDER 30 MINUTES / VEGETARIAN

PREP TIME: 10 minutes

COOK TIME: 20 minutes

ACCESSORIES: Cooking Pot

VARIATION TIP: Want to make these into pecan tassies? Use two 6-cup muffin tins and bake at 350°F for 15 minutes. The recipe makes 12 muffins.

6 ounces cream cheese, at room temperature

4 tablespoons (½ stick) unsalted butter

2 large eggs

1 teaspoon vanilla extract

1 cup light brown sugar, packed

1 cup all-purpose flour

½ cup pecan halves

1. Place the cream cheese and butter in a 7-inch silicone cake pan. Insert the Cooking Pot, place the cake pan in the pot, and close the hood. Select BAKE, set the temperature to 350°F, and set the time to 20 minutes. (If using a metal or glass cake pan, you may need to add 5 to 10 minutes to the baking time.) Select START/STOP to begin preheating. After 5 minutes of preheating (set a separate timer), open the hood and remove the cake pan. (The cream cheese and butter will be melted but not combined.) Close the hood to continue preheating.

2. While the unit is preheating, in a medium bowl, whisk together the eggs, vanilla, brown sugar, and 1½ tablespoons of the melted butter from the cake pan.

3. Transfer the remaining butter and cream cheese from the cake pan to a large bowl and mix to combine. (It may look a little like cottage cheese.) Slowly sift the flour into the bowl. Begin kneading and mixing the dough together with your hands. It may be sticky at first, but continue mixing until it forms into a smooth dough. Place the dough in the cake pan and press it into the bottom and up the sides of the pan to form a piecrust.

4. Pour the filling into the piecrust and top with the pecans.

5. When the unit beeps to signify it has preheated, place the cake pan in the Cooking Pot. Close the hood and bake for 20 minutes.

6. When cooking is complete, the crust edges will be golden brown. Remove the cake pan and let cool to room temperature before slicing and serving.

Mixed Berry and Cream Cheese Puff Pastries

When making these creamy, fruity pastry puffs, make sure to eat them right off the Foodi™ Grill, as they are even more delicious hot than after they've cooled down. Either way, you'll be amazed by how tasty these are, as if you ordered them from your favorite bakery. You can use fresh fruit for this one, but to save time, I use jam, which works just as well.

5 INGREDIENTS / NUT-FREE / UNDER 30 MINUTES / VEGETARIAN

PREP TIME: 10 minutes

COOK TIME: 8 minutes

ACCESSORIES: Grill Grate

VARIATION TIP: Prefer fresh fruit? Combine 2 cups of strawberries, blueberries, and blackberries together with 1 tablespoon of sugar.

1 sheet puff pastry (thawed if frozen)

4 tablespoons (½ stick) unsalted butter, melted

6 ounces cream cheese, at room temperature

1 cup mixed-berry jam

1. Insert the Grill Grate and close the hood. Select GRILL, set the temperature to LO, and set the time to 8 minutes. Select START/STOP to begin preheating.

2. While the unit is preheating, unfold the pastry dough on a flat surface. Cut the dough into four equal-size pieces. Brush each piece with the butter. Fold in ¼ to ½ inch of each side of each piece of dough to create a pocket for the filling. Spread a layer of the cream cheese across each pastry pocket and then add ¼ cup of jam on top of each.

3. When the unit beeps to signify it has preheated, place the pastries on the Grill Grate. Close the hood and grill for 8 minutes.

4. When cooking is complete, the puff pastry will be golden brown and the cream cheese and jam may be infused and melted together. Remove the pastries from the grill and serve.

Peaches-and-Cake Skewers

Skewers aren't just for vegetables and meats. You can grill fruits and cake on skewers, too! These skewers make dessert time a lot more portable and fun, and the warmed condensed milk tops them off nicely. Grilling these directly on the Grill Grate helps caramelize the sugars in the pound cake and in the condensed milk. If you want a more traditional pound cake recipe, be sure to check out Grilled Strawberry Pound Cake (page 234).

5 INGREDIENTS / NUT-FREE / UNDER 30 MINUTES / VEGETARIAN

PREP TIME: 10 minutes

COOK TIME: 8 minutes

ACCESSORIES: Grill Grate / Ninja® Foodi™ Grill Kebab Skewers

SUBSTITUTION TIP: Don't have fresh peaches? Use drained canned peaches. Don't have condensed milk? Use maple syrup to coat. You can also switch out pound cake for angel food cake.

1 loaf pound cake, cut into 1-inch cubes

4 peaches, sliced

½ cup condensed milk

1. Insert the Grill Grate and close the hood. Select GRILL, set the temperature to HI, and set the time to 8 minutes. Select START/STOP to begin preheating.

2. While the unit is preheating, alternate cake cubes and peach slices, 3 or 4 pieces of each, on each of 12 skewers. Using a basting brush, brush the condensed milk onto the cake and peaches and place the skewers on a plate or baking sheet.

3. When the unit beeps to signify it has preheated, place 6 skewers on the Grill Grate. Close the hood and cook for 2 minutes.

4. After 2 minutes, open the hood and flip the skewers. Close the hood to cook for 2 minutes more.

5. After 2 minutes, open the hood and remove the skewers. Repeat steps 3 and 4 with the remaining 6 skewers. Serve.

Sweet Potato Donuts

Donuts are either baked, which gives them a cakey texture, or fried, which can be deemed oily and unhealthy. These donuts are in between. On the Foodi™ Grill, the donuts are brushed with some avocado oil, which results in a chewy, airy, and crisp texture. If you've ever had mochi donuts, these are similar—the sweet potato gives that sticky, chewy, doughy texture that you cannot get using wheat flour. Give these a try— you'll be hooked!

5 INGREDIENTS / DAIRY-FREE / NUT-FREE / VEGETARIAN

PREP TIME: 15 minutes

COOK TIME: 52 minutes

ACCESSORIES: Cooking Pot

HACK IT: Don't have time to soften the sweet potato in the grill? Pierce the sweet potato and microwave it in 1-minute intervals for up to 5 minutes to achieve the desired softness.

VARIATION TIP: If you do not have a donut pan, you can form the dough into donut shapes and place them on the Grill Grate, flipping them after 4 minutes. You can also make these into donut holes (balls), but after grilling, they will be flattened and look more like cookies.

3 cups water

1 medium white sweet potato

⅔ cup all-purpose flour, plus more for dusting

½ cup granulated sugar

Avocado oil

1. Insert the Cooking Pot, pour in the water, and close the hood. Select BROIL, set the temperature to 500°F, and set the time to 20 minutes. Select START/STOP to begin preheating.

2. While the unit is preheating, peel the sweet potato and cut it into chunks.

3. When the unit beeps to signify it has preheated, add the sweet potato to the Cooking Pot, making sure the chunks are fully submerged in the water. Close the hood and cook for 20 minutes.

4. After 20 minutes, open the hood and pierce a potato chunk to check for doneness—it should be easy to slice into. Remove and drain the sweet potatoes.

5. In a large bowl, mash the sweet potato with a masher or fork. When it has cooled down, add ⅔ cup of flour and the sugar and mix until well combined. The dough will be sticky. Dust a clean work surface with some flour. Roll and knead the dough until it is no longer sticky and holds its form, using more flour as needed.

6. Divide the dough in half and then cut each half into 6 equal-size pieces. Roll each piece of dough into a cylinder about 4 inches long.

CONTINUED ▶

7. Insert the Cooking Pot and close the hood. Select GRILL, set the temperature to HI, and set the time to 16 minutes. Select START/ STOP to begin preheating.

8. While the unit is preheating, brush avocado oil on a 6-ring donut pan and place 6 donuts in the molds. Brush more avocado oil on top.

9. When the unit beeps to signify it has preheated, place the donut pan in the Cooking Pot. Close the hood and grill for 8 minutes.

10. When cooking is complete, remove the pan and transfer the donuts to a rack to cool.

11. Repeat steps 8 through 10 with the remaining donuts. Serve.

Vanilla Scones

MAKES 18 SCONES

These scones are a perfect grab-and-go treat to enjoy with tea or coffee in the morning or as a snack or dessert. The almond flour makes them gluten-free, but you can use all-purpose flour if you like. If you are watching your sugar content, you can also switch out the granulated sugar for erythritol or another sugar substitute.

GLUTEN-FREE / UNDER 30 MINUTES / VEGETARIAN

PREP TIME: 15 minutes

COOK TIME: 15 minutes

ACCESSORIES: Cooking Pot

VARIATION TIP: Add about ⅔ cup fresh blueberries to make these into blueberry scones, and switch out the vanilla extract in the icing with 1 to 2 tablespoons freshly squeezed lemon juice for a lemon glaze.

For the scones

2 cups almond flour

¼ cup granulated sugar

¼ teaspoon salt

1 tablespoon baking powder

2 large eggs

1 teaspoon vanilla extract

4 tablespoons (½ stick) unsalted butter, melted

2 tablespoons heavy (whipping) cream

For the icing

1 cup powdered sugar

2 tablespoons heavy (whipping) cream

1 tablespoon vanilla extract

To make the scones

1. In a large bowl, combine the almond flour, granulated sugar, salt, and baking powder. In another large bowl, whisk the eggs, then whisk in the vanilla, butter, and heavy cream. Add the dry ingredients to the wet and mix just until a dough forms.

2. Insert the Cooking Pot and close the hood. Select BAKE, set the temperature to 325°F, and set the time to 15 minutes. Select START/STOP to begin preheating.

3. While the unit is preheating, divide the dough into 3 equal pieces. Shape each piece into a disc about 1 inch thick and 5 inches in diameter. Cut each into 6 wedges, like slicing a pizza.

4. When the unit beeps to signify it has preheated, place the scones in the Cooking Pot, spacing them apart so they don't bake together. Close the hood and cook for 15 minutes.

CONTINUED ▶

To make the icing

5. While the scones are baking, in a small bowl, combine the powdered sugar, heavy cream, and vanilla. Stir until smooth.

6. After 15 minutes, open the hood and remove the scones. They are done baking when they have turned a light golden brown. Place on a wire rack to cool to room temperature. Drizzle the icing over the scones, or pour a tablespoonful on the top of each scone for an even glaze.

Ninja® Foodi™ Smart XL Grill
CHARTS

GRILL

INGREDIENT	AMOUNT	TEMP	COOK TIME	INSTRUCTIONS
POULTRY	Chart times are intended to cook poultry all the way through to an internal temperature of 165°F			
Chicken breasts	4 bone-in breasts (12–24 oz each)	HIGH	18–22 mins	Flip halfway through cooking
	6 boneless breasts (7–9 oz each)	HIGH	16–20 mins	Flip halfway through cooking
Chicken leg quarters	3 bone-in leg quarters (12–14 oz each)	HIGH	26–31 mins	Flip halfway through cooking
Chicken sausages, prepared	2 packages (8 sausages)	HIGH	6–8 mins	Flipping not necessary
Chicken tenderloins	9 boneless tenderloins (2–3 oz each)	HIGH	8–11 mins	Flip halfway through cooking
Chicken thighs	6 bone-in thighs (7–9 oz each)	HIGH	23–28 mins	Flip halfway through cooking
	6 boneless thighs (4–7 oz each)	HIGH	10–12 mins	Flip halfway through cooking
Chicken wings	2½ lbs, bone-in (drumettes & flats)	HIGH	15–18 mins	Flip halfway through cooking
Turkey burgers	6 patties (¼ lb each), 1 inch thick	HIGH	11–13 mins	Flipping not necessary

CONTINUED ▶

INGREDIENT	AMOUNT	TEMP	COOK TIME	INSTRUCTIONS
BEEF	Chart times are intended to cook beef to medium doneness with an internal temperature of 145°F			
Burgers	6 patties (up to 7 oz each), 1–1½ inches thick	HIGH	5–9 mins	Flipping not necessary
Filet mignon	6 steaks (6–8 oz each), 1¼–1½ inches thick	HIGH	12–15 mins	Flip halfway through cooking
Flat iron or flank steak	1 steak (18–24 oz), 1–1¼ inches thick	HIGH	11–15 mins	Flip halfway through cooking
Hot dogs	9 hot dogs	LOW	3–5 mins	Flip halfway through cooking
New York strip	4 steaks (10–12 oz each), 1¼–1½ inches thick	HIGH	9–12 mins	Flip halfway through cooking
Rib eye	3 steaks (14–16 oz each), 1¼ inches thick	HIGH	12–14 mins	Flip halfway through cooking
Skirt	4 steaks (10–12 oz each), ¾–1 inch thick	HIGH	7–11 mins	Flip halfway through cooking
Steak tips	2 lbs	MEDIUM	13–16 mins	Marinate as desired (see page 14 for inspiration)
T-bone	2 steaks (14–18 oz each), 1½ inches thick	HIGH	9–12 mins	Flip halfway through cooking

INGREDIENT	AMOUNT	TEMP	COOK TIME	INSTRUCTIONS
PORK, LAMB & VEAL	*Chart times are intended to cook pork, lamb & veal all the way through to an internal temperature of 145°F*			
Baby back ribs	1 rack, divided in half (10–13 bones)	HIGH	20–22 mins	Flip halfway through cooking
Bacon	8 strips, thick cut	LOW	7–9 mins	Flipping not necessary
Lamb rack	Full rack (8 bones)	HIGH	20–25 mins	Flip halfway through cooking
Pork chops	4 thick-cut, bone-in chops (10–12 oz each)	HIGH	15–19 mins	Flip halfway through cooking
	6 boneless chops (8 oz each)	HIGH	14–17 mins	Flip halfway through cooking
Pork tenderloins	2 whole tenderloins (1–1½ lbs each)	HIGH	15–20 mins	Flip halfway through cooking
Sausages	9 whole sausages (3–4 oz each)	LOW	7–10 mins	Flip halfway through cooking
Veal chops	6 bone-in chops (4–6 oz each)	HIGH	10–15 mins	Flip halfway through cooking
SEAFOOD	*Chart times are intended to cook seafood all the way through to an internal temperature of 145°F*			
Cod or haddock	6 fillets (5–6 oz each)	MAX	8–12 mins	Flipping not necessary
Flounder	3 fillets (5–6 oz each)	MAX	4–6 mins	Flipping not necessary
Halibut	6 fillets (4–6 oz each)	MAX	6–10 mins	Flipping not necessary

CONTINUED ▶

INGREDIENT	AMOUNT	TEMP	COOK TIME	INSTRUCTIONS
Oysters	12	MAX	5-7 mins	Shuck and place on grill, shell-side down
Salmon	6 fillets (6 oz each)	MAX	12-15 mins	Flipping not necessary
Scallops	18 (1½ lbs)	MAX	5-8 mins	Pat dry, season
Shrimp	2 lbs jumbo (approx. 30 count)	MAX	1-3 mins	Pat dry, season
Swordfish	2 steaks (11-12 oz each)	MAX	6-8 mins	Flipping not necessary
Tuna	4 steaks (4-6 oz each)	MAX	6-8 mins	Flipping not necessary
FROZEN POULTRY Chart times are intended to cook poultry all the way through to an internal temperature of 165˚F				
Chicken breasts	6 boneless breasts (7-9 oz each)	MEDIUM	20-25 mins	Flip 2 or 3 times while cooking
Chicken thighs	6 bone-in thighs (7-9 oz each)	MEDIUM	28-32 mins	Flip 2 or 3 times while cooking
Turkey burgers	6 patties (4-6 oz each)	MEDIUM	13-16 mins	Flip halfway through cooking, if desired
FROZEN BEEF Chart times are intended to cook beef all the way through to an internal temperature of 145˚F				
Burgers	6 patties (up to 7 oz each), 1 inch thick	MEDIUM	10-12 mins	Flip 2 or 3 times while cooking
Filet mignon	6 steaks (6-8 oz each), 1¼-1½ inches thick	MEDIUM	15-20 mins	Flip 2 or 3 times while cooking

INGREDIENT	AMOUNT	TEMP	COOK TIME	INSTRUCTIONS
New York strip	4 steaks (10–12 oz each), 1¼–1½ inches thick	MEDIUM	18–26 mins	Flip 2 or 3 times while cooking
Rib eye	3 steaks (14–16 oz each), 1¼ inches thick	MEDIUM	18–24 mins	Flip 2 or 3 times while cooking
FROZEN PORK Chart times are intended to cook pork all the way through to an internal temperature of 145°F				
Pork chops	6 boneless chops (8 oz each)	MEDIUM	22–26 mins	Flip 2 or 3 times while cooking
Pork tenderloin	2 whole tenderloins (1 lb each)	MEDIUM	22–28 mins	Flip 2 or 3 times while cooking
Sausage, uncooked	9 whole sausages	LOW	10–14 mins	Flip 2 or 3 times while cooking
FROZEN SEAFOOD Chart times are intended to cook seafood all the way through to an internal temperature of 145°F				
Halibut	6 fillets (6 oz each)	MAX	14–16 mins	Flip halfway through cooking, if desired
Salmon	6 fillets (4 oz each)	MAX	12–15 mins	Flip halfway through cooking, if desired
Shrimp	20 oz jumbo (approx. 30 count)	MAX	3–4 mins	Flipping not necessary
FROZEN VEGGIE BURGERS				
Veggie burgers	6 patties (4 oz each)	HIGH	8–10 mins	Flip halfway through cooking, if desired

CONTINUED ▶

INGREDIENT	AMOUNT	PREPARATION	TEMP	COOK TIME	INSTRUCTIONS
VEGETABLES					
Asparagus	2 bunches	Whole, trim stems	MAX	5–7 mins	Flipping not necessary
Baby bok choy	1½ lbs	Cut in half lengthwise, season	MAX	9–13 mins	Flip halfway through cooking
Bell peppers	4	Cut in quarters, season	MAX	6–9 mins	Flip halfway through cooking
Broccoli	2 heads (1¾ lbs)	Cut in 2-inch florets	MAX	10–12 mins	Flipping not necessary
Brussels sprouts	2½ lbs	Whole, trim stems	MAX	12–16 mins	Flip halfway through cooking
Carrots	10 (2 lbs)	Peel, cut in 2-inch pieces, season	MAX	12–14 mins	Flipping not necessary
Cauliflower	1 head (12–18 oz)	Cut in 2-inch florets	MAX	10–12 mins	Flipping not necessary
Corn on the cob	6	Whole ears, remove husks	MAX	10–13 mins	Flip halfway through cooking
Cremini mushrooms	1½ lbs	Cut in half, season	MAX	5–7 mins	Flipping not necessary
Eggplant	2 medium (16–24 oz)	Cut in 2-inch pieces, season	MAX	10–12 mins	Flip halfway through cooking
Green beans	24 oz	Trim stems, season	MAX	8–10 mins	Flipping not necessary

INGREDIENT	AMOUNT	PREPARATION	TEMP	COOK TIME	INSTRUCTIONS
Onions, white or red	6	Peel, cut in half, season	MAX	10–12 mins	Flip halfway through cooking
Onions, white or red	3	Peel, cut in 1-inch slices, season	MAX	4–6 mins	Flip halfway through cooking
Portobello mushrooms	6	Remove stems, scrape out gills with spoon, season	MAX	7–9 mins	Flip halfway through cooking
Squash or zucchini	2–3 (24 oz)	Cut in quarters lengthwise, season	MAX	12–16 mins	Flip halfway through cooking
Tomatoes	6–10	Cut in half, season	MAX	8–10 mins	Flipping not necessary
FRUIT					
Avocado	Up to 3	Cut in half, remove pit	MAX	4–5 mins	Flipping not necessary
Bananas	4	Peel, cut in half lengthwise	MAX	3 mins	Remove using silicone tipped tongs or spatula
Lemons and limes	5	Cut in half lengthwise, press down on grill grate	MAX	4 mins	Flipping not necessary
Mango	4	Skin and pit removed, press down gently on grill grate	MAX	4–6 mins	Flipping not necessary
Melon	6 spears (4–6 inches each)	Press down gently on grill grate	MAX	4–6 mins	Flipping not necessary

CONTINUED ▶

INGREDIENT	AMOUNT	PREPARATION	TEMP	COOK TIME	INSTRUCTIONS
Pineapple	6–8 slices or spears	Cut in 2-inch pieces	MAX	7–10 mins	Flip gently several times during cooking
Stone fruit (such as peaches and plums)	4–6	Cut in half, remove pit, press down on grill grate	MAX	10–12 mins	Flipping not necessary
BREAD AND CHEESE					
Bread (such as baguette or ciabatta)	12–16-inch loaf	Hand-cut, 1½-inch slices, brushed with canola oil	MAX	2–3 mins	Flipping not necessary
Halloumi cheese	24–36 oz	Cut in 1-inch slices	MAX	2–4 mins	Flipping not necessary

TIP: For less smoke, we recommend cleaning splatter shield after every use.

TIP: Use the Foodi™ Smart Thermometer with the proteins in the charts to cook to doneness without worrying about cooktimes.

AIR CRISP

INGREDIENT	AMOUNT	PREPARATION	TOSS IN OIL	TEMP	COOK TIME
VEGETABLES					
Asparagus	2 bunches	Whole, trim stems	2 tsp	390°F	12–14 mins
Beets	8 small	Whole	None	390°F	45–60 mins
Bell peppers (for roasting)	4–5 small peppers	Whole	None	400°F	20–25 mins
Broccoli	2 heads (1–1½ lbs)	Cut in 1-inch florets	1 Tbsp	390°F	12–16 mins
Brussels sprouts	2 lbs	Cut in half, remove stems	1 Tbsp	390°F	15–18 mins
Butternut squash	3 lbs	Cut in 1-inch pieces	1 Tbsp	390°F	26–28 mins
Carrots	2 lbs	Peel, cut in 1-inch pieces	1 Tbsp	390°F	18–22 mins
Cauliflower	2 heads (1–1½ lbs)	Cut in 1-inch florets	2 Tbsp	390°F	20–25 mins
Corn on the cob	6 ears	Whole ears, remove husks	1 Tbsp	390°F	11–15 mins
Green beans	2 lbs	Trim	1 Tbsp	390°F	11–13 mins

CONTINUED ▶

INGREDIENT	AMOUNT	PREPARATION	TOSS IN OIL	TEMP	COOK TIME
Kale (for chips)	8 cups, packed	Tear in pieces, remove stems	None	300°F	10–12 mins
Mushrooms	1½ lbs	Rinse, cut in quarters	1 Tbsp	390°F	11–13 mins
Potatoes, russet	3 lbs	Cut in 1-inch wedges	1–3 Tbsp, canola	390°F	25–30 mins
	2 lbs	Hand-cut fries*, thin	1–3 Tbsp, canola	390°F	22–26 mins
	2 lbs	Hand-cut fries*, thick	1–3 Tbsp, canola	390°F	24–29 mins
	5 whole (6–8 oz)	Pierce with fork 3 times	None	390°F	38–45 mins
Potatoes, sweet	1½ lbs	Cut in 1-inch chunks	1 Tbsp	390°F	20–25 mins
	6 whole (6–8 oz)	Pierce with fork 3 times	None	390°F	30–35 mins
Zucchini	2½ lbs	Cut in quarters lengthwise, then cut in 1-inch pieces	1 Tbsp	390°F	16–19 mins

*After cutting potatoes, allow raw fries to soak in cold water for at least 30 minutes to remove unnecessary starch. Pat fries dry. The drier the fries, the better the results.

INGREDIENT	AMOUNT	PREPARATION	TOSS IN OIL	TEMP	COOK TIME
POULTRY					
Chicken breasts	3 breasts (¾–1½ lbs each)	Bone in	Brushed with oil	375°F	25–35 mins
Chicken thighs	4 breasts (½–¾ lb each)	Boneless	Brushed with oil	375°F	20–24 mins
	6 thighs (6–10 oz each)	Bone in	Brushed with oil	375°F	25–30 mins
Chicken wings	6 thighs (4–8 oz each)	Boneless	Brushed with oil	375°F	16–18 mins
	2½ lbs (drumettes and flats)	Bone in	1½ Tbsp	390°F	22–26 mins

FOR BEST RESULTS, SHAKE OR TOSS OFTEN.

We recommend frequently checking your food and shaking or tossing it to ensure desired results.

Use these cook times as a guide, adjusting to your preference.

OR

Shake your food

Toss with silicone-tipped tongs

CONTINUED ▶

INGREDIENT	AMOUNT	PREPARATION	TOSS IN OIL	TEMP	COOK TIME
PORK AND LAMB					
Bacon	5 strips, cut in half	None	None	350°F	5–8 mins
Pork chops	3 thick-cut, bone-in chops (10-12 oz each)	Bone in	Brush with oil	375°F	17–20 mins
	6 boneless chops (8 oz each)	Boneless	Brush with oil	375°F	14–20 mins
Pork tenderloins	2 tenderloins (1–1½ lbs each)	Whole	Brush with oil	375°F	25–35 mins
Sausages	6 sausages	Whole	None	390°F	9–11 mins
FROZEN FOODS					
Chicken cutlets	6 cutlets	None	None	390°F	18–21 mins
Chicken nuggets	2 boxes (24 oz)	None	None	390°F	11–14 mins
Fish fillets	8 fillets, breaded	None	None	390°F	14–16 mins
Fish sticks	30 fish sticks (22 oz; approx. 2 boxes)	None	None	390°F	13–16 mins

INGREDIENT	AMOUNT	PREPARATION	TOSS IN OIL	TEMP	COOK TIME
French fries	1 lb	None	None	350°F	18–22 mins
	2½ lbs	None	None	360°F	25–30 mins
Mozzarella sticks	2 boxes (11 oz)	None	None	375°F	10–12 mins
Pizza rolls	1 large bag (40 oz, approx. 40 count)	None	None	390°F	12–15 mins
Popcorn shrimp	1½ boxes (approx. 24 oz)	None	None	390°F	10–13 mins
Pot stickers	1 bag (20 oz, 20 count)	None	None	390°F	12–15 mins
Sweet potato fries	1 bag (approx. 24 oz)	None	None	375°F	20–24 mins
Tater tots	1 bag (approx. 24 oz)	None	None	360°F	15–18 mins

FOR BEST RESULTS, SHAKE OR TOSS OFTEN.

We recommend frequently checking your food and shaking or tossing it to ensure desired results.

Use these cook times as a guide, adjusting to your preference.

OR

Shake your food

Toss with silicone-tipped tongs

DEHYDRATE

INGREDIENT	PREPARATION	TEMP	DEHYDRATE TIME
FRUITS AND VEGETABLES			
Apples	Cut in ⅛-inch slices, remove core, rinse in lemon water, pat dry	135°F	6–8 hours
Asparagus	Cut in 1-inch pieces, blanch	135°F	6–8 hours
Bananas	Peel, cut in ⅜-inch slices	135°F	6–8 hours
Beets	Peel, cut in ⅛-inch slices	135°F	6–8 hours
Eggplant	Peel, cut in ¼-inch slices, blanch	135°F	6–8 hours
Fresh herbs	Rinse, pat dry, remove stems	135°F	4 hours
Ginger root	Cut in ⅜-inch slices	135°F	6 hours
Mangos	Peel, cut in ⅜-inch slices, remove pit	135°F	6–8 hours
Mushrooms	Clean with soft brush (do not wash)	135°F	6–8 hours
Pineapple	Peel, cut in ⅜–½-inch slices, remove core	135°F	6–8 hours
Strawberries	Cut in half or in ½-inch slices	135°F	6–8 hours
Tomatoes	Cut in ⅜-inch slices; blanch if planning to rehydrate	135°F	6–8 hours

INGREDIENT	PREPARATION	TEMP	DEHYDRATE TIME
MEAT, POULTRY, FISH			
Beef jerky	Cut in ¼-inch slices, marinate overnight	150°F	5–7 hours
Chicken jerky	Cut in ¼-inch slices, marinate overnight	150°F	5–7 hours
Turkey jerky	Cut in ¼-inch slices, marinate overnight	150°F	5–7 hours
Salmon jerky	Cut in ¼-inch slices, marinate overnight	150°F	3–5 hours

MEASUREMENT CONVERSIONS

VOLUME EQUIVALENTS (LIQUID)

US Standard	US Standard (ounces)	Metric (approximate)
2 tablespoons	1 fl. oz.	30 mL
¼ cup	2 fl. oz.	60 mL
½ cup	4 fl. oz.	120 mL
1 cup	8 fl. oz.	240 mL
1½ cups	12 fl. oz.	355 mL
2 cups or 1 pint	16 fl. oz.	475 mL
4 cups or 1 quart	32 fl. oz.	1 L
1 gallon	128 fl. oz.	4 L

OVEN TEMPERATURES

Fahrenheit (F)	Celsius (C) (approximate)
250°F	120°C
300°F	150°C
325°F	165°C
350°F	180°C
375°F	190°C
400°F	200°C
425°F	220°C
450°F	230°C

VOLUME EQUIVALENTS (DRY)

US Standard	Metric (approximate)
⅛ teaspoon	0.5 mL
¼ teaspoon	1 mL
½ teaspoon	2 mL
¾ teaspoon	4 mL
1 teaspoon	5 mL
1 tablespoon	15 mL
¼ cup	59 mL
⅓ cup	79 mL
½ cup	118 mL
⅔ cup	156 mL
¾ cup	177 mL
1 cup	235 mL
2 cups or 1 pint	475 mL
3 cups	700 mL
4 cups or 1 quart	1 L

WEIGHT EQUIVALENTS

US Standard	Metric (approximate)
½ ounce	15 g
1 ounce	30 g
2 ounces	60 g
4 ounces	115 g
8 ounces	225 g
12 ounces	340 g
16 ounces or 1 pound	455 g

INDEX

ACKNOWLEDGMENTS

John: Thank you for always supporting and loving me. I can laugh and say this book is for you. Now start cooking!

Jaxon and Allexie: I missed you during these busy days and nights. This was all for you. I love watching you grow up and am proud to be your mommy.

My loving parents, Virginia and Manuel: You have taught me so much in and out of the kitchen. I am forever grateful for the sacrifices you've made for us.

Catalina and Bernard: Thank you for loving me as one of your own and giving me unconditional, never-ending support.

Mavelyn, Catherine, and Bryan, my confidants and the best siblings: Thankful for the advice, memories, and taste testing.

Family is everything. Estrada, Chico, Lacap, Tichi, De Leon, Maala, and Bihis families: Thank you for always encouraging and feeding me.

To my friends, online community, and editors: Thank you for all the motivation, development, and believing in me.

ABOUT THE AUTHOR

Mellanie De Leon studied exercise nutrition and wellness and later received her master's in education, knowing that we live in a world where we are constantly growing and learning something new every day. As a working, stay-at-home mother of two with busy days and nights, she calls for creativity in the kitchen to keep food interesting. Mellanie created an online following of those looking for food ideas, recipes, and motivation for losing weight, getting fit, and living a keto, low-carb, or sugar-free lifestyle.

When she's not cooking or baking, you'll find her crafting, looking for grocery sales to plan out her meals, working out, and doing event planning and decor, because things must always be presentable and orderly to logistically work with balancing life, work, family, wellness, and the kids.

You can chat with Mellanie by following her on Instagram (@KetoMommyMell), or check out her website at KetoMommyMell.com.

CPSIA information can be obtained
at www.ICGtesting.com
Printed in the USA
BVHW061450031121
620469BV00008B/8